D1557612

THE ESSENTIALS OF FLORIDA MENTAL HEALTH LAW

A STRAIGHTFORWARD GUIDE FOR
CLINICIANS OF ALL DISCIPLINES

Other Books in this Series

The Essentials of California Mental Health Law
Stephen H. Behnke, James J. Preis, R. Todd Bates

The Essentials of Massachusetts Mental Health Law
Stephen H. Behnke, James T. Hilliard

A NORTON PROFESSIONAL BOOK

THE ESSENTIALS OF FLORIDA MENTAL HEALTH LAW

A STRAIGHTFORWARD GUIDE FOR CLINICIANS OF ALL DISCIPLINES

STEPHEN H. BEHNKE, J.D., PH.D.
BRUCE J. WINICK, J.D.
ALINA M. PEREZ, J.D., L.C.S.W.

W. W. NORTON & COMPANY • NEW YORK • LONDON

Cases involving law and mental health can be exceedingly complex, highly specific, and require legal expertise that no book, pamphlet, or review will provide. In addition, laws change over time. You should therefore not use this book as a substitute for consultation with an attorney knowledgable in mental health law.

For information about permission to reproduce selections
from this book, write to
Permissions, W. W. Norton & Company, Inc., 500 Fifth Avenue,
New York, NY 10110

Composition by Tom Ernst.
Manufacturing by Haddon Craftsmen.

Library of Congress Cataloging-in-Publication Data
Behnke, Stephen H., 1958–
    The essentials of Florida mental health law : a straightforward guide for
clinicians of all disciplines / Stephen H. Behnke, Bruce J. Winick, Alina M. Perez.
        p.   cm.
    "A Norton professional book."
    Includes bibliographical references and index.
    ISBN 0-393-70309-6
    1. Mental health laws—Florida. I. Winick, Bruce J. II. Perez, Alina M. III. Title
KFF365.B44   2000
344.759′044—dc21

                                                                    99-054664

W. W. Norton & Company, Inc., 500 Fifth Avenue, New York, N.Y. 10110
www.wwnorton.com

W. W. Norton & Company Ltd., 10 Coptic Street, London WC1A 1PU

1 2 3 4 5 6 7 8 9 0

For My Uncle, the Reverend J. William Houran, from whom I have learned much.

—S.H.B.

To my dad, Milton Winick—though long gone, his spirit lives still within me.

—B.J.W.

To my parents, friends, and loved ones.

—A.M.P.

CONTENTS

ACKNOWLEDGMENTS

We would like to thank all our friends and colleagues who provided their encouragement and support for this project. We would like especially to acknowledge the invaluable contribution of Michael Feiler, Esq., and the research assistance of Cheryl Potter, J.D. We would also like to thank Professor Susan Stefan, J.D., for her helpful comments and others who read and commented on drafts of the manuscript: Douglas Webster, L.C.S.W., Gus Millor, L.C.S.W., Professor Kathy Cerminara, J.D., Richard Kaderman, Ph.D, Christina Pozo, Ph.D, and Patrick Reynolds, M.D.

James T. Hilliard, who coauthored the Massachusetts volume and is an enormously gifted mental health law attorney, has given the Essentials of Mental Health Law series a direction and focus. We are all indebted to him for his insight into mental health law, his clarity in thinking about these challenging questions, and his wisdom in knowing what it means to do the right thing.

Finally, we would like to thank our families and loved ones for their support and understanding.

INTRODUCTION

The idea for this book arose from our teaching mental health profession-als about how best to address problems in risk management. The most fre-quent comment from trainees and experienced clinicians alike—that it is enormously helpful to have laws relevant to clinical practice explained in a simple and straightforward way—suggested the need for a book to ori-ent mental health professionals to their legal rights and responsibilities.

The purpose of this book is to set forth, in a clear and concise manner, the laws most relevant to mental health practice in Florida. The book is also designed to explain and demonstrate how these laws apply to the many problems mental health professionals encounter on a day-to-day basis. The format will be useful both to the student trainee and to the more senior clinician; indeed, the majority of treaters find it difficult to keep up to date on how the Florida legislature and courts have changed the legal landscape of clinical practice. Lawyers, as well, may find the explanations of state laws governing mental health practice useful to their understanding of this interesting and ever-changing field.

The Essentials of Florida Mental Health Law is divided into two parts. The three chapters of part I serve as a general introduction to the law. The first chapter, A Brief Introduction to the Law, explains where the dif-ferent laws affecting clinical practice come from and, should a treater feel particularly bold, how she would go about finding an actual statute, court decision, or regulation.

The second chapter, *Tarasoff* and Its Florida Progeny, takes an actual statute and illustrates how a law "works." This chapter sets forth the phi-losophy of the Florida law, explains what the law requires, and demon-strates how different parts of the law fit together like building blocks to form a coherent whole. *Tarasoff* and Its Florida Progeny explains *why* the law was written, *what* the law says, and *how* the law goes about saying it. Any law can be analyzed in this manner, as we hope will become clear throughout the book.

The third and final chapter in part I discusses the set of laws and regulations perhaps most central to actual practice, those that pertain to privacy, confidentiality, and testimonial privilege. *Privacy* is an individual's right to make important life decisions—what to wear, whether to have children, which profession to pursue—without interference from the government. *Confidentiality* is the right to have communications with a therapist kept between the therapist and client. *Testimonial privilege*, often referred to simply as *privilege*, is the patient's right to prevent a therapist from divulging confidential information in a legal proceeding. Chapter 3 includes a discussion of mandatory reporting laws; these laws require a mental health professional to break confidentiality when certain circumstances are present. Appendix A contains the actual texts of the privacy, confidentiality, and privilege laws most central to clinical practice. By the end of part I the clinician should have a good sense of how a law can be read, understood, and applied in her work.

Part II consists of 200 questions clinicians often ask about Florida mental health law. We have divided the questions into nine topic headings. Topics range from the standard for placing an individual in a psychiatric hospital against his will, to the rules of confidentiality that govern consultations, to the wisdom of meeting with a family after a patient commits suicide. Answers to these questions describe in a clear, direct manner how the law affects clinical practice. In appendix B are several examples of written materials that clinicians may find helpful in their practice. These materials include an informed consent letter to begin a psychotherapy, a letter terminating a therapy with a difficult patient, and a reply to a board of registration letter of complaint. A sample subpoena is also included.

At the heart of this book is our belief that good patient care and knowledge of the law go hand in hand. Our experience is that, far from restricting or inhibiting clinical practice, knowing the essentials of Florida mental health law will free treaters from much undue—and unwarranted—anxiety about their legal rights and duties. We hope that such freedom will allow clinicians to concentrate on what they do best and enjoy most—treat patients.*

* A brief word about terminology. Solely for ease of reading, "client" and "patient" are used interchangeably, as are "clinician," "treater," "therapist," and "mental health professional." By "client" and "patient" we mean any individual who seeks services from a mental health professional. By the latter four terms we mean any individual who provides such services.

THE ESSENTIALS OF FLORIDA MENTAL HEALTH LAW

A STRAIGHTFORWARD GUIDE FOR CLINICIANS OF ALL DISCIPLINES

Part I

An Introduction to the Law

1

A Brief Introduction to the Law

The American system of law is divided into two layers: federal and state. Federal laws affect the United States as a whole, while state laws are specific to a particular state or commonwealth. As a citizen of Florida, you are also a citizen of the United States. You are thus accorded the rights and privileges, as well as the responsibilities, afforded by both federal and state law. While our discussion will focus primarily on laws made in Florida, we will also mention important federal laws that affect Florida citizens.

Florida laws may be similar to laws found in other states, but always keep in mind that any state law is binding only for that state. Because each state is its own sovereignty, each is free to decide for itself what laws to enact, which means that things can get a bit confusing, since the 50 states may have 50 different laws governing the same topic. Thus, always note whether a law is a *state* law; if so, then, should you reside in that same state, the law applies to you and you are bound to follow it. If the law belongs to another state, then it is not binding on you, although you will want to know what your state says about the particular topic.

Our discussion will address and explain how to cite five types of laws: (1) the constitutions; (2) statutes enacted by the legislature; (3) regulations promulgated by boards or agencies; (4) rules of court adopted by the judiciary; and (5) decisions made by courts.

Although the hierarchical relationships between the constitution, statutes, regulations, rules of court, and court decisions can be quite complicated, each of these five is nevertheless considered part of the law.

An outline of the discussion on how to cite Florida laws is found on pages 9–10.

The first and most important law in the state and in the federal government is the constitution. A constitution is that document whose provisions are sometimes referred to as "supreme," because no law in a given jurisdiction can conflict with anything in that jurisdiction's constitution—no state may pass a law that conflicts with the state constitution, and the federal government may not pass a law that conflicts with the United States Constitution. Many times a constitution will have a preamble that invokes its philosophical or moral basis. Both the Constitution of the United States and the Constitution of the State of Florida, for example, begin, "We, the People . . ." and thus make clear that their moral basis is found in the assent of the people. Simply put, a constitution is the touchstone by which a law will be deemed legitimate or illegitimate, and this is why our starting point for discussing law begins with recognizing the importance, indeed supremacy, of the constitution.

The second category of laws is "statutes." Generally, statutes are written by the legislature that we elect. The United States Congress is the legislature for the federal government. The representatives gather, spend much time collecting information, even more time arguing with one another, and then write a bill that, if signed by the Governor or the President, becomes a law. A Florida statute is sometimes referred to in an abbreviated form called a "citation." "Florida Statutes" is abbreviated (put in citation form) as "Fla. Stat." An example of a citation is "Fla. Stat. ch. 394.467 (1997)." This citation refers to section 467 of chapter 394 of the Florida Statutes. (The chapter reference comes first; the section number follows the period.) The date in the citation indicates that this statute can be found in the 1997 edition of a series of volumes that contains the Florida Statutes. The citation can be even further abbreviated by writing "section 394.467." Again, this refers to section 467 of chapter 394.

The third group of laws is not written by the legislature at all and, in fact, these laws are not even called laws. These laws are called "regulations." Different groups of people write regulations. Sometimes these people belong to boards or commissions that the legislature has created.

The Florida legislature created the Board of Psychology, for example, to adopt regulations that govern the practice of psychology in Florida. Regulations get their legitimacy through the legislature, which generally has neither the time nor the expertise to get into the nitty-gritty of running an administrative agency or of governing a highly specific profession. It is as if the legislature were to say, "Look, we really know very little about how things work in this profession or in this agency on a day-to-day basis. We therefore delegate to you broad authority to run this agency or to govern this profession in the way that makes most sense. You fill in the details about how things will get done." The details are the regulations. Generally, the legislature writes a statute authorizing a board, an agency, or a commission to write regulations. Regulations must be consistent with the statutes they are designed to carry out. A Florida regulation is referred to by the citation "Fla. Admin. Code Ann.," which stands for "Florida Administrative Code Annotated." An example of a citation to a regulation would be "Fla. Admin. Code Ann. r.65E-5.290 (1996)." This citation refers to the Florida Administrative Code Annotated, rule 65E, section 5.290, which appears in the volume published in 1996.

The fourth category of laws is "rules of court" adopted by the judicial branch of government. Rules of court apply to judges as they conduct judicial proceedings and to lawyers who practice before the judges. Rules of court are just what they sound like—rules that govern how things are to be done, somewhat like the rules of the road for drivers. Rules of court are important because they set forth the process by which a legal case moves forward. Failure to follow the rules of court can harm a client's case—perhaps seriously—and may even result in penalties. Examples of rules of court are the "Florida Rules of Civil Procedure" and the "Florida Rules of Criminal Procedure." As examples, Florida Rules of Criminal Procedure govern the evaluation and disposition of criminal defendants whose competence to stand trial has been questioned, while Florida Rules of Civil Procedure govern how one begins a malpractice lawsuit. Like statutes and regulations, rules of court have their own manner of citation. "Fla. R. Crim. P. 3.212," for example, refers to rule 3.212 of the rules of criminal procedure. "Fla. R. Civ. P. 1.390" refers to rule 1.390 of the rules of civil procedure. All these court rules are found in a volume appropriately called the "Florida Rules of Court."

The fifth and final group of laws are those found in court decisions. Laws that arise from court decisions are referred to as "case law." In some cases, courts simply interpret statutes, regulations, or court rules, but at other times courts actually make new law. As an example, courts have made new law in determining the scope of a mental health professional's duty in malpractice cases (see chapter 2).

In most instances relevant to our purposes, case law comes from a particular kind of court, an "appellate court." An appellate court is a court that deals with cases "on appeal," that is, when someone doesn't like the decision of a lower court (usually a trial court) and so asks a higher court to review the lower court's decision. The holding of an appellate court is referred to as "law" because, like the Constitution, statutes, regulations, and rules of court, the court's holding is legally binding. The court's holding is referred to as "case law" because it derives from a case. "Common law," a phrase you may have heard, is case law that has developed over a long, long time—many centuries, in fact.

The Florida court system is comprised of three tiers. The county and circuit courts are on the first tier. Most Florida trials take place in a county or a circuit court. The difference between a county and a circuit court rests on the type of case that each has the authority to decide (that is, has "jurisdiction over"; see question 6 in part II). For example, the county court has authority to decides cases where a sum of money less than $15,000 is at stake and cases that involve certain municipal and county ordinances. The circuit court, on the other hand, has jurisdiction over cases that involve guardianship, involuntary hospitalization, incompetence issues, and other cases that do not go before a county court.

The district court of appeals is on the tier above the county and circuit courts. There are five district courts of appeals in Florida. Each district court of appeals handles cases within a specific geographical location. As an example, the First District Court of Appeals covers the northwestern part of the state. The majority of cases brought in the Florida judicial system end when a district court of appeals has rendered a decision, that is, when a case reaches the second tier in the Florida judicial system. Put in the language of the law, the district court of appeals is the final court of decision for most Florida cases. In a word, the district court of appeals is usually the last stop on the litigation train.

The Supreme Court of Florida is the highest of the three tiers. In Florida, however, the State Supreme Court only has the authority to decide (only has jurisdiction over) cases that involve very specific matters. The Florida Constitution explicitly names which cases may come before the Florida Supreme Court. As examples, the Florida Constitution says that the Florida Supreme Court may hear cases that involve the death penalty, cases that involve conflicts between district courts of appeals (cases that arise when the district courts of appeals disagree among themselves), cases in which a district court of appeals "certifies" a question as being of great public importance and thus appropriate to be heard by the state's highest court, and cases that have come before a federal court but that concern Florida law. These cases, however, comprise only a small percentage of cases actually heard by Florida courts. In practice, the vast majority of cases in the state of Florida never get beyond a district court of appeals.

THE THREE TIERS OF THE FLORIDA COURT SYSTEM

I.   The first tier: **county and circuit courts**
     Most cases are heard by a county or a circuit court.

II. The second tier: **district court of appeals**
     There are five district courts of appeals in Florida, arranged according to their geographic location. Most Florida cases never go higher than a district court of appeals.

III. The third (and highest) tier: **Florida Supreme Court**
     The Florida Supreme Court only hears cases specified by the Florida Constitution.

The federal system operates in a similar fashion, in the sense of having three tiers. Federal district courts are the trial courts, the lowest tier in the federal system. A decision of a federal district court can be appealed first to a federal court of appeals and then to the United States Supreme Court. The United States Supreme Court is the highest federal court. The United States Supreme Court is not as restricted in what cases it may hear as is the Florida Supreme Court.

Legal cases from across the 50 states are grouped in volumes called "reporters" according to geography. Florida cases, naturally enough, are found in the *Southern Reporter*. The *Southern Reporter* has two editions. "So." in the citation to a legal case indicates that the case is found in the first edition of the *Southern Reporter*, while "So. 2d" indicates that the case is found in the second edition of the *Southern Reporter*. The citation will also indicate whether the case comes from the Florida Supreme Court, a Florida district court of appeals, or a county or circuit court. "Fla." is the abbreviation for cases of the Florida Supreme Court, while "Fla. Dist. Ct.

App." or "DCA" or "Fla. App. Dist." are abbreviations for cases from a Florida district court of appeals.* The numbers before and after the initials refer to the volume, page number, and date of the opinion. For example, "565 So. 2d 315 (Fla. 1990)" indicates that this opinion was written by the Florida Supreme Court (because of the "Fla.") in 1990. The citation further tells us that this opinion is found in volume 565, page 315 of the second edition of the *Southern Reporter.* The citation "582 So. 2d 784 (Fla. 5th Dist. Ct. App. 1991)" indicates that this opinion was written by the 5th District Court of Appeals in 1991. The opinion is found in volume 582, page 784 of the second edition of the *Southern Reporter.*

While cases heard by the Florida Supreme Court and the Florida District Court of Appeals are found in the *Southern Reporter* (either the first or second edition, depending upon when the case was written), cases decided by the county and circuit courts are found in a reporter called the *Florida Supplement.* Like the *Southern Reporter,* the *Florida Supplement* has two editions (Fla. Supp. and its second edition, Fla. Supp. 2d). Also like the *Southern Reporter,* citations in the *Florida Supplement* indicate which kind of court heard the case. As examples, "252 Fla. Supp. 351 (Fla. 5th Cir. Ct.) (1996)" indicates that the case is from the Fifth *Circuit* Court. "321 Fla. Supp. 823 (Miami-Dade County Ct.) (1999)" indicates that the case is from the *county* court of Miami-Dade.

The laws we have discussed—the constitutions, statutes, regulations, rules of court, and case law—can all be found in law libraries that are available to anyone who wishes to use them. Typically, each county in the state has a trial court with its own library. In addition, law schools have their own libraries, some of which are open to the public. If you would like to find a law, simply go to the reference librarians, people who can help you find what you are looking for. There are also numerous sites on the Internet that provide access to legal materials.

Our discussion of laws is not complete without mention of professional codes of ethical conduct. Codes of ethics are not considered law. They are written by private associations and may be amended without the consent or approval of an elected representative, judge, or government employee. Nevertheless, codes of ethics do establish acceptable standards of conduct

---

* "Fla. Dist. Ct. App." is the "official" way of referring to a district court of appeal's decision, and that is the way decisions of a district court of appeals will be cited in a law journal article. The other two ways of citation are also used, however, and in order to acclimate mental health professionals to what they might actually see when reading about cases, all three forms of citation are used interchangely throughout the book.

and may be adopted by state licensing boards. For this reason, it behooves a mental health professional to be intimately familiar with his or her profession's code of ethical conduct, and to think of that code as if it were law because, in a way, it is—it is the law of the profession.

One final comment. Should you find yourself faced with a legal question, *consult a lawyer who has expertise in mental health law.* Cases involving law and mental health can be exceedingly complex and require legal expertise that no book, pamphlet, or review will provide. Educating yourself about the law by reading statutes and court decisions is an enormously worthwhile endeavor. Educating yourself about brain surgery is enormously worthwhile as well. But don't go after that tumor with your Swiss army knife.

LAWS AFFECTING MENTAL HEALTH PRACTICE IN FLORIDA

I. Constitution
   A. Supreme law of the land
   B. No law may conflict with the Constitution

II. Statutes
   A. Written by the legislature
      1. United States Congress for federal laws
      2. Florida legislature for Florida laws
   B. Florida statutes referred to as, e.g., Fla. Stat. ch. 394.467 (section 467 of chapter 394 of the Florida Statutes; this citation may also be written as "section 394.467")

III. Regulations
   A. Written by agencies, with authority from the legislature
   B. Florida regulations referred to as, e.g., Fla. Admin. Code Ann. r.65E-5.290
      (Florida Administrative Code Annotated, rule 65E, section 5.290)

IV. Rules of court
   A. Adopted by the judiciary to govern judges and attorneys in court proceedings
   B. Serve as "rules of the road"
   C. Cited as, e.g.:
      1. Fla. R. Crim. P. 3.212
         (rule 3.212 of the Florida Rules of Criminal Procedure)
      2. Fla. R. Civ. P. 1.070
         (rule 1.070 of the Florida Rules of Civil Procedure)

continued

V. Cases
   A. Generally written by appellate courts
   B. Florida Supreme Court hears only cases specified by Florida Constitution
   C. Cases of the Florida Supreme Court and Florida district courts of appeals, found in the *Southern Reporter*, referred to as, e.g.:
      1. 582 So. 2d 784 (Fla. 5th Dist. Ct. App. 1991) [or "Fla. App. 5 Dist. 1991" or "Fla. 5th DCA 1991"]
         (1991 opinion of the Florida 5th District Court of Appeals, found in volume 582 of the second edition of the *Southern Reporter*, at page 784)
      2. 565 So. 2d 315 (Fla. 1990)
         (1990 opinion of the Supreme Court of Florida, found in volume 565 of the second edition of the *Southern Reporter*, at page 315)
   D. Cases of the circuit court and county courts, found in the *Florida Supplement*, referred to as, e.g.:
      1. 252 Fla. Supp. 351 (Fla. 5th Cir. Ct.) (1996)
         (1996 opinion of the Fifth Circuit Court of Florida, found in volume 252 of the *Florida Supplement*, at page 351)
      2. 321 Fla. Supp. 823 (Miami-Dade County Ct.) (1999)
         (1996 opinion of the Miami-Dade County Court, found in volume 321 of the *Florida Supplement*, at page 823)

VI. Codes of ethics
   A. Written by professional associations
   B. Establish standards of conduct for profession
   C. May be used as a guide for regulatory boards

2

TARASOFF AND
ITS FLORIDA PROGENY

Most clinicians have heard the word "Tarasoff," usually uttered with
some understandable, yet unfortunate, combination of anxiety and obligation. Of such magnitude is the aura surrounding *Tarasoff* that for many
clinicians the very word has become synonymous with the concept of
law and psychiatry. In reality, however, issues implicated by the *Tarasoff*
case and its legal progeny account for a small percentage of forensic
cases. Moreover, once the legal ruling is explained, much of the atten-
dant anxiety usually disappears. Indeed, unbeknownst to many, *Tarasoff*
entails a fascinating story.

Below is a discussion of the events that led to the *Tarasoff* case and an
analysis of the law that Florida enacted as a response. Our discussion
takes the Florida law apart, then puts it back together again, to show
how the various elements of this law form a coherent whole around a
particular set of values. The discussion then goes on to examine court
decisions that have elaborated the values behind Florida's particular
response to the *Tarasoff* decision.

The relevance of this discussion is that often a situation will arise that
has no clear corollary in the law—no case, statute, or regulation will
address directly what you should *do*. In fact, our experience is that most

situations fall into this category. When faced with such a situation, *the process by which a clinician decides what to do* becomes as important as the decision itself. The documentation of this process should show that the clinician appreciates what values are at stake and should demonstrate a thoughtful application of those values to the matter at hand. The appreciation and thoughtful application of the values embodied in a mental health law, together with the documentation of the decision-making process, will be a clinician's very best protection against liability. This chapter addresses the values important to a Florida mental health practitioner when a patient poses a threat to a third party.

THE LEGAL LANDSCAPE

To understand why the *Tarasoff* case has so captured the imagination of clinicians, one must examine two aspects of our legal system: first, how the law views legal obligations ("affirmative duties") to third parties; and second, the concept of negligence. In terms of the former, the American legal system rarely imposes affirmative duties unless two or more individuals have freely entered into a legal agreement that creates corresponding responsibilities. In legal terms, one rarely owes a duty to third parties. Take as an example that one morning I decide to go for a walk on the pier next to where I live and suddenly hear a cry for help. Should I see someone going under for the third time, there is no *legal* obligation that I do anything—I can simply keep on walking, without concern that I will be sued or charged with a crime.* Should there be a life preserver right beside me, a telephone for emergencies only feet away, I remain under no legal obligation whatsoever to act. I owe this third party no *duty*—he does not know me, I do not know him, and we have not entered into a relationship that creates affirmative duties to one another. From the law's point of view, our legal destinies are utterly independent.

An exception to this rule occurs should I begin a rescue, perhaps by picking up the life preserver and swinging it backward as if to throw it. In that case I have an obligation to make a reasonable attempt to complete the rescue. The reason behind the exception is that my commencing a rescue may serve to discourage others from acting. Hence, if I begin to

---

* This manner of behaving will not, however, get one nominated for many humanitarian awards.

act in this instance, I have an obligation to follow through. This exception notwithstanding, the overriding principle is that the law will not impose a duty to act unless and until the individuals have entered into some relationship recognized by law.

A second important concept upon which the *Tarasoff* case is built is that of *negligence*. Negligence is a form of tort. Tort is the legal term for the sort of mistake that gives rise to lawsuits in civil, as opposed to criminal, courts. Malpractice is a form of negligence, and hence is a tort.

A malpractice lawsuit is often said to consist of the "four Ds," defined as the Dereliction of a Duty Directly causing Damages. Each of the four Ds is an essential element of a malpractice claim. If any one D is missing, the lawsuit cannot succeed. You might think of the four Ds as the wheels on a car—if even one wheel is gone, the car stays put. In the example above, should the individual in the water drown and his estate attempt to sue me, my defense will be that I had no duty toward him and so cannot be held liable for negligence. One of the wheels is missing, so the suit cannot go anywhere. Likewise, in cases where there is dereliction of a duty, yet no damages, a suit for malpractice fails. This makes intuitive sense—no matter how bad my mistake, if you suffer no harm, you should not be able to collect moneys from me. Similarly, if I am derelict in my duty, yet my dereliction does not directly cause your damages, a suit in negligence cannot prevail. Again, this makes sense. If I make a mistake, and you happen to suffer a harm, yet it was not *my* mistake that caused your harm, I should not be held responsible for compensating you.

In a malpractice case, the plaintiff—the person who claims to have been harmed and is consequently bringing the lawsuit—must demonstrate by a preponderance of evidence, or more than 50% (see part II, question 4), that each of the four Ds is present. Each D has its own complexities; the manner in which one calculates damages, for example, can be enormously intricate, as can be showing direct causation. Dereliction of duty, also called "breach of duty," is somewhat unique, insofar as the standard by which to judge whether one is derelict remains constant— for those in the medical profession, one must provide care that is *reasonable*. One need not provide the best, most expensive, or most up-to-date care available; one only need provide care that is within the standard of practice of an average member of the profession practicing within her specialty. Should one provide care that falls below this standard, one can be considered derelict in one's duty.

Defining the fourth D, that of duty, involves answering two questions.

The first question is: *What* duty is owed? That is to say, I must determine precisely what my legal obligation entails. The second question is: *To whom* is the duty owed? Now that I know what I must do, to whose benefit must I do it? It was in answering these two questions that the *Tarasoff* case broke new ground.

THE FOUR "D'S" OF NEGLIGENCE

I. Dereliction
    A. The mental health professional must provide care that is **reasonable**.
    B. Care is considered reasonable if it is **within the standard of practice of an average member of the profession practicing within her specialty**.
    C. If the care falls below what is reasonable, the mental health professional is derelict in his or her duty.

    No dereliction = The lawsuit for malpractice fails

II. Duty
    The mental health professional **has a legal relationship** with an individual that gives rise to a duty.
    A. What is the duty? (An important point in *Tarasoff*)
    B. To whom is the duty owed? (An important point in *Tarasoff*)

    No duty = The lawsuit for malpractice fails

III. Directly causing
    The dereliction of duty must **directly cause** the damages.

    No direct causation = The lawsuit for malpractice fails

IV. Damages
    The person bringing a negligence suit must have **suffered harm**.

    No damages = The lawsuit for malpractice fails

THE FACTS OF THE CASE

Early in July of 1969 a young man named Prosenjit Poddar arrived at an appointment to see a clinician at the University of California, Berkeley, student health center. Poddar, a 25-year-old graduate student, had come to the student health center at the urging of a friend who had become concerned over Poddar's obsession with a 19-year-old undergraduate, Tatianna Tarasoff. By the time Poddar arrived at the student health center that summer he had been transformed from a student with enormous potential and industriousness into a loner who spent hour upon hour in his room listening to secretly recorded audiotapes of his conversations with Tatianna. After meeting at a folk dance for international students nearly a year earlier, Poddar and Tatianna had shared a lingering flirtation but, to Poddar's great disappointment, no more.

Following his initial appointment at the student health center, Poddar began treatment with a clinical psychologist, Dr. Lawrence Moore. Poddar told Dr. Moore that he was going to kill a girl whom he did not name, but who was identifiable as Tatianna. Shortly thereafter, Poddar left therapy, almost certainly in response to Dr. Moore's statement that he would have to restrain Poddar should Poddar continue to talk of killing Tatianna. After consulting with colleagues, Dr. Moore wrote a letter to the Berkeley police that read, in part:

> He is at this point a danger to the welfare of other people and himself. That is, he has been threatening to kill an unnamed girl who he feels has betrayed him and has violated his honor. He has told a friend . . . that he intends to go to San Francisco to buy a gun and that he plans to kill the girl. . . . Mr. Poddar should be committed for observation in a mental hospital. (Winslade & Ross, 1983)

The campus police found and questioned Poddar. After extracting from Poddar a promise to stay away from Tatianna, however, the police released him. The director of the department of psychiatry then ordered that Poddar not be committed to a psychiatric hospital. Neither the campus police nor anyone at the student health center warned Tatianna or her parents of Poddar's threat. A short time later, on October 27, Poddar went to Tatianna's home and killed her.

Tatianna's parents brought a lawsuit against a number of individuals at UC Berkeley, including Dr. Moore and his colleagues. Their claim was based upon an action in negligence: The treaters had been derelict in their duty to warn Tatianna of Poddar's threat, a dereliction that directly caused Tatianna's death. The therapists—now defendants in the lawsuit—responded that they had no relationship with Tatianna, and so had no duty toward her. In the absence of a duty, they reasoned, a lawsuit could not succeed. They argued that, in addition to owing no duty to Tatianna, therapist-patient confidentiality prohibited them from disclosing this information. The defendants argued that the case was open and shut: What happened to Tatianna was a tragedy but, with one of the four Ds (duty) missing and with the constraints of confidentiality, a tragedy that had no place being decided in a court of law.

The lawsuit had an extremely high profile because of its possible impli-cations. If Tatianna Tarasoff's parents were to prevail, therapists could have a duty toward people with whom they had no professional relationship, per-haps whom they had never met nor even seen. While courts had held psy-chiatrists responsible for damage done when their patients were prematurely released or had escaped from an inpatient psychiatric facility, this case was different: Poddar was an outpatient and Dr. Moore was a psy-chologist, raising the specter that the ruling would encompass all mental health professionals, who could henceforth be held responsible for harms committed by *any* of their patients. The American Psychiatric Association judged the case to be of such import that it entered the fray as an *amicus curiae*, Latin for "friend of the court." An amicus curiae is an organization which, while neither a plaintiff nor a defendant, nevertheless has an interest in the outcome of a case. The APA, fearing that with the stroke of a pen the court might significantly increase the number of individuals who could sue a therapist and win, argued "that even when a therapist does in fact predict that a patient poses a serious danger of violence to others, the therapist should be absolved of any responsibility for failing to act to protect the potential victim" (*Tarasoff* at 345). Put in other words, the APA wanted a blanket rule that a therapist is not liable to third parties whom a patient injures, even if the therapist could predict that the patient would be violent.

The court's first order of business was to examine whether there was any sort of relationship between Dr. Moore and Tatianna that the law would recognize. Such a relationship would give rise to a duty and so sup-ply the missing D. To address this question the court reviewed case law that held that a duty may arise when there is a "special relationship" between two individuals. A special relationship, the court explained, could give rise to affirmative duties toward third persons in cases where a third person is the foreseeable victim of some harm. The court examined the doctor-patient relationship between Dr. Moore and Poddar and con-cluded that it was indeed this sort of special relationship. Thus, the court reasoned, because of Dr. Moore's special relationship to Poddar, Dr. Moore owed a duty to Tatianna Tarasoff, the foreseeable victim of Poddar's harm. Put another way, the court concluded *that Dr. Moore had a duty to Tatianna Tarasoff because she was the foreseeable victim of his patient's harm.* In less than two pages, the court had supplied the absent D.*

* Part of the court's thinking may well have been that the "special" nature of the therapist-patient relationship makes it likely that a patient would tell a therapist about feelings of wanting to hurt someone.

Having concluded that Dr. Moore and his colleagues did owe Tatianna a duty, the court's next order of business was to determine how that duty should be defined. Perhaps the greatest misunderstanding about the *Tarasoff* case is on precisely this point. The court stated,

> [O]nce a therapist does in fact determine, or under applicable professional standards reasonably should have determined, that a patient poses a serious danger of violence to others, he bears a duty to exercise reasonable care *to protect* [italics added] the foreseeable victim of that danger. (345)

The *Tarasoff* case held that the duty a therapist owes to third parties is the duty *to protect*—not, as is commonly misunderstood, the duty *to warn*.

The court was then presented with the question of how broad a circle of potential victims the duty to protect should encompass. Again the APA weighed in, arguing "that warnings must be given only in those cases in which the therapist knows the identity of the victim." The APA's approach could be characterized as, "Therapists should not be liable to third parties at all, but if the court decides they are, they should be liable only to those third parties who have been identified." The *Tarasoff* court was not so restrictive in its thinking. Addressing the question of whether a therapist must know exactly who the potential victim is before a duty arises, the court explained,

> [I]n some cases it would be unreasonable to require the therapist to interrogate his patient to discover the victim's identity, or to conduct an independent investigation. But there may also be cases in which a moment's reflection will reveal the victim's identity. The matter thus is one which depends upon the circumstances of each case, and should not be governed by any hard and fast rule. (345)

The court left open the possibility that the duty to protect could extend to individuals whom the therapist had not yet identified, yet who could be known after "a moment's reflection." This seemingly innocuous comment has given rise to an enormous debate over the extent to which a therapist must know, or be able to determine, who the potential victim is before a duty to that third person arises. Some states, for example, require that the potential victim be identified before any duty arises. Other states have been far more expansive, creating a duty to protect when it becomes clear that anyone—regardless who—will be harmed. Below we will see how Florida has dealt with this issue.

The *Tarasoff* case examined the second of the four Ds—duty—in a way that no court had done before. The court answered the two central questions about the duty owed by a therapist to a third party: The duty owed is the duty *to protect,* and the duty is owed to *foreseeable victims of harm who can be identified after "a moment's reflection."* The heart of the case, however, lies in how it directly pitted two values—confidentiality and public safety—against one another. There was no way to finagle. Given the way the court framed the issue, it had to choose one value at the expense of the other. The court came down decidedly in favor of public safety. In perhaps its most famous quotation, the *Tarasoff* court concluded,

> the public policy favoring protection of the confidential character of patient-psychotherapist communications must yield to the extent to which disclosure is essential to avert danger to others. *The protective privilege ends where the public peril begins* [italics added]. (347)

The balance struck by the court—that confidentiality must yield to public safety—is the foundation of the *Tarasoff* ruling. Before turning to see how the state of Florida has addressed the issues raised by the *Tarasoff* decision, we leave the reader with two historical notes on what happened to those most intimately involved with Tatianna's murder.

In the criminal matter, Poddar was charged with first degree murder. After a trial, at which much evidence concerning his mental status was heard, he was found guilty of second-degree murder and sent to a state prison. Poddar appealed and, five years later, the California Supreme Court overturned his conviction. The state was then in the position of putting Poddar on trial again for Tatianna's murder; instead, however, the prosecutor struck a bargain with Poddar's attorney. In exchange for not retrying the criminal case, Poddar's attorney would ensure that Poddar would return home and not come back to the United States. Today Poddar is married and living in India.

In the civil matter, the California Supreme Court announced its rule of law—that therapists have a duty to protect foreseeable victims of harm who can be identified after a moment's reflection—and instructed the trial court to apply this rule of law to determine whether Dr. Moore and his colleagues had been negligent in fulfilling their duty. Questions of fact before the trial court would therefore have been: Was Tatianna Tarasoff a foreseeable victim of Poddar's harm? If so, did Dr. Moore and his colleagues fulfill their duty to protect Tatianna by notifying the campus police? If notifying the police did *not* suffice to fulfill their duty to protect, did their failure to take additional steps to fulfill their duty to protect directly cause Tatianna's death? Before the case could make it back to the trial court, however, the parties reached a settlement. For a sum of money (that was never disclosed) Tatianna's parents agreed to dismiss the lawsuit. As a consequence, no clinician involved in Prosenjit Poddar's care was ever held liable for negligence in a court of law.

THE FLORIDA *TARASOFF* STATUTE

Section 455.671*

Communications between a patient and a psychiatrist . . . shall be held confidential and shall not be disclosed except upon the request of the patient or the patient's legal representative. . . . Notwithstanding any other provision of this section . . . where:

(1) A patient is engaged in a treatment relationship with a psychiatrist;
(2) Such patient has made an actual threat to physically harm an identifiable victim or victims; and
(3) The treating psychiatrist makes a clinical judgment that the patient has the apparent capability to commit such an act and that it is more likely than not that in the near future the patient will carry out that threat, the psychiatrist may disclose patient communications to the extent necessary to warn any potential victim or to communicate the threat to a law enforcement agency. No civil or criminal action shall be instituted, and there shall be no liability on account of the disclosure of otherwise confidential communications by a psychiatrist in disclosing a threat pursuant to this section.

* Before July 1, 1997, section 455.671 was section 455.2415. Materials written before July 1, 1997, will therefore refer to section 455.2415 when discussing disclosures of confidential information following a patient's threat. Our discussion uses section 455.671 throughout.

An outline of the essential elements of section 455.671 is found on page 26.

FLORIDA AND THE ISSUE OF *TARASOFF*

There are nine aspects of Florida law on this issue that are important to discuss. First, each major mental health discipline has its own statute. Section 455.671 applies to psychiatrists, section 490.0147 applies to licensed psychologists, and section 491.0147 applies to licensed social workers, licensed marriage and family therapists, licensed mental health counselors, and certified masters social workers. A mental health professional should be sure to read the statute that applies to his or her discipline. This discussion will focus on section 455.671, because that statute is the most complex and has been the subject of important court decisions. The same analysis that will be used to examine section 455.671, however, can be applied to sections 490.0147 and 491.0147 (which can be found in appendix A) as well.

Second, Florida district courts have directly commented upon the meaning and scope of these statutes. What is interesting and important from a mental health law perspective is that the *common law* rule concerning a mental health professional's duty, as set forth by Florida courts, is consistent with the rule the Florida legislature has enacted through *statutes*. That is to say, Florida courts and the Florida legislature are in agreement about what the rule is—the common law duty and the statutory duty go hand-in-hand. If, however, the Florida legislature changed the rule, Florida courts would be bound to follow the new statute. Because both courts and the legislature have explicitly addressed this issue, it is important for Florida mental health professionals to read the statute itself and to be aware of what Florida courts have said about a mental health professional's duty when a patient threatens a third party. Below we discuss section 455.671 and four district court cases that have made important rulings.

Third, section 455.671 begins by emphasizing that communications between a patient and a psychiatrist are confidential. The statute therefore represents an exception to the rule of confidentiality. As a consequence, only when the specific conditions set forth in the statute are met can confidential communications be disclosed. Mental health professionals must therefore check to ensure that all the provisions of section 455.671 are present before discussing any confidential information outside the treatment relationship.

Fourth, the language in paragraph (1) of section 455.671 applies narrowly to a psychiatrist who has a treatment relationship with a patient. Florida courts have read this language expansively by holding that it applies to *any* practicing mental health professional (see the discussion of the *Boynton* case below). Moreover while section 455.671 does not define "treatment relationship," one of the leading cases in this area (see below) discusses section 455.671 in the context of a relationship that consisted of a single visit to a psychiatrist's office. As a consequence, it seems that Florida courts might well also take an expansive view of what constitutes a treatment relationship.

Fifth, paragraph (2) of section 455.671 sets forth the nature of the threat that permits a disclosure of information. The threat must be an "actual" threat to "physically harm" an "identifiable victim." Note both the specificity and ambiguity of this clause. The threat must be "actual," but section 455.671 does not require that it be in words. Presumably a patient could communicate an actual threat without using words, by making clear an intent to harm without using language to convey that intent. Likewise, the language "identifiable victim" suggests that the victim's actual name need not be known. What appears important is that the victim is *able* to be identified through information provided by the patient. The effect of paragraph (2) is to provide guidance, but not definitive answers. The clinician should ask—has my patient actually threatened physically to harm someone whom I can identify? If so, the clinician should go on to ask whether the conditions in paragraph (3) are present.

Sixth, paragraph (3) contains the final set of conditions that must be met before section 455.671 will permit a disclosure of information. Paragraph (3) requires a clinical judgment. The judgment is that the patient has the "apparent capability" to carry out the threat and that it is "more likely than not" that the threat will be carried out in the "near" future. Note that paragraph (3) is asking the clinician to do several things: assess whether the patient is capable of carrying out the threat; assess the likelihood that the patient will actually carry out the threat; and assess whether the harm will occur soon. If the clinician judges that the patient does not have the capability of carrying out the threat, or that there is less than a 50% chance the threat will be carried out, or that the harm will not occur in the near future, section 455.671 will not permit a disclosure of information.

Seventh, *if* all the conditions in paragraphs (1), (2), and (3) are present, section 455.671 permits the clinician to disclose otherwise confidential information. Note that the statute's language is permissive—unlike in many other states, mental health professionals in Florida are not *required* to disclose information in the face of a patient's threat to harm a third party. Florida law does not impose a duty to act. Section 455.671 is not a mandatory reporting statute. A Florida mental health professional cannot successfully be sued for failing to warn a third party. Section 455.671 states that when a certain set of conditions are present, a mental health professional *may*, if she chooses, disclose certain information to a potential victim or to a law enforcement agency. Whether she will do so resides in her professional discretion. Note the shift from the *Tarasoff* decision. *Tarasoff* said that when faced with a choice between confidentiality and public safety, the mental health professional has a *duty* to choose public safety. Florida takes this choice out of the hands of the law and places it in the hands of the clinician. Florida does not so much rearrange the values struck by *Tarasoff* as it relocates where that decision will be made—in the mental health professional's office, rather than in the state legislature or courthouse.

Eighth, section 455.671 states that information may be disclosed "to the extent necessary" to provide an appropriate warning. This language is consistent with the Parsimony Principle (see chapter 3). Any disclosure of otherwise confidential information should be limited to the purpose for which the disclosure is made. If the purpose of the disclosure is to provide a warning, the disclosure should consist of the information necessary for the victim to protect him or herself, or for the police to protect the victim. The disclosure of any other information falls outside the scope of section 455.671 and is therefore not permitted by this statute.

Ninth, section 455.671 states that should the conditions set forth in paragraphs (1) through (3) be present, the clinician cannot be held liable for disclosing confidential material. This element restates the balance struck in *Tarasoff*—confidentiality yields to matters of safety—and, as a corollary to this balance, releases clinicians from liability when they further safety at the expense of confidentiality.

In several important cases Florida district courts have addressed the question of whether a mental health professional is under a legal obligation to warn third parties of a patient's threat. Perhaps the most well known of these cases is *Boynton v. Burglass*, 590 So. 2d 446 (Fla. App. 3 Dist. 1991). The facts of the *Boynton* case were straightforward. Milton Burglass, a psychiatrist, had been treating Lawrence Blaylock on an outpatient basis. In May of 1986, Blaylock shot and killed Wayne Boynton, Jr. Boynton's parents then brought a lawsuit against Dr. Burglass, in which they alleged that Dr. Burglass had failed to warn Wayne Boynton, Jr. or the police that Blaylock had threatened serious harm and was prone to violence. According to the lawsuit, Dr. Burglass was negligent in this respect, and his negligence had caused Wayne Boynton Jr.'s death. The 3rd District Court of Appeals took the case as one of "first impression," that is, as an issue that no Florida Court had ruled on before. The Court's analysis was brief and its conclusion unambiguous: Mental health professionals in Florida have no duty to warn a potential victim of danger posed by a voluntary outpatient. The court based its conclusion on three reasons.

First, the district court of appeals explored the history behind the concept of a "special relationship" that had figured so prominently in the *Tarasoff* decision. As sometimes happens when different state courts address the same issue, the Florida court came to a different conclusion than had the California court about what circumstances constitute a special relationship. According to the California court, a special relationship creating a duty arises when a third party is the foreseeable victim of a patient's harm. According to the Florida district court of appeals, a duty can arise out of a special relationship only when the person upon whom the duty is to be imposed has the ability or the right to control the patient's behavior. The Florida district court of appeals was thus "linking" two conditions: the ability or right to control the patient, and the liability that flows from harm that a patient inflicts on a third party. The court reasoned that where there is no ability or right to control, there can be no liability for what the patient does.

Second, the court reasoned that "[b]ecause psychiatry is, at best, an inexact science, courts should be reluctant to impose liability upon psychiatrists" (*Boynton* at 449). The court was extremely skeptical of psychiatry's ability to predict dangerousness. Remarking that "the internal workings of the human mind remain largely mysterious" (at 450), the court explained that:

> To impose a duty to warn or protect third parties would require the psychiatrist to foresee a harm which may or may not be foreseeable, depending on the clarity of his crystal ball. Because of the inherent difficulties psychiatrists face in predicting a patient's dangerousness, psychiatrists cannot be charged with accurately making those predictions and with sharing those predictions with others. (at 450)

Thus, the court concluded, psychiatrists should be under no legal duty to predict when a patient will harm a third party.

Finally, the court looked to how imposing a duty to warn or protect would affect the treatment relationship. The court began by noting that "[c]onfidentiality is the cornerstone of the psychiatrist-patient relationship" (at 451), and then said that a duty to warn would "not only run afoul of the psychiatrist-patient confidentiality privilege, but would also severely hamper, if not destroy, the relationship of trust and confidence that is crucial to the treatment of mental illness" (at 451). The court concluded that "[r]equiring a psychiatrist to breach that privilege in order to warn a third party would inhibit the free expression vital to diagnosis and treatment and would, thus, undermine the very goals of psychiatric treatment" (at 451).

The court ruled that a psychiatrist has no duty to warn or protect a third party from the harm posed by a voluntary outpatient. The ruling was based on three reasons: first, a psychiatrist has neither the ability or the right to control a voluntary outpatient; second, predicting dangerousness is an inherently unreliable endeavor; and third, imposing a duty to warn would undermine effective psychiatric treatment. In refusing to impose a duty to warn or protect, the court made an additional point that mental health professionals should note: The decision applies "equally to psychologists, psychotherapists, and other mental health practitioners" (at 448). The *Boynton* ruling should therefore be read as applying to all practicing clinicians.

Two other district court cases that speak to the issue of a duty to warn or protect third parties are worthy of note. In *Santa Cruz v. N.W. Dade Com. Health Ctr.* 590 So. 2d 444 (Fla. App. 3 Dist. 1991), the district court of appeals reasoned that " '[o]ne who takes charge' is one who has the right and the duty to control the [patient's] behavior, as would be true in the case of a committed inpatient" (*Santa Cruz* at 445). The court ruled that because Northwest Dade Community Health Center had not taken charge of a patient (did not have custody of a patient) who shot a third party, Northwest Dade did not owe a duty to the third party to control the patient's behavior. Note how *Santa Cruz* and *Boynton* both link the issue of *control* to the issue of *duty*—if a mental health professional cannot exercise control over a patient, then the mental health professional cannot be held responsible for what the patient does to a third party.

Green v. Ross, 691 So. 2d 542 (Fla. App. 2 Dist. 1997), follows from *Boynton* and *Santa Cruz*. In *Green*, the court made two points relevant to the question of a mental health professional's duty to warn a third party. First, the court emphasized that the language of section 455.671 is *permissive*. Mental health professionals *may*, but are *not required*, to disclose confidential material to warn a third party or the police of a patient's threat. Second, the court said that the legislature, rather than a court, should make any change in the law that would bring about a duty to warn victims of a patient's possible violence. Put another way, the court reasoned that a change in the law should occur in the State House, rather than in a court house.

One case decided by a district court of appeal, *O'Keefe v. Orea*, 731 So. 2d 680 (Fla. App. 1 Dist. 1998), appears to stray from the Florida rule that mental health professionals do not have a duty to warn third parties of a patient's threat. *O'Keefe* involved a psychiatrist, Dr. Orea, who was treating Christopher O'Keefe, a 17-year-old boy, for a variety of symptoms, which included abrupt, out-of-character, and violent attacks on individuals whom Christopher knew well and apparently liked and respected a great deal. Part of the treatment involved Dr. Orea consulting to Christopher's parents. Following three such attacks, Christopher was hospitalized; when Dr. Orea determined that Christopher was stable enough for discharge, Christopher returned to live with his parents. Four days after his discharge—and following a telephone call in which Mrs. O'Keefe told Dr. Orea that Christopher appeared out of control and could not be contained in the family home—Christopher attacked both his parents and killed his father. Mrs. O'Keefe then brought a negligence lawsuit against Dr. Orea, in which she claimed that he had an obligation to warn or protect her and her husband because of Christopher's propensity for violence.

The court held that Dr. Orea did owe a duty to warn Christopher's parents about their son's condition. In its opinion, however, the court stated explicitly that it was "unnecessary to reach the *Boynton/Tarasoff* 'duty to warn' issue" in order to decide the case. Rather, the court reasoned that "Dr. Orea's duty to warn the O'Keefes concerning their son's condition derives *from the fiduciary relationship* between Dr. Orea and the parents of his minor patient, as well as [from] *the physician-patient relationship* between Dr. Orea and Mr. and Mrs. O'Keefe." The court explained that "[i]n view of these fiduciary relationships," Dr. Orea had a legal duty to Christopher's parents. Note that in reaching its decision, the court limits its ruling—that Dr. Orea had a duty to warn—to treatments that involve a child and that include the parents. While *O'Keefe* can be interpreted as straying from the general rule that a mental health professional has no duty to warn or protect third parties, the court's language—especially the statement that it would *not* reach the *Boynton/Tarasoff* duty to warn issue—limits its relevance to child cases where parents are part of the treatment.*

* For a discussion of *Paddock v. Chacko*, 522 So. 2d 410 (Fla. App. 5 Dist. 1988), see question 49.

FLORIDA AND THE ISSUE OF *TARASOFF*

Section 455.671

I.   Communications between a mental health professional and a patient are confidential. A disclosure of confidential information is permitted when the conditions set forth in section 455.671 are met.

II.   Section 455.671 should be read in the context of Florida court opinions that address the issue of a patient's threats to harm a third party.
   A.   Common law and statutes agree.
   B.   Florida legislature could rewrite statute and courts would be bound to follow new rule.

III.   Section 455.671 applies to a psychiatrist in a treatment relationship.
   A.   The statute has been interpreted by courts to apply to all mental health practitioners.
   B.   "Treatment relationship" may be understood in a similarly broad fashion.

IV.   To fall under the provisions of section 455.671, the threat must be:
   A.   an **actual** threat
   B.   to inflict **physical** harm
   C.   an **identifiable** victim.

V.   If a patient makes an actual threat to inflict physical harm on an identifiable victim, the mental health professional must make a clinical judgement that:
   A.   the patient has the **apparent capability** to carry out the threat,
   B.   it is **more likely than not** the patient will carry out the threat, and
   C.   the threat will be carried out in the **near** future.

VI.   If all the conditions set forth in section 455.671 are met, the mental health professional has the discretion to disclose confidential information to:
   A.   the potential victim or
   B.   a law enforcement agency.

VII.   Disclosures should be made only "to the extent necessary" to achieve purpose of warning a potential victim so that victim's safety may be protected.

VIII.   A clinician will not be held liable for disclosing confidential information if acting in accordance with the provisions of section 455.671.

IX.   Other statutes contain similar language and pertain to other mental health disciplines.
   A.   Section 490.0147 for psychologists
   B.   Section 491.0147 for social workers, marriage and family therapists, and mental health counselors

CONCLUSION

Each state is its own sovereignty. Each state may decide for itself what laws to enact and how to balance important values against one another in writing its laws. California held that a mental health professional has a duty to protect an identifiable third party when a patient has threatened that person harm. Florida has decided that a mental health professional is free to use her own judgment about how best to balance public safety and confidentiality. Both statutes and court decisions make clear that mental health professionals in Florida are under no *duty* to protect a third party from harm inflicted by a voluntary outpatient. A malpractice case based on such a duty therefore cannot succeed.

Having examined the *Tarasoff* decision and Florida's response, we now turn to a series of statutes and regulations central to mental health law, those governing privacy, confidentiality, and testimonial privilege. Our discussion of these laws forms the body of the following chapter; the actual texts of important privacy, confidentiality, and privilege laws are found in appendix A. As you read, notice both what the laws say and how they are put together. Your understanding of how these statutes and regulations embody a coherent set of values will be an invaluable resource when confronted with a dilemma in your own practice.

3

PRIVACY, CONFIDENTIALITY, AND TESTIMONIAL PRIVILEGE

Privacy, confidentiality, and testimonial privilege affect the day-to-day life of a clinician perhaps more than any other area of mental health law, yet they remain elusive concepts. We sense that each of these words captures something important, but also feel a general fuzziness about what they share with one another and, perhaps more important, what is unique to each. And so we begin with definitions.

DEFINITIONS

Privacy is a right that stems from an underlying value central to our society, that of individual autonomy. Autonomy is a highly valued right because, as a society, we believe in self-determination: Individuals have the right to lead their lives however they choose, provided their choices do not unreasonably interfere with the choices others wish to make. Autonomy is therefore an active concept.

The privacy right that flows from the value of individual autonomy is more passive. In *Olmstead v. United States*, 277 U.S. 438 (1928), Justice Brandeis, a famous Justice of the United States Supreme Court, remarked that the right to privacy is "the right to be let alone—the most compre-hensive of rights and the right most valued by civilized men." Justice Brandeis's definition captures the notion that privacy is a right that pre-vents others, especially the government, from unduly interfering with our lives. Because the active right of autonomy (an individual's right to deter-mine the course of her life) is so completely intertwined with its passive compliment, the right to privacy (the right to be let alone), many aspects of autonomy, such as the right to decide how to educate one's children, the right to decide upon a profession, the right to travel where one pleases, the right to choose "what [one] eats, wears, or reads," (*Kent v. Dulles*, 357 U.S. 116 (1958), at 125–126), are commonly referred to as "privacy rights." Our focus, however, will be on the privacy right that allows us to be "let alone."

Confidentiality is an aspect, or subset, of privacy. Confidentiality in the clinical context is the right to have things that are communicated to a mental health professional kept in confidence, that is, not revealed to individuals outside the professional relationship. We refer to such indi-viduals as "third parties." Confidentiality has legal, ethical, and interper-sonal dimensions. From a *legal* perspective, a mental health professional has an obligation to ensure that what a patient communicates to her stays with her. From an *ethical* perspective, confidentiality is premised upon values our society holds dear, those of privacy and individual autonomy. Confidentiality ensures that patients are free to decide for themselves with whom they will share what is most intimate to them and that what they choose to share will remain private. From an *interper-sonal* perspective, confidentiality goes to the very heart of the profes-sional relationship. Protecting the sanctity of a patient's communications provides a safe haven for the patient to share the most intimate aspects of her life experience. To keep communications confidential is to treat the patient with dignity and respect and so to build trust. Trust is the foundation that creates and defines the space where two people may work together toward a mutual goal. The promise of confidentiality and privilege is thus the foundation of a successful clinical relationship.

Testimonial privilege, often referred to simply as "privilege," flows from the very same values as does confidentiality—the values of privacy and individual autonomy—but is a concept narrower in both theory and prac-tice. Testimonial privilege is the patient's right to keep confidential com-munications from being disclosed in a legal proceeding. When the privilege applies, a patient has the prerogative to prevent a mental health professional from testifying or releasing records in a court of law, a deposition, or an administrative hearing (in short, any sort of legal proceeding). When a patient decides not to allow a mental health professional to disclose confidential information, the patient is said to "invoke privilege." When a patient invokes privilege, the mental health professional may not discuss the patient or release any of the patient's records in a legal proceeding unless a statute creates an exception to privilege or a court orders the mental health professional to disclose otherwise confidential information. A client who voluntarily authorizes a mental health professional to testify or release records in a legal proceeding is said to "waive privilege."

Note the tension between the values that lie behind testimonial privilege and the truth-finding mission of a court. The tension arises because testimonial privilege keeps information out of the judicial system. When an individual invokes privilege, information that may be relevant to a legal proceeding is not admitted into evidence, which is why lawyers say that "privilege suppresses truth." Put another way, we could seek complete candor and truth in all legal proceedings were we willing to expose the most intimate details of relationships our society holds dear. However, because of the value we place on preserving the sanctity of certain relationships (such as that between a husband and a wife, a psychotherapist and a patient, a priest and a penitent, an attorney and a client), we declare these relationships "off limits" to the law. We call these relationships "privileged." Because testimonial privilege limits the amount of information available to the legal system, judges tend to stick very close to the letter of the law when they interpret testimonial privilege statutes. Generally, a judge will deem privileged only those relationships explicitly named by the statute. For the most part, a relationship not named in the law cannot hide behind the cloak of privilege to avoid exposure in a legal proceeding.

THREE GUIDELINES

The laws that govern privacy, confidentiality, and testimonial privilege can be enormously complex when applied in practice. It is therefore helpful to have certain general principles in mind when assessing your legal responsibilities to keep confidential—or to disclose—something your client has communicated to you. These three guidelines will help as you make your way through this important, yet complicated, area of mental health law.

First, the statutes that deal with privacy, confidentiality, and testimonial privilege are based on a presumption: With respect to privacy, a mental health professional's foremost obligation is to her client. A mental health professional's first instinct should *always* be to keep client communications confidential. The presumption of confidentiality, however, is not absolute. In certain circumstances, the obligation a mental health professional owes to keep private what a patient reveals must be balanced against interests of our society as a whole. An example of an important societal interest is the safety of children. Sometimes the law determines that a societal interest outweighs the client's right to privacy and confidentiality and so creates an exception to confidentiality. A mental health professional will disclose confidential information only when the law explicitly creates an exception to the general presumption of confidentiality.

Second, a mental health professional must pay attention not only to whether patient communications will be kept in confidence or disclosed; a mental health professional must also consider *how* she will disclose information if the necessity of doing so arises. Neither state laws nor principles of professional ethics fully address how mental health professionals should behave in these circumstances. We suggest two principles to guide professional conduct whenever a mental health professional is called upon to disclose information a patient has communicated. We refer to these two principles as the "Law of No Surprises" and the "Parsimony Principle."

The Law of No Surprises says simply that a clinician should take every reasonable step to inform a client about the circumstances that will warrant a disclosure of confidential information to a third party. The Law of No Surprises is founded upon a clinical truism: You never want your client to be surprised when you disclose confidential information. Explaining the limits to confidentiality at the beginning of your work will lay the groundwork should the need to disclose confidential information arise and will not leave your client feeling as if you were working behind her back. (Words you never want a client to begin a sentence with are: "You didn't tell me you were going to tell . . .") The Law of No Surprises is consistent with statutes and codes of ethics that require a mental health professional to tell a client at the beginning of the relationship what circumstances will necessitate a breach of confidentiality. A corollary to the Law of No Surprises says that, in order to minimize any possibility of surprise or confusion, a disclosure of information should be done together with the client whenever possible.

Our second rule that governs the disclosure of confidential information is the Parsimony Principle. The Parsimony Principle says that a mental health professional only discloses that information necessary to achieve the purpose of the disclosure, and no more. If, for example, you receive a call from an emergency room physician who needs to have certain information about a suicidal client, you provide information that will help the physician assess and formulate a plan to protect your client's safety. No more. If you are making a referral for an MRI, you may choose to share that your client suffers from an anxiety disorder since her anxiety may make it difficult for her to tolerate lying in a long, dark tube. There is no reason to share that she also suffers from an eating disorder. To put the Parsimony Principle another way: Determine what information is necessary and sufficient to address the need for disclosure and disclose only that information. The Law of No Surprises and the Parsimony Principle are guides for all mental health professionals when they must disclose confidential information.

The third and final guideline is that every mental health professional must look to her profession's code of ethics before disclosing confidential information. Each major mental health discipline has its own code of ethics, and every ethics code speaks to the issue of confidentiality. If, in disclosing confidential information, a mental health professional violates that code, she runs the risks of being disciplined by her professional association, of being considered negligent for deviating from her profession's standard of care and, because certain ethical principles are reflected in statutes that regulate mental health professions, of being disciplined by the state's regulatory board. Often codes of ethics require a more stringent standard of behavior than does the law (see question 128 for a discussion of a circumstance in which what is legally permissible might not be ethically permissible). For this reason, read and become familiar with your profession's code of ethics.

LAWS THAT GOVERN PRIVACY

The right to privacy is found in the United States Constitution. While the word "privacy" is not mentioned in the actual text of the Constitution, the Supreme Court has said that a number of the Constitution's amendments have penumbras—a word whose Latin roots mean "almost a shadow"—under which the right to privacy falls. As an example, the Supreme Court has read the word "liberty" in the Fourteenth Amendment's due process

CONFIDENTIALITY: DISCLOSURES OF INFORMATION

I. Presume that everything a patient communicates to you is confidential.

II. If a question of disclosing a patient communication arises, consider whether any exception to confidentiality created by law permits or requires the disclosure.

III. If the disclosure is to take place in a legal proceeding, consider whether any exception to testimonial privilege permits or requires the disclosure.

IV. Law of No Surprises, Parsimony Principle, and professional codes of ethics govern all disclosures of patient communications.
   A. Law of No Surprises
      1. Inform client at outset that there are limits to confidentiality.
         a. Give general contours of limits to confidentiality at initial session.
         b. Emphasize that client will be notified of any disclosures.
         c. Document your discussion.
      2. Whenever possible, make client part of disclosure process, up to and including having the client make the actual disclosure when appropriate.
      3. Consider giving client informed consent letter at first session.
   B. Parsimony Principle
      1. Determine what information is necessary and sufficient to meet purpose of disclosure.
      2. Disclose only that information.
   C. Professional codes of ethics
      1. Each major mental health discipline has a code of ethics.
   2. Florida statutes that regulate mental health professions embed some ethical principles. These ethical principles may then be used to evaluate whether professional misconduct has occurred.
      3. Often codes of ethics require a more stringent standard of behavior than does the law.

clause broadly to encompass a variety of rights never mentioned in the actual wording of the Amendment, or anywhere else in the Constitution. The Supreme Court has said that the privacy rights protected by the

Constitution—although not found in the Constitution's actual language—include an individual's decisions concerning whom to marry, how best to educate one's children, and whether to accept medical treatment.

The Florida Constitution explicitly recognizes a right to privacy. Article I, section 23 of the Florida Constitution, titled "Right to Privacy," states in part that "[e]very natural person has the right to be let alone and free from governmental intrusion into the person's private life." Thus, both the United States and the Florida Constitutions protect privacy (although, because of its more explicit wording, the Florida Constitution gives Florida courts wider latitude in protecting privacy than does the U.S. Constitution). One note: While the right to privacy protected by the United States and Florida Constitutions provides the foundation for confidentiality and testimonial privilege, in practice it is the Florida legislature and courts that provide most of the actual protections in this area for Florida mental health professionals.

LAWS THAT GOVERN CONFIDENTIALITY

Important Florida confidentiality laws discussed in this section are found in appendix A.

Statutes, regulations, and court decisions that cover each of the mental health professions, including sexual assault counselors and domestic violence advocates, protect the confidentiality of communications made by a patient in the course of the professional relationship. Florida statutes also protect the confidentiality of records of patients who receive services in either mental health treatment facilities or substance abuse facilities, or from health maintenance organizations. Insurance companies are legally bound to protect the confidentiality of psychotherapy records. Taken together, these statutes create an overriding presumption that all information concerning a mental health client is confidential. A mental health professional should assume that a patient's communications and a patient's records are to be kept confidential and should disclose confidential information only when a clear exception to confidentiality arises.

When an exception to confidentiality does arise, it is the result of a balance between patient's right to privacy (the autonomy interest) and a competing societal interest (such as a child's safety). Some exceptions to confidentiality are permissive, others are mandatory. Whether an exception is permissive or mandatory generally depends on the importance of the societal interest at stake; as an example, because society places great value upon protecting children, the duty to break confidentiality is mandatory when a child's safety is at issue. Note when reading the statutes that the permissive exceptions use the language "may" disclose and the mandatory exceptions use the language "shall" disclose.

EXCEPTIONS TO CONFIDENTIALITY

Despite the arguments that the exceptions to confidentiality swallow the rule, confidentiality is maintained in the majority of treatments conducted by mental health professionals. Essential to your work is a clear understanding of when you are and when you are not bound by confidentiality, as well as when you are bound to break confidentiality.

Keep in mind that every exception to confidentiality represents a balance of some value against the value of keeping clinical material confidential. Put another way, whenever the law authorizes or requires a breach of confidentiality, there is another interest at stake that is equal to or outweighs confidentiality. If you can hold on to this point as you read through the exceptions to confidentiality, you are well on your way to understanding this area of law. The occasions outlined by the Florida statutes that permit or require treaters to disclose otherwise confidential patient information (see appendix A for the actual texts) fall into the following eight categories:

1. client consent
2. treatment emergencies
3. public safety
4. facilitation of treatment
5. provision of mental health services
6. the legal system
7. research
8. mandatory reporting statutes

CLIENT CONSENT
The value behind confidentiality is individual autonomy. Autonomy dictates that an individual is free to decide for herself with whom she will communicate and what the content of her communications will be. The first exception to the rule of confidentiality is entirely consistent with individual autonomy: An adult client who is competent may consent to allow the mental health professional to share communications with

specified third parties. In the case of client consent, the disclosure of information furthers the client's wishes and so reinforces the value of individual autonomy. In Florida all the statutes regulating mental health practitioners contemplate a client's waiver of confidentiality as an exception to confidentiality, and this underscores an important, yet often overlooked, point: *Confidentiality belongs to the client.* Consistent with the value of autonomy, in virtually all cases it is for your client—not you—to decide with whom to share otherwise confidential information.

Many of the statutes and regulations require that a patient's consent to release confidential information or records be in writing. Written consent makes clear the nature and extent of the disclosure and will serve as a record if any unclarity or disagreement about the consent arises. A client's written consent must be legible and must give the name of the individual who is authorized to disclose the information, the individual or agency to whom the disclosure may be made, the date on which the consent to release ceases to be valid, and any limitations on how the released information may be used. When your client is a couple or a family, statutes require that you obtain the consent of each adult participant before disclosing any information. In practice, many clinicians, especially when they have a good working relationship with a client, rely on an oral consent and perhaps would even consider it patronizing or demeaning to ask a client to sign a release. While the vast majority of these clinicians will never encounter any clinical or legal difficulties from releasing information without a written consent, it is important to remember that should any misunderstanding arise the dispute will degenerate into the clinician's word against that of the client, and the clinician may be found not to have abided by her statutory obligation to obtain the client's written consent (see appendix A).

TREATMENT EMERGENCIES

The second exception to confidentiality, that of a treatment emergency, is likewise consistent with the value of autonomy. Whereas client consent is the direct expression of a client's wishes, the disclosure of confidential information in an emergency is presumed to be the expression of a client's wishes. The presumption is that most people would give the emergency precedence over confidentiality. This presumption is honored for the duration of the emergency—even if the client expressly states a wish that confidentiality not be broken. The idea behind this exception is that an emergency is no time to sort these things out, to decide whether a client's judgment is intact or whether his words are a true expression of his desires—all that can wait until after the emergency is resolved. During the course of the emergency, confidentiality will yield to treatment; that is the way most people would want it.

A treatment emergency is a circumstance in which information is necessary to protect the individual's health and physical well-being from immediate harm. In practice, you can go by the rule that an emergency is a circumstance in which a reasonable person would judge that an individual's health and physical well-being are at risk. You may disclose confidential information for the purpose of attenuating that risk; let the Parsimony Principle be your guide as you do so. As an example of an emergency communication, paramedics in an ambulance may talk to medical personnel in an emergency room regardless of whether the patient has authorized the communication.

Two points about the emergency exception to confidentiality merit discussion. First, beware of strangers claiming "emergency." Many a clinician has been duped into disclosing confidential information by a caller stating that an "emergency" necessitates releasing client information. Before discussing any client on an "emergency" basis, ask who needs to know, and what emergency necessitates disclosure. If a true emergency exists, this information can be passed on in a matter of seconds. If you have doubts, attempt to confirm the emergency before discussing your client.*

Second, when faced with a possible emergency, pay attention to the process by which you decide what to do. Your protection from a breach-of-confidentiality claim will be your documentation of the process by which you come to a decision about whether to break or to maintain your client's confidentiality. As your decision-making process unfolds, you should consider the facts as they are known to you; the reliability of your sources; the imminence of harm; alternatives to breaking confidentiality; consultations that, in an ambiguous situation, agree with the degree of the emergency and the necessity of breaking confidentiality. Your documentation should indicate that you have made a reasoned decision about what to do. What will not help is a note in the record that reads, "Emergency, disclosed confidential patient information." Although there may be very good reasons for doing so, your protection from liability—the documentation of how you came to your decision—is nowhere

* We owe a debt to Jay Patel, M.D., for emphasizing this important point to us.

to be found in such a note. Rather, your note should indicate clearly why you shared information with a third party, "Received call from emergency personnel at approximately 3 P.M. Patient P.B. was found unconscious at her residence; attempts to revive P.B. were under way at that time. EMT asked what medication P.B. was prescribed and whether I was aware of any other substances P.B. may have ingested. I provided EMT names and doses of medication, and stated that P.B. had a recent history of abusing benzodiazapenes." The necessity of disclosing confidential information is immediately apparent upon reading such a note.

PUBLIC SAFETY
A third category of exceptions to confidentiality balances the state interest in public safety against the patient's privacy interest. Perhaps the most well-known safety exception to patient confidentiality arises when a patient presents a threat of danger to a third party. In the case *Boynton v. Burglass,* 590 So. 2d 446 (Fla. 3d Dist. Ct. App. 1991), a Florida district court of appeal expressly rejected a duty to warn. The court noted that the legislature had written a statute creating a duty of confidentiality; the district court of appeals reasoned that a court should not override this statute by creating an exception to confidentiality. The district court of appeal also noted that section 455.671 (Fla. Stat. ch. 455.671) provides mental health professionals with the *option* to disclose patient communications in certain circumstances: when the patient has made an "actual" threat to "physically harm" an "identifiable victim." In such a case, the mental health professional may, if she chooses, warn the victim or the police of the patient's threat. Statutes that regulate psychologists (Fla. Stat. ch. 490.0147), and social workers, marriage and family therapists, and mental health counselors (Fla. Stat. ch. 491.0147) indicate that confidentiality may be waived "when there is a clear and immediate probability of physical harm to the patient, or to the society" (see appendix A for the texts of these statutes). Note that all these statutes use the permissive "may," rather than the mandatory "shall." Note also that if a psychotherapist does decide to breach confidentiality, he must be sure to comply with provisions of the relevant statute in order to avoid exposure to liability for breach of confidentiality.

Section 455.674 (Fla. Stat. ch. 455.674) creates another public safety exception to confidentiality when an individual is in danger of spreading HIV. According to this statute, if a physician is acting "reasonably and in good faith," he is permitted to disclose a patient's HIV positive status to the patient's sexual or needle-sharing partner, provided the patient has disclosed the identity of the partner and refuses either to notify the partner himself or to refrain from engaging in sexual or drug activity in a manner that is likely to transmit the virus. Before disclosing any information, however, the physician must first discuss the HIV test results with the patient, offer the patient educational and psychological counseling, and try to obtain the patient's consent to the disclosure. The physician must also inform the patient of his intent to notify the partner. Note that the language of section 455.674 is permissive and applies only to physicians. (See question 176 for the applicability of this statute to other mental health professionals.)

FACILITATION OF TREATMENT
The fourth category of exceptions to confidentiality is designed to facilitate the treatment process. Section 455.667 (Fla. Stat. ch. 455.667[5]) allows a mental health professional to disclose patient information "to other health care practitioners and providers involved in the care or treatment of the patient." Section 455.667(5) is designed to promote treatment by allowing mental health professionals involved in a particular client's care to discuss important treatment information. Note that because treatment information can be shared without the client's consent, this exception to confidentiality places the value of providing treatment ahead of the patient's autonomy. In a similar manner, section 394.4615 (Fla. Stat. ch. 394.4615) authorizes a mental health professional who works in a facility to release records to an "aftercare treatment provider, or an employee or agent of the department [Department of Children and Family Services] if necessary for treatment of the patient." Through these exceptions to confidentiality the law recognizes that good treatment sometimes requires that treaters communicate with one another. Treatment exceptions to confidentiality allow a clinician to do so regardless of whether the client consents, if the treater believes that sharing information is necessary for good treatment.

PROVISION OF MENTAL HEALTH SERVICES
The fifth category of exceptions to confidentiality ensures that clients will receive mental health services of an acceptable quality. Exceptions necessary to achieve this end involve peer and administrative review. Administrative review serves a number of essential purposes. First, by monitoring the ethical and legal standards to which health professionals are subject, administrative review helps make sure that patients receive adequate care and treatment. In addition, review agencies serve as watchdogs to help

prevent professional misconduct. Agencies such as the Human Rights Advocacy Committee, licensing boards, the Department of Children and Family Services, and the Agency for Health Care Administration investigate treatment practices (see Fla. Stat. ch. 394.4615[5]). When appropriate, such agencies can take remedial action based on their review of clinical records. By investigating reports of misconduct, review boards also help protect against mental health practice that falls below the standard of care. Also, federal law allows organizations such as the Advocacy Center for Persons with Disabilities to protect the rights of individuals with mental illness by examining records relevant to charges of abuse, neglect, or exploitation.

THE LEGAL SYSTEM
The legal system needs information to work effectively. This need sometimes conflicts with the value of keeping client communications confidential. The exceptions to confidentiality that involve the legal system thus represent a balance: In certain, specific situations, the needs of the legal system will outweigh a client's right to privacy.

Sections 394.4615 and 397.501 (Fla. Stat. ch. 394.4615[2][c] and 397.501[7][5]) explicitly state that a mental health professional must provide information when ordered to do so by a court. Other legal system exceptions to confidentiality arise when a court issues a search warrant or an order for criminal arrest or when a patient's lawyer needs records for adequate representation (see Fla. Stat. ch. 394.4615[2][b]), in which case the lawyer may consent to a release of the client's records. In addition, the law allows psychiatric records to be released without a patient's consent when the patient is committed or is to be returned to the Department of Corrections from the Department of Children and Family Services, and the Department of Corrections requests such records (see Fla. Stat. ch. 394.4615[2][d]). These exceptions to confidentiality recognize that, at times, the needs of the legal system will outweigh a client's right to privacy—the balance swings away from privacy and toward the societal interest of our legal system. (See chapter 7 for specific questions regarding how a mental health professional should respond to a subpoena or a court order.)

Another very limited legal system exception to confidentiality arises when a client commits or threatens to commit a crime at a mental health professional's workplace or against a mental health professional's employee. Section 397.501 (Fla. Stat. ch. 397.501[7][5][b]) and section 415.608 (Fla. Stat. ch. 415.608[3][a]) permit disclosure of limited information to law enforcement officers when an individual receiving substance abuse services or services at a domestic violence shelter is involved in such a crime. In keeping with the Parsimony Principle, these statutes limit disclosure to information directly related to the facts of the crime or threatened crime and other basic identifying information. No information regarding the patient's mental status or treatment may be released. Under section 397.501 (Fla. Stat. ch. 397.501[7][j]), a court may authorize the disclosure and use of the records of a client receiving substance abuse services for the purpose of conducting a criminal investigation only if the court finds that the crime involved is extremely serious (such as homicide or assault with a deadly weapon).

RESEARCH
Effective medical research relies on information. Without sharing information, advances due to research would cease. Section 394.4615 (Fla. Stat. ch. 394.4615[3][b]) states that information from a clinical record may be released to a "qualified researcher" if necessary to gather treatment data or to evaluate programs. Section 394.4615 (Fla. Stat. ch. 394.4615[4]) also specifies, however, that the information must be abstracted in such a way as to protect the individual's identity.

MANDATORY REPORTING STATUTES
The final exceptions to confidentiality are found in Florida's mandatory reporting statutes. To the extent the law serves as a balance for competing interests, mandatory reporting statutes provide an excellent illustration of our jurisprudence at work. Mandatory reporting statutes require that information pertaining to certain groups of individuals not be kept confidential. These are groups that society has deemed particularly vulnerable—children, the elderly, and disabled adults. Because these groups are less able to protect themselves than other groups in society, we place a higher value on ensuring their health and well-being than we do on keeping information revealed in a clinical setting confidential. As a consequence, information about harm or abuse to individuals in these groups is made available to agencies charged with their protection. Mandatory reporting statutes make clear the societal balance of values: For individuals belonging to especially vulnerable groups, well-being and safety trump confidentiality. Thus, mandatory reporting statutes reside on the furthest end of a continuum—the interests of society outweigh the individual's right to privacy.

MANDATORY REPORTING LAWS

Florida's two mandatory reporting statutes are remarkably similar in both structure and content. We will comment upon eight elements of these statutes.

An outline of the essential elements of the mandatory reporting laws is found on page 44.

The first of the eight elements is perhaps the most obvious, and for that reason all the more likely to be overlooked: Individuals are *required* to report when certain criteria are met. That is why these statutes are called "mandatory," rather than "discretionary," reporting statutes. The statutes are quite specific about both the mandatory nature of the reporting and the nature, circumstances, and timing of the reports that must be made.

The second of the eight elements is the list of individuals upon whom the statutes impose a duty to report. Any individual *may* contact the central abuse hot line to report suspected abuse or neglect of a child, an elderly person, or a disabled adult. The law imposes the *obligation* to report on individuals identified at the beginning of each statute. These lists of mandated reporters (see question 29) cover virtually any person who, in a professional capacity, would come into contact with a child, an elderly person, or a disabled person. As a consequence, any individual whose work brings him or her into contact with any of the individuals in these groups should consider him or herself a mandated reporter.

The third element involves the definition of the individuals on behalf of whom a mandatory report is made. Section 39.01 (Fla. Stat. ch. 39.01[12]) defines a child as an individual under the age of 18 who has not been emancipated (see question 185). Section 415.102 (Fla. Stat. ch. 415.102[10] and [12]) sets forth the definitions of a "disabled adult" and an "elderly person." For the purposes of the mandatory reporting statute, an elderly person is an individual who is 60 years of age or older, who suffers from the infirmities of old age (for example, from organic brain damage or other physical, mental, or emotional dysfunctions), and whose ability to care for or protect him or herself is impaired as a result. Section 415.102 (Fla. Stat. ch. 415.102[10]) defines a disabled adult as an individual who is 18 years of age or older, who has a mental or physical disability, and who, as a result of the mental or physical disability, is "substantially" restricted in performing the normal activities of daily living.

The fourth element involves the definition of the conditions that must be reported. For children, the law requires that any incidents of known or suspected abuse, abandonment, or neglect be reported. Sections 39.01 (Fla. Stat. ch. 39.01[2]) and 827.03 (Fla. Stat. ch. 827.03[c]) define these terms. As examples, section 39.01 defines abuse as "any willful act or threatened act that results in a physical, mental, or sexual injury or harm that causes or is likely to cause the child's physical, mental, or emotional health to be significantly impaired," while section 827.03 includes in the definition of abuse the active "encouragement of any person to commit an act that results or could reasonably be expected to result in physical or mental injury to a child." Both statutes define neglect as a caregiver's failure both to provide a child with necessary care, supervision, and services and to make a reasonable effort to protect a child from abuse, neglect, or exploitation. Section 39.01 (Fla. Stat. ch. 39.01[30][a–k]) provides a detailed list of examples that constitute child abuse and neglect. Included in this list are physical injuries such as cuts, bites, burns, or scalding; excessively harsh discipline that is likely to result in physical injury; and failure to provide a child with adequate food or clothing. According to section 39.01 (Fla. Stat. 39.01[1]), "abandonment" occurs when a parent sufficiently fails to support and nurture a child so as "to evince a willful rejection of parental obligations."

For elders and disabled adults, any incidents of abuse, neglect, or exploitation must be reported. Section 415.102 (Fla. Stat. ch. 415.102[1]) defines abuse as the "nonaccidental infliction of physical or psychological injury or sexual abuse," and neglect (Fla. Stat. ch. 415.102[22]) as "the failure or omission . . . to provide care, supervision and services necessary to maintain the physical and mental health of the disabled adult or elderly person." Section 415.101 (Fla. Stat. ch. 415.101[2]) includes financial exploitation and misuse of funds in the definition of exploitation.

The fifth element identifies the standard by which reports must be made. The language of the statutes is virtually identical: Any mandated reporter who "knows or has reasonable cause to suspect" that harm has occurred must report. The statutes do not require that a reporter confirm that the reportable condition—be it abuse, neglect, sexual abuse, or exploitation—is occurring or has occurred. Rather, the statutes only require that the reporter "knows or has reasonable cause to suspect" that the necessary conditions are present. Once a reporter reasonably suspects, she will turn the matter over to a state agency that will initiate an investigation. Mandated reporters are thus encouraged to act without

MANDATORY REPORTING STATUTES

I. **Mandated** reporting for certain groups:
    A. Children (individuals under the age of 18) (Fla. Stat. ch. 415.503[2])
    B. Elderly (individuals over the age of 60 who suffer from the infirmities of old age and whose ability to protect or care for self is impaired) (Fla. Stat. ch. 415.102[12])
    C. Dependent adults (individuals over 18 years of age with a mental or physical disability that significantly impairs their ability to perform activities of daily living) (Fla. Stat. ch. 415.102[10])

II. **Any individual** can report. Statutes list **mandated reporters.** Any individual who, in a professional capacity, comes into contact with a person in one of the groups to whom mandatory reporting statutes apply should consider self a mandatory reporter.

III. Conditions for reporting:
    A. Children
        1. Abuse
        2. Abandonment
        3. Neglect
    B. Elderly and disabled persons
        1. Abuse
        2. Neglect
        3. Exploitation (including financial exploitation and misuse of funds)

IV. Standard for reporting: A mandated reporter knows or has reasonable cause to suspect condition for reporting is present.

V. When reports must be made:
    A. Immediately when mandated reporter has reasonable cause to suspect.
    B. Reports can be written or oral.
    C. Counselor at the central registry will assign a response priority to the report: immediate, 24 hours, or next working day.

VI. To whom reports must be made:
    A. Florida's statewide central abuse registry and tracking system, available 24 hours a day, 7 days a week
    B. Central abuse registry telephone number: 1-800-96-ABUSE

VII. Failure to report: Possible criminal sanctions, civil sanctions, and professional discipline.

VIII. Release from liability: No civil or criminal sanctions attach when report is made in good faith.

IX. Confidentiality and privilege do not apply to mandatory reports.

waiting for definitive evidence, thereby increasing the likelihood that the state may intervene sooner rather than later.

The sixth element involves the timing of the report. The state of Florida has a statewide central abuse registry and tracking system, open 24 hours a day, 7 days a week. All reports of suspected child, elderly, and disabled person abuse, neglect, or exploitation are made to the registry through a single toll-free telephone number: 1-800-96-ABUSE. When a report of child abuse is made, the counselor at the central registry will determine if the case requires immediate or 24-hour response priority, that is, if the department shall commence an investigation immediately, regardless of the time of day or night, or if the investigation shall be commenced within 24 hours after the receipt of the report. In cases of child abuse or neglect, the central registry will contact the Department of Children and Family Service's designated district staff responsible for investigations. In cases of elderly person or disabled adult abuse, neglect, or exploitation, the registry will notify the Department of Children and Family Services designated adult protective investigative district staff. Reports of elderly and disabled person abuse, neglect, or exploitation have 24-hour or next–working day priorities.

The seventh element is the penalty for not reporting when one is mandated to do so and the release from liability when a report is made. Each statute states that if a mandated reporter "knowingly and willfully" fails to report suspected abuse or neglect, or prevents another mandated reporter from reporting, that individual will be guilty of a second degree misdemeanor. Other penalties may also follow. For example, sections 490.009 and 491.009 (Fla. Stat. ch. 490.009[h] and 491.009[h]) regulating psychologists, social workers, mental health counselors, and marriage and family therapists make a mental health professional subject to disciplinary proceedings for "failing to perform any statutory or legal obligation." While failing to report when one is required to do so may lead to civil and criminal penalties, sections 39.203 and 415.111 (Fla. Stat. chs. 39.203 and 415.111[b]) protect any individual who makes a report in good faith. The clear message is that penalties will attach if a mandated reporter has reasonable cause to suspect a reportable condition and does nothing, whereas such an individual who goes forward in accordance with the law and contacts the appropriate agency will not incur a penalty.

The eighth and final element involves the waiver of confidentiality. Each of the mandatory reporting statutes states that any individual who makes a report is not bound by confidentiality or testimonial privilege. That is, the privileged nature of the psychotherapist-client relationship does not apply to any situation involving known or suspected abuse. This provision makes explicit the balance of values behind this set of laws: Confidentiality will yield when the health, well-being, and safety of individuals we deem specially vulnerable and in need of protection are at issue.

LAWS THAT GOVERN TESTIMONIAL PRIVILEGE

The purpose of testimonial privilege is to allow a sacred space—a hallowed ground—that is protected from the scrutiny of the legal system. Since 1976 the Florida Evidence Code has recognized the psychotherapist-patient privilege. The Florida testimonial privilege statutes (Fla. Stat. ch. 90.503, 90.5035, and 90.5036) explicitly cover:

- licensed physicians who diagnose mental or emotional disorders;
- licensed psychologists;
- licensed or certified social workers, mental health counselors, and marriage and family therapists;
- treatment personnel of mental health facilities, community mental health centers, hospitals, and substance abuse treatment centers that engage primarily in the diagnosis or treatment of mental and emotional disorders;
- sexual assault counselors who work in rape treatment centers; and
- domestic violence advocates who are employees or trained volunteers in domestic violence programs.

Testimonial privilege is created by statute and only when a statute specifically names a discipline should a mental health professional assume that testimonial privilege applies. In other words, only when a statute explicitly names your discipline should you assume that your client may rely on privilege to prevent you from disclosing information in a legal proceeding. As an example of how testimonial privilege statutes are exclusive, the psychotherapist-patient privilege outlined in section 90.503 (Fla. Stat. ch. 90.503[1]) states that privilege applies to *licensed* clinical social workers. Confidential communications shared with an *unlicensed* social worker might not be covered by privilege; that is, a client may not have the prerogative to prevent an unlicensed social worker from discussing what he said in a treatment, if the social worker were given a subpoena to do so. So—know whether the privilege statute applies to your discipline.

Two additional points about testimonial privilege are important. First, privilege, like confidentiality, is not absolute. Exceptions to privilege allow patient communications to be disclosed in a legal proceeding. If you think of testimonial privilege as a cloak that hides confidential communications from the scrutiny of the legal system, you can think of the exceptions to testimonial privilege as holes in the cloak that let the law "peak through" and see what happened in a relationship normally hidden from its eyes. Second, keep the concept of testimonial privilege separate from the concept of mandatory reporting. A mandatory reporting statute tells a mental health professional to do something. Privilege, on the other hand, indicates whether a patient's communication can be revealed in a legal proceeding. Privilege has to do with lawyers, courts, and judges. Mandatory reporting tells a mental health professional to pick up the phone.

EXCEPTIONS TO TESTIMONIAL PRIVILEGE

The exceptions found in the testimonial privilege statutes are perhaps more appropriately referred to as "potential exceptions." The reason for this qualification is that no exception to testimonial privilege is automatic; when the possibility of an exception is raised, a judge will review the materials in his chambers (called an "in camera" review). In the review the judge will determine first, whether the materials are relevant to the matter before the court, and second, whether some exception to privilege will allow the materials to be disclosed in the legal proceeding. Only when the materials are both relevant and fall under an exception to privilege will the judge order that they be disclosed.

The first exception to privilege arises under section 90.503 (Fla. Stat. ch. 90.503[4][a]) when a psychotherapist, during the course of diagnosis or treatment, reasonably believes that the patient is in need of hospitalization. When an involuntary commitment proceeding is commenced (see chapter 5), the clinician may be called to testify or his records may be subpoenaed and information that otherwise would be privileged can be revealed. This exception represents a judgment by the legislature that when civil commitment is involved, the *parens patriae* and *police power* interests of the state (see the introduction to chapter 5) outweigh the patient's interest in confidentiality.

A second exception arises under section 90.503 (Fla. Stat. ch. 90.503 [4][a]) when a court orders that an individual be examined by a mental health professional. As an example, a court may order that a criminal defendant be examined to determine whether he was insane at the time of the crime or whether he is competent to proceed (see chapter 6). A court may also order an examination in a civil case, as sometimes happens in custody proceedings or when child abuse or neglect is alleged. This exception to testimonial privilege represents the judgment that society's interest in accurate decision making sometimes requires information that would otherwise be kept completely confidential be disclosed in a legal proceeding. Mental health professionals who perform court-ordered evaluations should make clear at the outset of an interview that anything said will be disclosed to the court, and the clinician should work to dispel any notion that what is said will remain confidential. At that point, the individual being assessed has at least the option of not providing any information. In this sense, this exception to testimonial privilege can be seen as a waiver by an individual who knowingly chooses to participate in an evaluation without the usual expectation of confidentiality.

A third exception to privilege arises under section 90.503 (Fla. Stat. ch. 90.503[4][a]) when a client introduces her mental or emotional condition into a legal proceeding. The reason behind this exception is straightforward: If an individual wishes to make his mental or emotional state an issue in a legal matter, that claim must be given a full and fair hearing. A full and fair hearing requires that information gathered by a mental health professional be made available to all the parties involved in the case. Thus, if following an accident of some sort, a patient makes a claim based on emotional suffering, his therapy records may no longer be protected by privilege. Why? Because he has made his emotional state an issue in a legal matter and it would be unfair to the opposing party to allow the patient to hide behind the cloak of privilege to protect information that might help the other side.

Two comments about this exception to privilege are important. First, for the exception to apply the client herself must have introduced her mental or emotional condition into the legal proceeding. The opposing party cannot do so in order to have the client's privilege disappear. Second, there must be a reasonably clear relationship between the legal issue raised by the client and his mental or emotional condition. As an example, a client seeking custody of a child in a divorce proceeding may claim that she is a "fit and proper parent." According to the Fourth District Court of Appeals in *Roper v. Roper*, 336 So. 2d 654 (Fla. 4th Dist. Ct. App. 1976), that claim alone does not mean that the client has waived her privilege. The *Roper* decision is important, because otherwise any time one parent in a divorce proceeding claimed to be a fit and proper parent, the other parent could demand to see any records from the first parent's mental health treatment. That is not to say, however, that mental health records might never be introduced in a custody proceeding. In *Miraglia v. Miraglia*, 462 So. 2d 507 (Fla. 4th Dist. Ct. App. 1985), for example, a parent had attempted suicide, and in *Critchlow v. Critchlow*, 347 So. 2d 453 (Fla. 3rd Dist. Ct. App. 1977), the individual had admitted herself into a mental hospital. In *these* cases courts have ruled that there is a close connection between one's fitness as a parent and one's mental and emotional health, so that a claim about the former necessarily implicates the latter. Courts have therefore ruled that an exception to privilege applies, and have allowed confidential communications to be introduced at trial when individuals in these circumstances claimed to be "fit and proper" parents.

The mental condition exception to privilege also applies after the patient's death, when any party relies on the emotional or mental condition of the deceased person as an element of the party's claim or defense. This situation may arise in disputes over whether a deceased person was competent at the time of making a will.

Other statutes create exceptions to testimonial privilege. As examples, section 490.0147 (Fla. Stat. ch. 490.0147[1]) and section 491.0147 (Fla. Stat. ch. 491.0147[1]) create an exception to privilege for psychologists, social workers, marriage and family therapists, and mental health counselors when a client has raised an allegation of wrongdoing against a treater. These statutes say that one of these mental health professionals may rely on otherwise confidential information if that information is necessary, or even relevant, to the mental health professional's defense in a civil, criminal, or disciplinary action. As an example, if a patient brings a legal action against his treater and the treater needs confidential information to defend herself, the patient cannot then invoke privilege in order to prevent that information from being admitted into the legal proceeding. The law will thus not permit a client to use testimonial privilege as a way of rendering the mental health professional defenseless against the client's accusation.

The above discussion of the exceptions to testimonial privilege applies to Florida courts. What would happen if a mental health professional were asked—or ordered—to testify in a *federal* court? In one set of cases, the federal court will simply apply Florida law, so that the above discussion would be relevant to privilege. Under the Federal Rules of Evidence, the federal trial court (known as federal district court), will apply Florida law concerning issues of testimonial privilege in a case of "diverse citizenship," that is when one party is a citizen of Florida and the other is a citizen from another state. In other cases, the Federal Rules of Evidence will apply.

Federal Rule of Evidence 501 (cited as Fed. R. Evid. 501) provides that questions of privilege shall be guided by "reason and experience." While this somewhat enigmatic phrase does not explicitly recognize a psychotherapist-patient privilege, certain federal courts have ruled that there is a privilege between a mental health professional and a patient. The United States Supreme Court approved this development in *Jaffee v. Redmond*, 116 S. Ct. 1923 (1996). In recognizing the existence of a psychotherapist-patient privilege in *Jaffee*, the Supreme Court applied testimonial privilege to a licensed psychiatric social worker. Thus, in both state and federal court a psychotherapist may assert a client's testimonial privilege. The exact contours of the privilege may differ somewhat in federal court, however, and if called to testify in a federal proceeding a mental health professional will want to learn how privilege applies in federal court.

Part I, our introduction to the law, closes here. Part II, 200 questions about Florida mental health law, is really nothing more than the application of the concepts put forth in the first part of the book. As you read part II, keep in mind that behind every statute or regulation lies an important value; behind every exception to a statute or regulation lies another important value. When faced with a problem that has no clear solution, think through what values are at stake. Remember as you do so that any statute or regulation can be analyzed in the same way as we've done in chapters 2 and 3. If you can break a law down into its smaller parts, the law's mystique will soon evaporate. So will lingering anxieties about your legal rights and responsibilities.

OVERVIEW OF PRIVACY, CONFIDENTIALITY, AND TESTIMONIAL PRIVILEGE

I. **Privacy**: The right to decide how to live one's own life
   A. Constitution of the United States (penumbras of amendments to the Constitution)
   B. Article I, section 23, of the Florida Constitution

II. **Confidentiality**: The client's right to have communications kept within the bounds of the professional relationship
   A. All mental health professionals should assume client communications and client records are to be kept confidential.
   B. Confidential information should be disclosed only when:
      1. A client waives confidentiality, or
      2. A court orders the mental health professional to disclose confidential material, or
      3. A statute explicitly creates an exception to confidentiality.
   C. Exceptions to confidentiality:
      1. Client consent
         a. Should be in writing
         b. Obtain from each adult participant in treatment
      2. Treatment emergencies
      3. Public safety
         a. No duty to warn in Florida
         b. Physicians may disclose client's HIV status under appropriate circumstances.
      4. Facilitation of treatment
      5. Provision of mental health services
      6. The legal system
      7. Research
      8. Mandatory reporting statutes
         a. Children
         b. Elderly persons
         c. Disabled adults

III. **Testimonial privilege** (or simply **privilege**): The client's right to prevent the mental health professional from revealing confidential communications in a legal proceeding
   A. Psychotherapists (Fla. Stat. ch. 90.503)
      1. A licensed physician engaged in the practice of treating or diagnosing mental or emotional conditions
      2. Licensed psychologists
      3. Licensed mental health counselors
      4. Licensed clinical social workers
      5. Licensed marriage and family therapists
   B. Sexual assault counselors (Fla. Stat. ch. 90.5035)

continued

C. Domestic violence advocates (Fla. Stat. ch. 90.5036)
D. A client is said to "waive privilege" when she allows a mental health professional to reveal communications in a legal proceeding.
E. A client is said to "invoke privilege" when she does not allow a mental health professional to reveal communications in a court of law, a deposition, or a legal proceeding. If the client is unavailable, the mental health professional may invoke privilege on the client's behalf.

Part II

200 Questions on Florida Mental Health Law

Part II consists of 200 questions mental health professionals often ask about the law. For the most part, the questions are self-explanatory, so only a brief word of introduction is in order.

First, our questions represent a fraction of what could be asked—the list is virtually endless. What we have done is to divide the questions into ten topic headings that cover the essential areas of Florida mental health law and then to present those questions that, in our experience, most concern clinicians. Familiarity with these answers will provide an excellent overview of what clinicians need to know in Florida. If, after reading part II, you don't have a particular answer you are looking for, you will at the very least have a way to think about the question.

Second, the questions refer to a number of statutes, regulations, rules of court, and court cases. We therefore thought it would be helpful briefly to review how important Florida laws are cited:

- *Statutes*: "Fla. Stat. ch. 394.467" refers to section 467 of chapter 394 of the Florida Statutes. This citation can also be written as "section 394.467."

- *Cases of the Florida Supreme Court:* "565 So. 2d 315 (Fla. 1990)" refers to the 1990 opinion of the Supreme Court of Florida found in volume 565 of the second edition of the *Southern Reporter,* at page 315.
- *Cases of the Florida Courts of Appeals:* 582 So. 2d 784 (Fla. 5th Dist. Ct. App. 1991 [or Fla. App. 5 Dist. 1991 or Fla. 5th DCA 1991]) refers to the 1991 opinion of the Florida 5th District Court of Appeals, found in volume 582 of the second edition of the *Southern Reporter,* at page 784.
- *Florida Administrative Code:* Fla. Admin. Code Ann. r. 65E-5.290 (1996) refers to rule 65E, section 5.290 of the *Florida Administrative Code Annotated.*
- *Rules of Court:* e.g., Fla. R. Civ. Proc. 1.420 refers to rule 1.420 of the *Florida Rules of Civil Procedure.* Fla. R. Crim. Proc. 3.212 refers to rule 3.212 of the *Florida Rules of Criminal Procedure.*

Finally, don't read all the questions at once. It's too much. Part II covers a lot of territory, much more than can be absorbed in one sitting. At most, read a single topic at a time. Responses are designed for easy access and are well suited as references—but they can be dense. Take your time, enjoy what you read, and let us know what you think. Part II of this book will serve its purpose well if our readers find our responses to these questions helpful in their clinical practice.

4

THE LEGAL SYSTEM AND LEGAL PROCESS

Mental health professionals find no topic more shrouded in mystery than the legal system and legal process: the law's way of doing things. Remember, though, that lawyers find what mental health professionals do equally mystifying—and intriguing. The questions below, which discuss particular aspects of how the legal system works, are written to illuminate the rationale behind the law's requirements. As you read, try to keep in mind both the legal rule and whatever value the rule, or its exception, is designed to promote.

QUESTIONS DISCUSSED IN THIS CHAPTER

1. What is the difference between civil law and criminal law?
2. What is a tort?
3. What does it mean to say that our system of law is "adversarial"?
4. What is a standard of proof?
5. What is a burden of proof?
6. What does it mean to say that a court has "jurisdiction"?
7. Why do lawyers seem so different from mental health professionals?

8. What is a deposition?
9. Why is a deposition important?
10. What is an interrogatory?
11. What is the difference between an expert witness and a fact witness?
12. Who decides who qualifies as an expert witness?
13. It seems that expert witnesses sometimes attempt to pass off "junk science" as real science in the courtroom. How does a judge decide what science is good enough science to allow an expert witness to testify in court?
14. If I receive a subpoena and must testify at a deposition about a therapy case, am I an expert witness or a fact witness?
15. What should I know if I am called to testify as a fact witness?
16. Does whether I am an expert witness or a fact witness make any difference in what I am paid?
17. I've heard that a "writ of habeas corpus" can play an important role in protecting the rights of a psychiatric patient. What is a writ of habeas corpus?
18. What is a statute of limitations?
19. What is the statute of limitations for malpractice lawsuits in Florida?
20. How does the statute of limitations apply to cases involving minors?
21. Does Florida law allow additional time for an individual to bring a lawsuit against a perpetrator of abuse or incest?
22. What is the Americans with Disabilities Act?
23. Is it legal for an employer to ask during a job interview whether an applicant suffers from a mental illness or has ever received care from a mental health professional?
24. A job applicant may be asked to have a physical examination as part of the employment process. If asked about prescription medication, is it necessary to tell the individual conducting the examination about antipsychotic medication the applicant may be taking?
25. Who has access to medical information revealed during a job-related physical examination?
26. Lawyers frequently say that competent adults have a right to informed consent. What is "informed consent" and when is an adult "competent" to give informed consent?
27. Lawyers sometimes make reference to "judicial review" and "administrative review." What is the difference between judicial and administrative review?
28. What is the role of hypnosis in legal proceedings?

DISCUSSION

1. What is the difference between civil law and criminal law?

Criminal law is based on the notion of *moral blameworthiness*. In a criminal court a person may be found guilty, given a fine, and sentenced to jail or prison because he has violated the criminal law and so must be morally sanctioned. Murder and manslaughter are two examples of crimes for which society punishes wrongdoers.

The civil law is much further removed from the notion of moral blame-worthiness. The purpose of a civil lawsuit is to assign responsibility for harm and to provide an appropriate "remedy" for that harm. The typical remedy is an award of damages designed to make a victim whole (although a remedy can also include an "injunction" that prevents a party from engaging in some activity such as spewing noxious fumes into the air). For example, the purpose of a malpractice suit is to determine whether a treater is responsible—in civil court parlance, "liable"—for the harm suffered by a patient. If the treater is found liable, the civil court will then determine the remedy for that harm, that is, the award of damages required to make the patient whole. The remedy is referred to as the "award of compensatory damages." In the very limited circumstances where it is appropriate not only to make the aggrieved party whole, but to punish the wrongdoer as well, there can also be an award of "punitive damages."

2. What is a tort?

In the words of Black's Law Dictionary, a tort is "A private or civil wrong or injury . . . for which a court will provide a remedy in the form of an action for damages." To explain, a tort is a *civil* wrong—a private individual has been harmed and goes to court to seek compensation. A tort action differs from a criminal action, which is brought by a prosecutor to redress a wrong against society. At times the parties in a tort action will agree to *settle*. To settle a case means that the parties agree to some amount of damages without waiting for a court to decide for them. Malpractice is a type of tort (the elements of a malpractice claim are discussed in chapter 2).

3. What does it mean to say that our system of law is "adversarial"?

Legal actions, whether civil or criminal, pit one party against another. The parties to a lawsuit are thus *adversaries*. Our adversarial system of law is built on the assumption that having two parties on opposite sides of an issue, each motivated to advance its own position, is the way most likely to yield what is true, right, and fair. In the adversary process (as distinguished from the inquisitorial process used in some other countries, such as France) the judge plays a relatively passive role and must remain neutral and detached.

In criminal cases, one party is the government. The idea is that an individual has harmed society as a whole by his crime and the government has the responsibility of ensuring that the individual is held accountable for what he has done. Note how, by taking on this responsibility, the government also precludes private individuals from taking the law into their own hands and exacting retribution—vengeance belongs to the state. Thus, the title of a criminal case in Florida is always along the lines of *State v. Saks*, showing that the State of Florida is the aggrieved party bringing suit. Saks is the criminal *defendant*, who may go to jail if she is found guilty. (The state is also referred to as "*the prosecution*.") In civil law, private individuals who have been harmed may bring the action, and are referred to as *plaintiffs*. The second name in the title of both civil and criminal lawsuits, the name of the party on the other side of the "v." (for "versus") is the *defendant*. What's important to remember is that lawsuits consist of adversaries, two parties with competing interests, only one of whom will prevail.

4. What is a standard of proof?

Think of a "standard of proof" as a hurdle. If someone told you that on your way to work tomorrow you would have to jump over a hurdle, you might well ask, "How high is the hurdle?" Exactly the same question is asked in law. The height of the "proof hurdle" in a legal proceeding is called the standard of proof. The standard of proof depends on the importance of the issues at stake. For example, criminal trials, in which society may condemn the actions of some individual and which may involve depriving a citizen of his personal liberty, require our system's highest standard of proof, *beyond a reasonable doubt*. The reason for this strict standard of proof is that our society will deprive an individual of his liberty only when his guilt is certain—under tradition of jurisprudence it is better to free ten guilty people than to imprison one innocent person. Thus, society's values are reflected in the choice of the standard of proof. Proof *beyond a reasonable doubt* is considered proof in the 95%–99% range. Proof *by clear and convincing evidence,* by contrast, is a lower standard of proof, often described as proof in the 75% range. Proof by clear and convincing evidence is required in civil commitment cases. The lowest standard of proof, *a preponderance of the evidence*, is proof by more than 50%, or "more likely than not." Civil cases generally, including malpractice cases, involve the lowest standard of proof, a preponderance of the evidence.

5. What is a burden of proof?

While the *standard* of proof refers to the height of the proof hurdle, the *burden* of proof refers to which party must jump the hurdle to win the case. In every case one party will bear the burden of proof—that is, one of the parties will have to be prepared to jump as high as the proof hurdle requires. In a criminal case, the prosecutor—the attorney for the government—bears the burden of proof. It is therefore the prosecutor who must prove beyond a reasonable doubt that the defendant is guilty. In a civil case (such as a malpractice case), the plaintiff bears the burden of proof. It is therefore the plaintiff who must show by a preponderance of the evidence that all the elements of a malpractice claim (see chapter 2) are present. Similarly, in a civil commitment case, the state (as the party seeking to commit the patient) must bear the burden of proof. The state must carry that burden by clear and convincing evidence when it seeks to place an individual in a hospital involuntarily because of mental illness and dangerousness.

Any legal proceeding will involve both a standard and a burden of proof. A mental health professional who becomes involved in a legal proceeding will therefore want to know what standard of proof the case requires and which party bears the burden of proof. In other words, the mental health professional will ask, "How high is the hurdle?" and "Who must jump the hurdle to win the case?"

6. What does it mean to say that a court has "jurisdiction"?

Jurisdiction is the legal way of saying "who gets to decide." The person with the T.V. clicker has jurisdiction over which programs are watched; the person in the driver's seat has jurisdiction over what radio station is played in the car; the birthday boy or girl has jurisdiction over what kind of cake gets served. Jurisdiction indicates in which court's domain a particular matter rests. The legislature has created different kinds of courts and assigns different matters to each of them. Generally, a statute will indicate which court has jurisdiction over a given type of case. Florida statutes, for example, provide that the circuit court has jurisdiction over guardianships and involuntary civil commitment. Jurisdiction is always relevant because a party must determine *which* court has jurisdiction before it can proceed with a legal action.

7. Why do lawyers seem so different from mental health professionals?
Lawyers, by training, are professional skeptics who take nothing at face
value and will insist that a mental health professional support a position
with concrete evidence. In addition, lawyers see themselves as representing the patient's wishes. To a lawyer, representing the patient's wishes
translates into what the patient *says* he wants at a given time.

The skepticism displayed by lawyers is part of their professional training
and serves them well in legal proceedings, where evidence must be supported by standards of proof. Recall that the *lowest* standard of proof is a
preponderance of the evidence. That standard requires lawyers to marshal
enough evidence to demonstrate that their argument is *more likely than
not* correct. Mental health professionals are rarely held to even the lowest
legal standard of proof—appropriately, since their work is different.
Perhaps, however, mental health professionals sacrifice thoroughness by
not being more rigorously challenged.

A number of years ago one of us attended a clinical case conference in
the Midwest. A consultant was interviewing a patient who had been
admitted to a psychiatric hospital for having jumped off a rather high
bridge. Despite the height of the bridge, the patient had suffered no
injuries whatsoever. The discussion following the interview centered on
the level of this patient's suicidality. As the case conference went on, one
of the clinicians rather timidly asked whether there was any independent
confirmation that this young woman had indeed jumped off the bridge.
There was not. The patient had shown up at an emergency room in soak-
ing wet clothes, and every clinician from that point on had simply taken
her story at face value. The remarkable issue was not that this young
woman did—or did not—jump off the bridge. Rather, it was that her treating clinicians did not know, and did not attempt to find out or confirm
whether she had or hadn't, yet were proceeding as if this part of her history
were certain. Clearly the clinical assessment would be quite different
depending on whether this woman actually jumped off the bridge, or
whether she *claimed* that she jumped off the bridge, but had not. A bit of
lawyerly skepticism at the outset might have been useful for the treatment.

Lawyers apply their skepticism all the time. They will ask how a clinician *knows* that a patient will hurt himself if released from the hospital,
how a clinician *knows* that a particular treatment will work, or how a clinician *knows* that a patient cannot perform a certain job or task. While the
questions may seem abrasive, insensitive, and not fully appreciative of the
mental health professional's expertise, it is based on the legal model: At

least a preponderance of the evidence, or more than 50% of the available data, must supply the foundation for any position, statement, or opinion.

Another matter to consider is that a lawyer is a patient's (and, for that matter, a mental health professional's, should the need arise) legal representative. For a lawyer, proper representation means advocating for what the client says he wants. Therein lies a friction with mental health professionals. Clinicians are trained in the complexity of human behavior. They regard a patient's oral expression of a desire as only one aspect of what the person truly wants. Often mental health professionals will counsel an individual to delay acting until ample time has been devoted to exploring all the advantages and disadvantages of a particular course of action. Other times, mental health professionals will probe a patient's unexpressed feelings. Thus, the posture of the mental health professional—to delay and to explore—may be directly at odds with that of the lawyer— to act. This difference can be intensified by the lawyer's skepticism, by virtue of which the lawyer may discount a mental health professional's reasons for caution and delay. The consequences of this friction are mental health professionals who feel devalued professionally and frustrated that lawyers are helping patients accomplish what mental health professionals consider not necessarily in the patient's best interests.

Despite these differences, there are many successful lawyer-clinician teams who do excellent work. If you are called upon to work with an attorney, try to keep three things in mind: First, both you and the lawyer are working on behalf of the patient. While you may disagree about goals, each of you has been trained to assist your client within the scope of your expertise. Second, find the time to ask yourself the sort of questions the lawyer might ask. Clinicians rarely engage in this sort of activity, partly because they are rarely called upon to explain the rationale behind their treatment. Ask yourself questions like: What is my treatment plan? What facts in the client's history support my use of this plan? What facts in the client's history would be *inconsistent* with this plan? Might there be other plans that I have not considered and that may be helpful? If I have made an intervention, such as an involuntary hospitalization, on what basis have I made that intervention? How certain am I that the intervention will be successful? On what facts or observations do I base my certainty? In other words, try to place yourself in the shoes of the lawyer and ask the skeptical questions she would ask. Third, find a time to sit with the lawyer to understand better what she thinks about the case. Ask what the lawyer intends to do and why she intends to do it. Explore the reasons behind her plan of action. As you discuss the case with the lawyer, remember that she will hold your reasoning to a standard of evidence, so be prepared to explain the reasons behind *your* thinking as well. Above all, keep in mind that the more you and the lawyer work *together*, the better each of you will serve your mutual client.

8. What is a deposition?

Depositions are part of a legal process called "discovery." "Discovery" is just that—a process whereby one party in a lawsuit discovers facts and information from the opposing party in the lawsuit. Discovery serves an important function in preparing for a trial that is to take place. At the very beginning stage of a legal case an attorney may have only a partial understanding of the facts. The attorney will need to develop further her understanding of what took place in order to refine her legal theory and to marshal the evidence for presentation at trial.

The discovery process has several purposes: The facts and information garnered during discovery allow the parties to focus on the issues that will be addressed at trial; facts and information that may be lost or forgotten before the trial actually takes place are recorded and thereby preserved; the parties may be more disposed to settle the lawsuit after certain facts and information come to light. The process of discovery allows a party literally *to discover* the nature, strengths, and weaknesses of the lawsuit. Depositions are an important part of the discovery process. The purpose of taking a deposition is consistent with the purpose of discovery—for a party to learn *what it does not know*.

In a deposition, a witness is interrogated in the presence of attorneys for both sides and must answer questions under oath. Depositions are particularly well-suited to uncovering unknown facts and information. Depositions consist of oral questions and oral responses. Lawyers can ask questions from a wide range of topics. Furthermore, the rules of admissibility—rules that can exclude certain evidence from a trial—are much less strict for depositions. Wide latitude is given to lawyers regarding the types and scope of the questions. If an objection is raised to a particular question, the objection is noted and reviewed at trial. The question itself is answered during the deposition.

Most depositions take place at an attorney's office—the attorney who wants the deposition—at a time that all the parties agree on (although sometimes attorneys will take a deposition at a health care provider's office both for the provider's convenience and to save expense). Testimony at a deposition takes place under oath and a court reporter is present to record the proceedings. A deposition may last from half an hour to several days, depending on the importance of the testimony being taken.

It is wise to consult your malpractice carrier any time you testify to determine whether the presence of a lawyer is indicated. If you receive a subpoena, be sure to check with your malpractice carrier and follow their advice on whether you should have legal representation. One instance will always require an attorney's presence: when you are the defendant (that is, the person being sued). When an issue of confidentiality or testimonial privilege is likely to arise, you should seriously consider having a lawyer present (although one may not be absolutely necessary), insofar as answering a question may expose you to a claim that you have breached your client's confidentiality (see chapter 7, Subpoenas and Court Orders). When you are serving as an expert witness you will often be deposed beforehand so that the opposing attorney can see ahead of time what you intend to say at the trial.

9. Why is a deposition important?
Deposition testimony is taken under oath. Consequently, false or misleading statements can lead to a charge of perjury. In addition, if what you say at trial differs from what you said at a deposition, the opposing counsel can use your deposition to contradict—in legal parlance, "impeach"—you at trial. Frequently, one or both of the parties to a lawsuit will order a transcript of a deposition. The transcript will be prepared by the stenographer (who will be present at the deposition) and a witness will sometimes be asked to sign the transcript to attest to its accuracy. It is extremely useful for you to obtain a copy of the transcript following the deposition, for two reasons: First, to verify its accuracy and to correct any mistakes for the final version; second, having a copy of the transcript will allow you to review what you said at the deposition before you testify at trial.

10. What is an interrogatory?
An interrogatory is the *written* equivalent of a deposition. An interrogatory is sent only to the parties in the lawsuit, not to expert witnesses. When a party receives the interrogatory, she must respond in writing and sign a sworn statement that the responses are true.

11. What is the difference between an expert witness and a fact witness?
A fact witness is an individual who has *personal knowledge* of some situation or event relevant to a legal proceeding. An expert witness need not have personal knowledge of the matter. Rather, an expert witness is

called to testify because he has *special knowledge that can help the jury in making its decision.* While a fact witness testifies to *facts,* of which he has direct knowledge, an expert witness gives expert *opinions* that derive from his unique expertise.

As an example, consider that one day you are walking down the aisle of the grocery store. You slip on a banana peel and aggravate that old knee injury so that you are unable to participate in the big golf tournament this weekend. You decide to sue the store for your injury.

You will call as a *fact witness* anyone present in the store who witnessed the events surrounding your accident, such as the baker who saw the banana on the floor immediately before you fell, the person at the cash register who saw you go down, the butcher who heard your blood-curdling scream. All of these people have personal knowledge of what happened—they will testify about the events that led to your injury based on what they personally saw and heard. Courts allow fact witnesses to testify solely about what they personally experienced. If a fact witness attempts to testify to matters of which he has no direct experience, the lawyer on the other side will immediately object.

Your attorney will call as an *expert witness* Dr. Peel, the world-famous authority on injuries suffered during banana falls. Dr. Peel did not see or hear you fall, but he has special knowledge regarding how the knee turns in an unusual manner during a banana fall and the injuries unique to those dreadful contortions. Dr. Peel will testify about the severity of your injury, your likely prognosis, and your inability to participate in the upcoming golf tournament. Note that Dr. Peel was not in the store when you fell and he has no personal knowledge of what occurred. Rather, Dr. Peel's knowledge about your injury derives almost entirely from secondhand information: your description of the fall, the X-rays, the report of the emergency room physician, and the reports submitted by your treating physician.

Two comments about expert witnesses. First, the expert is allowed to speak only on those matters his expertise covers. Dr. Peel will not be allowed to speak about the sorts of injuries that result from garbanzo bean falls, because he is only a banana fall expert. Garbanzo bean falls lie outside his area of expertise. Note how this restriction is somewhat like the restriction on fact witnesses, who are allowed to testify only as to matters of which they have personal knowledge. All witnesses—fact and expertise—may speak solely to those matters that lie within their direct experience (fact) or within their expertise (expert).

Second, the expert must testify as to the facts that underlie his expert opinion. Describing the facts upon which the expert opinion is based is called "laying the foundation." Dr. Peel, for example, will base his expert opinion—that you must wait one year before you play golf again—on his examination of your knee and his review of your knee's medical record. He will begin his testimony by describing in great detail his examination and his review. He will then say, "Based on these facts, I am of the opinion that . . ." Your attorney has laid the foundation for Dr. Peel's expert testimony.

12. Who decides who qualifies as an expert witness?

The trial judge decides who will qualify as an expert witness. Section 702 in chapter 90 (Fla. Stat. ch. 90.702) provides that a witness is qualified as an expert by "knowledge, skill, experience, training, or education." The party who presents the expert witness must establish to the judge's satisfaction that the witness has specialized knowledge that will help the jury make its decision. There isn't any list of names or qualifications that determine who is an expert. Rather, the trial judge asks two questions: Does the expert know things that the jury most likely does not? Will what the expert knows help the jury in making its decision? If the answer to both these questions is "yes," the judge is free to qualify the person as an expert and allow her to give expert opinions at trial (see also the following question).

13. It seems that expert witnesses sometimes attempt to pass off "junk science" as real science in the courtroom. How does a judge decide what science is good enough science to allow an expert witness to testify in court?

The Florida Supreme Court addressed this question in *Flanagan v. State*, 625 So. 2d 827 (Fla. 1993). *Flanagan* involved a man who had been convicted of sexually battering his 9-year-old daughter. At the trial, a psychologist had testified about the profile of a person who would batter his minor child; the defendant was said to fit this profile. Following his conviction the defendant appealed and claimed that the scientific principles that underlay the psychologist's testimony were not valid.

The Florida Supreme Court said that to be admissible in court, "novel scientific evidence" must meet the standard set forth by a federal court in *Frye v. United States*, 293 F. 1013 (D.C. Cir. 1923). According to the "Frye test," scientific testimony must be based on a principle or discovery that is "sufficiently established to have gained general acceptance in the particular field in which it belongs" (*Frye* at 1014). The Frye test has come to be known as the "general acceptance" test. Before an expert can testify to scientific evidence, such evidence must be based on a principle or discovery that is "generally accepted" by the scientific community. The Court ruled that because profile evidence was not generally accepted by the scientific community, it did not meet the Frye test, and so should not have been admitted at the trial.

14. If I receive a subpoena and must testify at a deposition about a therapy case, am I an expert witness or a fact witness?
You can be subpoenaed as either, so be clear about whether you are being called to testify as an expert or as a fact witness. A lawyer will not send a subpoena to his own witness. Therefore, if you receive a subpoena, it is from the *other* side. A lawyer would subpoena you as an expert only if you had already been identified as an expert by *your* side. So if you receive a subpoena and are confused about whether you are an expert or a fact witness, you are almost certainly a fact witness.

15. What should I know if I am called to testify as a fact witness?
The following five points may be helpful if you receive a subpoena to testify as a fact witness.

First, you are not required to prepare for a deposition, either by reading your notes or reviewing the therapy. Preparing may lessen your anxiety, but time so spent will not be compensated. So if you do decide to prepare, it's on your own time.

Second, should you decide to prepare, know that any documents you make regarding your patient's treatment—including personal notes made in contemplation of your testimony—are subject to a subpoena! In addition, an attorney can question you about *conversations* you had in preparation for the deposition, with whomever, including your patient and your patient's attorney. The sole exception is that you do not have to answer questions about conversations you had with your own attorney.

Third, respond only to the questions. Volunteer nothing and speculate even less. "I don't recall" or "I don't know" are fine answers, if true. A deposition is neither an intelligence test nor a memory competition. Attempts to impress the opposing attorney with your memory may get you into trouble at trial, when written documents show exactly the opposite of what you testified under oath at the deposition.

Fourth, although you are being called as a fact witness, the opposing attorney will very likely ask you to give an expert opinion. If you are asked a question that demands *more than your personal knowledge of this treatment and this patient,* give your attorney time to object before beginning your answer. If, for example, you are asked to explain the usual prognosis for patients with this diagnosis, to discuss the controversy surrounding what medication should be given to such patients, or to give your opinion on the debate over the treatment of choice, you are being asked to provide expert testimony. Because this testimony is not based on your knowledge of this singular treatment and this particular patient, your attorney will object. The court will limit your testimony to the facts of which you are personally aware.

Finally, in the absence of a specific exception created by the law (see chapter 3), you must have written permission from your patient or an order from the court (see chapter 7, Subpoenas and Court Orders) before you disclose any information or release any records. Only your patient's written permission or an order from the court will allow you to disclose confidential information or communications that are protected by testimonial privilege. A subpoena alone will not suffice.

16. Does whether I am an expert witness or a fact witness make any difference in what I am paid?

Whether you are a fact witness or an expert witness makes an *enormous* difference in how much you are paid. An expert witness negotiates a fee with the lawyer on behalf of whose client he will testify or consult. Services provided by the expert witness may consist of interviewing the patient, reviewing the record, speaking with current or former treaters, discussing the case with lawyers, and traveling to and from where the testimony is taken. The expert's fee will generally be set before the expert begins work. Expert witnesses can make a lot of money.

Fact witnesses are paid a fee established by statute. The fee in Florida is $5.00 per day (*not* per hour) and $.06 per mile of traveling. That said, many clinicians who are called as fact witnesses attempt to negotiate a reasonable hourly fee—often through an attorney—for time spent at the deposition and any time spent in preparation for the deposition. Both sides have an incentive to negotiate in these circumstances. The clinician who is testifying would obviously like to get paid more than $5.00 per day, especially since she will almost certainly have to cancel appointments. The attorney who has issued the subpoena does not want a clinician who is angry at having to cancel appointments, frustrated about pay, and eager to say as little as possible to expedite the process and get back to her office. The negotiated payment may be the clinician's hourly treatment fee.

17. I've heard that a "writ of habeas corpus" can play an important role in protecting the rights of a psychiatric patient. What is a writ of habeas corpus?

A writ of habeas corpus is a procedure that comes from centuries-old English law. The writ of habeas corpus, often referred to as the "Great Writ" because of its enormous legal and social significance, was used to request that a judge review the legality of an individual's incarceration. The drafters of the United States Constitution included the Great Writ as a means of having a judge review the decision of a state to incarcerate an individual.

The writ of habeas corpus was incorporated into Florida law to allow for a judge to review an individual's involuntary hospitalization. The power of a writ of habeas corpus is that it affords an individual the opportunity to go before a judge and say, "I am being confined illegally. I should be set free." The judge will then review the detention and ask the party responsible to justify the detention. A writ of habeas corpus can be used in child custody matters (where the judge will determine the child's proper custodian); in incompetency cases (where the judge will determine whether the alleged incompetent adult should be released from detention); and in civil commitment cases (where the judge will determine whether the patient has been appropriately placed in the hospital, or whether the patient is being denied a right or privilege).

18. What is a statute of limitations?

The law seeks to promote justice. If one individual injures another, justice requires that the injured party be allowed to seek compensation for that injury. But how long should the injured party be allowed to wait before she brings a lawsuit? Some might argue that she should be able to wait as long as she likes. She was harmed and therefore deserves compensation, regardless of when she seeks it.

The law takes a different position. The law limits the amount of time that may pass before you bring a suit, for two reasons. First, even though someone harmed you, that person has a right eventually to proceed with her life, without fear of being brought into court. A limitation on when a plaintiff can bring suit allows people to continue with their lives without worrying that events from the distant past could return to burden them. Thus, laws that limit the time within which a plaintiff can bring suit promote efficiency. Second, evidence becomes stale or disappears with time. A lawsuit affords a plaintiff an opportunity to prove that another person harmed her. The accused, in turn, has the opportunity to defend herself. If too much time elapses before a plaintiff files the suit, the accused person's ability to defend herself proportionately diminishes—memories fade, physical evidence deteriorates, and people helpful to a defense become old and die. For these reasons, the law imposes a time limit following an injury within which a plaintiff must bring suit. If the time expires, the lawsuit will not be heard. The statute of limitations specifies the length of this time period.

19. What is the statute of limitations for malpractice lawsuits in Florida?
Section 95.11 (Fla. Stat. ch. 95.11[4][a] and [b]) sets forth the statute of limitations in malpractice actions. Section 95.11 makes a distinction between *medical* and *professional* malpractice. In *Weinstock v. Groth*, 629 So. 2d 835 (Fla. 1993), the Florida Supreme Court ruled that psychologists are not considered to be health care providers. The logic of the *Weinstock* ruling would seem to apply to other mental health professionals who do not have a medical degree, such as social workers, marriage and family therapists, and mental health counselors. The implication is that these mental health professionals are considered to be mental health *practitioners*. Malpractice by a mental health practitioner is considered to be *professional* malpractice rather than *medical* malpractice. Thus, the statute of limitations set forth in section 95.11(4)(a) governs malpractice for these non-M.D. mental health professionals.

According to section 95.11(4)(a), an action for professional malpractice must be brought within two years of when the act that constitutes malpractice occurs. The twist is that the two-year statute of limitations begins to run when "the cause of action is discovered *or should have been discovered with the exercise of due diligence.*" Thus, a patient has two years from when she discovered that malpractice may have occurred—or with "due diligence" should have discovered that malpractice occurred—to bring a lawsuit against her treater. Section 95.11(4)(a) therefore sets as the time to begin counting the two-year statute of limitations period the time that an individual would recognize something constituting malpractice may have happened.

Section 95.11(4)(b), on the other hand, addresses the issue of *medical* malpractice. Section 95.11(4)(b) sets the same two-year period as the statute of limitations, and has the same twist as does (4)(a)—the two-year period begins to run from when the individual knew of the incident, or should have known of the incident "with the exercise of due diligence." Section 95.11(4)(b) adds another two twists, though. First, a lawsuit based in medical malpractice must be brought *within four years total* of when the incident occurred. Thus, if the individual did not discover the incident—even were she to exercise due diligence—she still only has a total of four years to file a lawsuit (not two years from whenever she learns of the incident). If a patient discovers that she has been harmed by her physician three and a half years after a medical procedure, she only has six months left within which to file suit. In one single instance an adult patient has more than four years to file suit—and this is the second twist to 95.11(4)(b). When the patient can prove that the injury was not discovered because of fraud, concealment, or intentional misrepresentation, she has up to seven years to file a lawsuit. (See the following question for how the statute of limitations applies to injuries to children.)

One note: Under section 766.106 (Fla. Stat. ch. 766.106), a patient must notify a health care provider 90 days prior to filing a medical malpractice lawsuit. This 90-day period allows the health care provider time to review the case, in order to see whether the case can be settled without going to trial.

20. How does the statute of limitations apply to cases involving minors?
Section 95.11 (Fla. Stat. ch. 95.11[4][b]) permits a minor to bring a negligence action against a health care provider either within two years of the injury, or anytime prior to the minor's eighth birthday—whichever period is longer. Note that the seven-year-period for malpractice actions involving fraud, concealment, and intentional misrepresentation (discussed in the question above) does *not* preclude the minor or the minor's representative from bringing the action on or before the minor's eighth birthday, even if the minor's eighth birthday is over seven years from when the injury occurred.

21. Does Florida law allow additional time for an individual to bring a lawsuit against a perpetrator of abuse or incest?
In April of 1992, the Florida legislature passed section 95.11(7) (Fla. Stat. ch. 95.11[7]). Section 95.11(7) states that an individual who has suffered abuse or incest has three different ways to gauge how much time she has to bring a lawsuit against the perpetrator:

- within seven years of when she reaches the age of majority (that is, until she is 25);

- within four years of when she ceases to be dependent on the abuser;
- within four years from the time she discovers *both* the injury (how she has been hurt, for example, an inability to enjoy sex) *and* the causal relationship between the injury and the abuse (the fact that the abuse or incest caused her injury).

Section 95.11(7) says that whichever of these three occurs latest—that is, gives the *most* time to bring the lawsuit—is the appropriate gauge.

A problem arises when the lawsuit is based on abuse or incest that occurred *before* April of 1992, when section 95.11(7) became law. In *Hearndon v. Graham*, 710 So. 2d 87 (Fla. App 1 Dist. 1998), the First District Court of Appeals ruled that cases occurring before section 95.11(7) was made law are governed by the old statute of limitations, which is four years. The court then paused, however, and said that this seemed unfair, given that many people simply don't remember that they have been abused, or don't connect the abuse to current symptoms, within that four-year period. The court considered whether it should apply the "delayed discovery" rule, a rule that allows the statute of limitations to stop running for a period of time in order to avoid an unjust result (an example of which would be not allowing a woman to sue the perpetrator of sexual abuse simply because more than four years had passed before she remembered what had happened). While the court ruled that it was bound to apply the four-year statute of limitations, because that's what the previous statute (in effect when the abuse in the *Hearndon* case had occurred) said, it was troubled enough by the result (not allowing the lawsuit to go forward) that it "certified" (see chapter 1) a question to the Florida Supreme Court. That question—which the Court has not yet ruled on—asks whether courts should apply the delayed discovery rule in cases that involve "traumatic amnesia caused by the abuse" (*Hearndon* at 92). The delayed discovery rule would serve to stop the statute of limitations from running ("toll" the statute, in legal parlance) until the individual realized that she had been abused and that the sexual abuse caused her injury.

22. What is the Americans with Disabilities Act?

The Americans with Disabilities Act was signed by President Bush in 1990. This Act provides sweeping federal protection for individuals with disabilities, including mental disabilities, in areas of employment, public services, and private services that accommodate the public. To be eligible for protection under the Act, an individual must have an impairment, a record of an impairment, or be regarded as having an impairment that substantially limits one or more major life activities. Thus, it protects both individuals who have an actual impairment and individuals who, because of stereotypes, may be kept out of the mainstream of their community's social and economic life.

Under the Americans with Disabilities Act, an employer may not refuse to hire and may not fire an individual because of a disability, if that individual can perform the "essential functions" of the job, either with or without "reasonable accommodation." The essential functions of the job are those duties that are necessary to the task. It would be necessary for an individual working as a hotel receptionist, for example, to interact with hotel guests. A reasonable accommodation is a modification that allows the individual to perform the essential functions of the job. A person with a mental disability, for example, may need time during working hours to see a therapist. Such time would be a reasonable accommodation. A more severe mental disability may require several days off for a brief inpatient stay. Additional unpaid leave for the purpose of a hospitalization could also be considered a reasonable accommodation.

23. Is it legal for an employer to ask during a job interview whether an applicant suffers from a mental illness or has ever received care from a mental health professional?
No. No excuses, no exceptions.

24. A job applicant may be asked to have a physical examination as part of the employment process. If asked about prescription medication, is it necessary to tell the individual conducting the examination about antipsychotic medication the applicant may be taking?
An employer may require a prospective employee to take a job-related physical only after the employer has made an initial offer of employment. In addition, the employer may require the physical only if all other successful applicants are required to take the same physical. The results of the examination must be kept confidential, and in a separate file. As part of a physical, the prospective employee will usually be asked to list all medications he is taking or has been prescribed. It is necessary for the employee to answer this question fully, and so to include any antipsychotic medication in his response. The employer may take back his offer of employment only if the results of the examination reveal that the indi-

vidual is not capable of performing the essential elements of the job he
has been offered.

25. Who has access to medical information revealed during a job-related physical examination?

The results of the physical examination are confidential and treated as
medical records (see chapter 10). Only with the written consent of the
employee may these records be released to third parties.

26. Lawyers frequently say that competent adults have a right to "informed consent." What is informed consent and when is an adult "competent" to give informed consent?

A value held dear in our society is that of individual autonomy. We
believe that individuals should be free to decide for themselves about a
whole range of life choices. The decision involving treatment is an example of the kind of choices people are free to make in our society. The
requirement of informed consent supports the value of individual autonomy in the context of treatment decisions. Informed consent means that
an individual makes a voluntary, knowing choice to accept or to reject a
certain course of treatment.

One question that frequently arises in discussions about informed
consent is: "What degree of information must a treater provide for the
consent to be truly informed?" According to section 394.455 (Fla. Stat.
ch. 394.455[9]), a treater must provide enough information for the
patient to make a "knowing" decision. Typically this will include information concerning the patient's diagnosis, the nature of the proposed
procedure, the risks and benefits of the proposed procedure, alternative
procedures along with their risks and benefits, and the risks of no treatment at all.

Once the patient has been provided the appropriate information, he
must then consent in a manner that is "voluntary and competent."
According to section 394.455 (Fla. Stat. ch. 394.455[9]), voluntary consent is consent devoid of "any element of fraud, deceit, duress, or other
form of constraint or coercion." According to section 765.101 (Fla. Stat.
ch. 765.101[7]), competent consent requires an individual to be physically and mentally able to communicate a willful and knowing decision.
Thus, competent consent requires the individual to express a choice
about treatment and to have at least a rudimentary understanding of the
information that has been provided.

In certain circumstances consent to treatment must be in writing. The Baker Act (Fla. Stat. ch. 394.459[3]; see chapter 5), for example, requires written consent for voluntary admissions to a psychiatric facility. If the patient has been adjudicated incompetent or is unable to provide informed consent to treatment, a surrogate decision-maker (such as a guardian, guardian advocate, health care surrogate, or proxy; see chapter 8) will make a decision on the patient's behalf. Parents or guardians generally consent to treatment on behalf of minors.

27. Lawyers sometimes make reference to "judicial review" and "administrative review." What is the difference between judicial and administrative review?

Decisions that affect the rights and entitlements of individuals are often made by administrative agencies, such as the Agency for Health Care Administration. When an individual is not satisfied with the decision of an agency, that individual may seek administrative review. Generally, a hearing officer will conduct an administrative hearing which may be held in a city, county, or state administrative agency having authority over the matter in question. For example, if an individual is denied Medicare coverage of a hospital stay because of the hospital's interpretation of Medicare guidelines, he may seek review of the decision through the Florida Quality Assurance agency, which will determine if the hospital's decision was correct. Generally, administrative hearings are less formal in their proceedings than are courts.

When administrative remedies have been exhausted and the individual is still not satisfied with the outcome, he may go to court and ask for a court to review the agency's decisions. The matter will then go before a judge, and hence will be one for judicial review.

28. What is the role of hypnosis in legal proceedings?

Hypnosis was long thought to improve memory, and so it is natural that the legal system would have an interest in what role hypnosis might play in discovering forgotten facts relevant to a legal proceeding. Research, however, has changed our fundamental understanding about how memory works, and our view of the relationship between hypnosis and memory has changed accordingly. Today, courts are extremely skeptical of the view that hypnotizing a witness will yield an accurate and objective account of past events. Court decisions reflect this changed view.

The courts have made three important rules about what happens when an individual who has been hypnotized wants to testify at trial. While these decisions were all in the context of criminal trials, their reasoning and analysis applies with equal force to civil trials. First, in *Bundy v. State*, 471 So. 2d 9 (Fla. 1985), the Supreme Court of Florida said that "the concerns surrounding the reliability of hypnosis warrant a holding that this mechanism, like polygraph and truth serum results, has not been proven sufficiently reliable by experts in the field to justify its validity as competent evidence in a criminal trial" (at 18). The court concluded that "hypnotically refreshed testimony is *per se* inadmissible in a criminal trial [in Florida]" (at 18). Thus, memory that has been enhanced by hypnosis is not admissible as evidence in a criminal court—an individual who has been hypnotized cannot testify about any memories that arose during or after the hypnosis.

Second, in *Stokes v. State*, 548 So. 2d 188 (Fla. 1989), the Supreme Court of Florida ruled that while an individual who has been hypnotized cannot testify as to facts that came out following hypnosis, such an individual can testify about statements made *prior* to having been hypnotized, provided the statements were "properly recorded." The court explained that for a statement to have been properly recorded, it "must be taken down on paper, or recorded on video or audio tape, or reduced to writing in a police officer's notes or report" (at 196). This second point is consistent with the court's general discomfort over any memories that arise from hypnosis: memories of an individual who has been hypnotized are admissible *only if* those memories were documented *before* the hypnosis took place.

Finally, in *Morgan v. State*, 537 So. 2d 973 (Fla. 1989), the Supreme Court of Florida ruled that the rule of *per se* inadmissibility could be applied to witnesses, but not to criminal defendants. Following an important decision of the United States Supreme Court, the Florida Supreme Court reasoned that because criminal defendants have a right to testify at trial, it was not permissible to have an absolute bar against their testimony, even if that testimony folows hypnosis. The court was clear, though—the exception to the rule of inadmissibility applied only to criminal defendants. The *Morgan* court's limitation of its ruling served to reemphasize the court's general suspicion of memories that arise from hypnosis and the court's extreme reluctance to have any such memories be introduced as evidence at trial.

5

INVOLUNTARY HOSPITALIZATION AND TREATMENT

Civil commitment refers to the process by which the state deprives an individual of his civil liberties because a risk of harm arises from his mental illness. The term "civil" distinguishes this sort of commitment from a criminal commitment, that is, a commitment that follows a finding of guilt in a criminal court of law. When placing individuals in a psychiatric facility, mental health professionals act under the authority of a state statute. In Florida this statute is the Baker Act, which allows mental health professionals to deprive an individual of his civil liberties when a substantial risk of serious bodily harm arises from his mental illness.

Just as in the criminal context, a deprivation of civil liberties because of mental illness is limited by procedural safeguards called "due process." Due process requires that when we deprive an adult of his liberty, whether because that individual is a suspected criminal or because that individual is mentally ill and dangerous, we make sure that certain procedures, such as the right to be represented by a lawyer and the right to a hearing before a judge or hearing officer, are in place. The amount of process—that is, how many safeguards—the Constitution requires depends on a balance of the individual's interest to be free and the state's interest to promote public health and to protect the safety of its citizens. The state protects its interests by invoking two separate types of power: the parens patriae *power, the authority to act as a parent and care for a citizen who is not able to care for himself, and the* police *power, the authority to detain an individual who is a danger to himself or to someone else.*

For many years in this country, mental illness alone was enough to justify depriving an individual of his liberty. Thus, were an individual simply "in need of treatment," he could be placed against his will in a psychiatric hospital. Times have changed, however, and today an individual's mental illness must present an issue of safety before he may be placed involuntarily in a hospital. Put another way, the state (often directed by court decisions) has grown less comfortable in using its parens patriae *power to govern the involuntary treatment of psychiatric patients; the* police *power now provides the basis for most state interventions into the lives of individuals who suffer from mental illness.*

QUESTIONS DISCUSSED IN THIS CHAPTER

29. Where does one find the statutes and regulations that govern psychiatric hospitalizations?
30. How does the Baker Act provide for involuntary psychiatric hospitalizations?
31. What is the criteria for taking an individual to a receiving facility for involuntary examination?
32. The requirements for involuntary examination, hospitalization, and treatment under the Act are based on a person's "mental illness." Does the law define "mental illness"?
33. What actually happens during the 72-hour examination period?
34. Who can authorize a 72-hour hold for involuntary examination?
35. Which court has jurisdiction over cases that involve an involuntary psychiatric examination in a receiving facility?
36. If someone believes that he has been wrongfully taken to a receiving facility for an involuntary examination, can he ask a court to review that decision?
37. What are the criteria that govern involuntary hospitalization beyond the 72-hour examination?
38. A hearing, called a "Baker Act involuntary placement hearing," determines whether a person should be confined for involuntary treatment following the 72-hour examination period. How does such a hearing work?

39. What happens if at the end of a six-month period an individual continues to meet the criteria for involuntary treatment?
40. What judicial review is available if a person believes he has been unlawfully confined for treatment following the initial 72-hour hold or that his period of involuntary treatment has been incorrectly continued for another six months?
41. Which court has jurisdiction over cases involving detention beyond the 72-hour examination?
42. What is the standard of proof in involuntary hospitalization cases? Who bears the burden of proof?
43. How does a person receive *voluntary* psychiatric hospitalization and treatment?
44. When may a voluntary patient be held against his will?
45. What rights does a psychiatric inpatient have?
46. Can any rights of a psychiatric inpatient ever be denied?
47. Do psychiatric patients have the right to refuse antipsychotic medication?
48. The Baker Act gives a great deal of authority to psychiatrists, psychologists, psychiatric nurses, clinical social workers, and police officers. Could a patient who has been involuntarily hospitalized ever have cause to sue one of these individuals?
49. Does a mental health professional have a legal duty to hospitalize an outpatient who appears to meet the criteria for involuntary hospitalization?
50. Can alcohol or substance abuse (rather than mental illness) provide the basis for involuntary hospitalization?
51. May seclusion and restraint be used for therapeutic purposes?
52. If a client who clearly meets the criteria for involuntary hospitalization gets up to walk out of my office, should I attempt physically to restrain him?
53. Does Florida have a law providing for outpatient commitment?

DISCUSSION

29. Where does one find the statutes and regulations that govern psychiatric hospitalizations?

The statutes and regulations relevant to psychiatric hospitalizations are found in two places. First, the Florida Mental Health Act, more commonly known as the Baker Act (named after a former State Representative from Miami, Maxine Baker, who sponsored and advocated for the bill), contains all the statutory provisions that relate to hospitalizations based on mental illness. The Baker Act thus addresses topics such as voluntary and involuntary treatment, patients' rights, and confidentiality. The Baker Act is found in chapter 394, part I of the Florida Statutes. Whenever a reference is made to a section of the Baker Act, that section is therefore found in chapter 394 of the Florida Statutes. Second, the Florida Administrative Code, Rule 65E-5, contains the administrative rules that interpret the statutes and provide guidance to state institutions.

30. How does the Baker Act provide for involuntary psychiatric hospitalizations?

Involuntary psychiatric hospitalization is provided for by a two-stage process. First, an individual who is believed to meet certain criteria may be placed in a receiving facility, which could be a hospital or a crisis center, for 72 hours (weekends and holidays are not counted as part of the 72-hour period, so that the actual time an individual is involuntarily detained can be longer than 72 hours). The purpose of this 72-hour period is to examine the individual and to determine whether he or she is a danger to self or others. These examinations take place at "receiving facilities" designated by the state for involuntary examination and subsequent hospitalization. Receiving facilities are generally hospitals and crisis stabilization units located at certain community mental health centers. Second, if it appears during the 72-hour examination period that an individual meets another set of more stringent criteria, the administrator of the facility may "petition" (file a written request) that asks a court to order an involuntary hospitalization for the purpose of protecting the individual or others whom the individual might harm, and for providing treatment. (Note that, if competent, the individual must first be given the option of entering the hospital on a *voluntary* basis). Thus, the Baker Act provides for two stages:

• an examination stage; and
• a hearing stage in which a court determines whether hospitalization beyond the initial 72-hour period is warranted.

31. What is the criteria for taking an individual to a receiving facility for an involuntary examination?

The Baker Act defines the circumstances under which an adult may be taken to a psychiatric hospital designated by the county for examination and subsequent hospitalization. According to section 463 of the Baker Act (Fla. Stat. ch. 394.463), there are three requirements for a 72-hour involuntary examination:

- The individual has a mental illness; *and*
- As a result of that mental illness, the individual refuses *or* is unable to determine whether examination is necessary; *and*
- the person is likely to suffer from self-neglect *or* cause harm to him or herself or others.

Note three things about section 394.463's criteria. First, the criteria are applicable *only* to individuals with a mental illness. Second, the mental illness must be the *cause* of the individual's refusal to be examined or inability to determine whether an examination is necessary. Third, as a result of the mental illness the person is likely to suffer harm, or to injure himself or someone else. If section 394.463's criteria are met, the individual may be placed in a receiving facility for up to 72 hours for the purpose of determining whether further hospitalization is appropriate.

32. The requirements for involuntary examination, hospitalization, and treatment under the Act are based on a person's "mental illness." Does the law define "mental illness"?
The Baker Act defines mental illness as "an impairment of the emotional processes that exercise conscious control of one's actions or of the ability to perceive or understand reality, which impairment substantially interferes with a person's ability to meet the ordinary demands of living." Note how the impairment must "substantially" interfere with the person's ability to function in everyday life. Also, the statute specifically excludes retardation, developmental disabilities, intoxication, substance abuse, and antisocial behavior from the definition of mental illness.

33. What actually happens during the 72-hour examination period?
Section 394.463 (Fla. Stat. ch. 394.463[2][f]) sets what happens during the 72-hour examination period. Upon arriving at the receiving facility, the patient must be examined by a physician or clinical psychologist "without unnecessary delay"; this is generally considered to mean within 24 hours. On the basis of this examination, one of the four following things must happen: (1) the patient is released entirely (unless he has been charged with a crime, in which case the release is to a law enforce-

ment officer; (2) the patient is released with a recommendation for outpatient treatment; (3) the patient is asked to consent to voluntary treatment; (4) the patient is believed to meet the criteria for involuntary hospitalization, refuses to consent to voluntary hospitalization, and the administrator of the receiving facility files a petition (a written request), asking a court to order continued hospitalization.

If, at the end of the 72-hour examination period, a petition for involuntary placement is filed with a court (option 4), the petition must be supported by the opinion of a psychiatrist and the second opinion of a clinical psychologist or another psychiatrist. Both of these mental health professionals must have personally examined the patient within the preceding 72 hours. The opinions must state that the criteria for continued involuntary placement are met (see question 37). (In certain rural counties, with populations of less than 50,000, the second opinion may be provided by a physician or psychiatric nurse who has special training and experience.)

34. Who can authorize a 72-hour hold for involuntary examination?

An involuntary examination is a way to have a person placed in a hospital (a receiving facility) to assess that individual and determine whether further hospitalization and treatment is appropriate. Often the situation is an emergency and the necessity of getting the person to a safe place is paramount. Section 463 of the Baker Act (Fla. Stat. ch. 394.463) provides for the possible emergency nature of the situation by allowing three ways to place an individual in a receiving facility for an examination. First, while courts generally must hear two sides to every story, in this situation a judge may issue an *ex parte* order. An *ex parte* order occurs when a court hears only one side to a story and issues a directive on the basis that action must be taken immediately. If a court receives sworn testimony—someone comes before a judge and speaks under oath—the court can issue an *ex parte* order that directs a police officer to pick an individual up and take him to the nearest receiving facility. Second, a police officer may take into custody a person who appears to meet the criteria for involuntary examination and deliver him to the nearest receiving facility. Third, a physician, clinical psychologist, psychiatric nurse, or clinical social worker (these terms are defined in section 394.455) may sign a certificate stating that he or she has examined the person within the past 48 hours and that the person appears to meet the criteria for involuntary examination. The certificate must state the observations on which this conclusion is based. A police officer may then take the individual into custody and deliver him to a receiving facility.

35. Which court has jurisdiction over cases that involve an involuntary psychiatric examination in a receiving facility?

The circuit court for the county in which the receiving facility is located has jurisdiction over cases that involve involuntary examination. Thus, a circuit court judge for that county would be the appropriate judge to issue an *ex parte* order that an individual be placed in a receiving facility for a 72-hour examination. Likewise, a petition for continued hospitalization is filed in the circuit court for the county in which the receiving facility is located.

36. If someone believes that he has been wrongfully taken to a receiving facility for an involuntary examination, can he ask a court to review that decision?

Yes. An individual can file a writ of *habeas corpus* to challenge confinement for the purpose of involuntary examination.

37. What are the criteria that govern involuntary hospitalization beyond the 72-hour examination?

Section 463 of the Baker Act (Fla. Stat. ch. 394.463) sets forth the criteria that govern whether it is appropriate to place an individual in a receiving facility for an involuntary examination (see question 31). Section 467 of the Baker Act sets forth the criteria that govern whether it is appropriate to confine an individual involuntarily for a longer period of time than the initial 72 hours, for the purpose of providing treatment and protecting the patient's safety as well as the safety of others. The criteria that govern hospitalizations beyond the 72-hour examination period are more stringent because they allow hospitalizations for a much longer period of time, up to six months.

According to section 467 of the Baker Act, a person may be involuntarily placed for treatment beyond the initial 72-hour examination period if the court finds that a person is mentally ill and, because of his mental illness, has refused voluntary placement or is unable to determine whether placement is necessary. In addition, the individual must be:

- incapable of surviving alone or with the help of others and without treatment is likely to suffer from neglect that poses a real and present threat of substantial harm to his or her well-being; *or*

- There is substantial likelihood that in the near future he or she will inflict serious bodily harm on himself or another person, as evidenced by recent behavior causing, attempting, or threatening such harm.

Finally, all available less restrictive treatment alternatives, which would offer an opportunity for improvement of his or her condition, have been judged to be inappropriate.

Note six things about the criteria for involuntary treatment found in section 394.467. First, the individual must be mentally ill to meet the section's criteria. Second, the individual must be given the option of voluntary treatment, or must be unable to determine whether placement is necessary, before involuntary placement is appropriate. Third, there must be a *causal link* between the individual's mental illness and his inability to care for himself or the likelihood that he will harm himself or someone else. Fourth, a likelihood of harm to oneself or others must be supported by actual behaviors—mere conjecture that an individual is likely to harm himself or someone else will not suffice. Behaviors offered in support of a likelihood to harm must be "recent." Fifth, before involuntary hospitalization is appropriate an individual's incapacity to survive alone must pose a "*real* and *present* threat of *substantial* harm" to his well-being. In the alternative, there must be a "*substantial* likelihood that in the *near* future" the person will inflict "*serious* bodily harm" on himself or someone else. Sixth, no appropriate alternative less restrictive than hospitalization can be available.

Hospitalization for the purpose of treatment above and beyond the 72-hour examination period is appropriate only when all the criteria set forth by section 467 of the Baker Act are met.

38. A hearing, called a "Baker Act involuntary placement hearing," determines whether a person should be confined for involuntary treatment following the 72-hour examination period. How does such a hearing work?

During the course of the 72-hour hold for an examination, mental health professionals will determine whether the individual meets the criteria for involuntary admission. If the mental health professionals conclude that continued hospitalization is indeed appropriate, they will offer the patient hospitalization on a voluntary basis. If the patient refuses, the administrator of the facility will file a petition (a written request) with the circuit court that requests continued hospitalization on an involuntary basis. In response to this petition, the court will hold a hearing. The hearing must be held within five days from when the petition is filed.

At the hearing to determine whether involuntary placement is warranted beyond the 72-hour period allotted for examination, the stakes have dramatically increased. An individual can now be confined in a psychiatric hospital for six months against his will. As a consequence, the law provides for certain protections designed to safeguard the individual's legal rights. These safeguards include the right to an attorney (to a public defender if the individual does not have a private lawyer). The patient's attorney must be allowed to see the patient, to interview witnesses, and to review records relevant to the case. The individual also has the right to be examined by an independent expert, and the law requires that the patient or his attorney be notified of this right. If it is determined that the patient is not competent, section 4598 of the Baker Act (Fla. Stat. ch. 394.4598) says that a guardian advocate will be appointed to protect his rights (see question 109).

The hearing is usually held in a hospital room. The state attorney represents the facility that has filed the petition requesting continued hospitalization. Testimony is given under oath and the proceedings must be recorded. According to Florida law, the circuit court has jurisdiction over the proceeding, but may appoint a "special master" to preside. All evidence relevant to the necessity of involuntary treatment must be admitted. At least one of the mental health professionals whose opinions formed the basis for the petition for continued confinement is required to testify (although this requirement is often not observed). If the judge or hearing officer concludes at the hearing that the patient meets the criteria for involuntary placement found in section 467 of the Baker Act, the court orders that the patient be retained or transferred to an appropriate facility for a period of up to six months.

39. What happens if at the end of a six-month period an individual continues to meet the criteria for involuntary treatment?

The criteria for involuntary treatment following the initial six-month commitment are the same criteria set forth in section 467 of the Baker Act (Fl. Stat. ch. 394.467). If the patient continues to meet these criteria, the administrator of the treatment facility must, prior to the expiration of the six-month period, file a petition requesting authorization for continued involuntary placement. The request must be accompanied by a statement from the patient's physician or clinical psychologist that justifies the request, a brief description of the patient's treatment during the time he was involuntarily placed, and an individualized plan of continued treatment. Hearings on petitions for continued involuntary placement are administrative rather than judicial in nature (see question 27) and so may be (and usually are) conducted by a hearing officer. As in the initial placement process, the patient has the right to an attorney. If the administrative judge concludes that the criteria are met for continued involuntary placement, the judge will sign an order for continued involuntary placement. Like the initial order, the order for continued placement is for up to six months. The same procedure is followed prior to the expiration of each period in which the patient is retained. Patients may continue to be confined as long as they continue to meet the commitment criteria set forth in section 467 of the Baker Act.

40. What judicial review is available if a person believes he has been unlawfully confined for treatment following the initial 72-hour hold or that his period of involuntary treatment has been incorrectly continued for another six months?
Because of the six-month period of confinement, the Baker Act specifically provides that individuals may request a court to review their confinement beyond the 72-hour examination. In addition, section 459 of the Baker Act (Fla. Stat. ch. 394.459) provides that individuals may seek a writ of habeas corpus (see question 17) from the circuit court at any time to challenge the cause and legality of their detention, or to challenge the legality of the conditions under which they are detained. Finally, if no reasonable mental health professional would think that an individual meets commitment criteria, then keeping that individual in this hospital against his will may constitute false imprisonment and even battery, if the individual is physically restrained from leaving. (See *Garcia v. Psychiatric Institutes of America,* 638 So. 2d 567 [Fla. App. 5 Dist. 1994] concerning this last point.)

41. Which court has jurisdiction over cases involving detention beyond the 72-hour examination?
The circuit court has jurisdiction to decide whether the individual requires hospitalization following the 72-hour examination. According to section 394.467(6)(a)(2), a special master may preside over this hearing. In 1997, the Florida Supreme Court, in *Onwu v. State,* 692 So. 2d 881 (Fla. 1997), stated that "an involuntary commitment under the Baker Act may only be entered by the circuit court" (at 883), so the circuit

court actually issues the order for involuntary commitment. (Note, however, that in *Liebman v. State,* 555 So. 2d 1242 [Fla. App. 4 Dist. 1989]), the Fourth District Court of Appeals ruled that a hearing officer may make decisions about *continued* hospitalization, following the initial determination by a circuit court; see question 39).

42. What is the standard of proof in involuntary hospitalization cases? Who bears the burden of proof?

In cases that involve involuntary hospitalization, the state bears the burden of proof to show that the individual meets the criteria for involuntary hospitalization. Section 467 of the Baker Act (Fla. Stat. ch. 394.467[1]) provides that the standard of proof is clear and convincing evidence. (See questions 4 and 5 for discussions of the standard and burden of proof.) Thus, the state must jump a "mid-level" proof hurdle before an individual may be hospitalized against his will above and beyond the initial 72-hour placement. The language found in the Baker Act concerning the standard of proof squares Florida law with *Addington v. Texas,* 441 U.S. 418 (1978), in which the United States Supreme Court ruled that clear and convincing evidence is the federal Constitutional standard required for involuntary hospitalization and treatment.

INVOLUNTARY HOSPITALIZATON

The Baker Act: Chapter 394 of the Florida Statutes

I. 72-hour examination period
    A. Governed by section 463 of the Baker Act (Fla. Stat. ch. 394.463).
    B. May be arranged for by:
        1. A court's *ex parte* order
        2. A police officer
        3. A physician, clinical psychologist, psychiatric nurse, clinical social worker
    C. Standard for:
        1. Individual has a mental illness
        2. As a result of mental illness:
            a. individual refuses or is unable to determine whether examination is necessary; *and*

continued

       b.   person is likely to suffer from self-neglect or cause harm to himself or others.

D.   Mental illness is defined as impairment of an emotional process that **substantially** interferes with the person's ability to meet the **ordinary demands of living.**

E.   Habeas corpus available for judicial review.

F.   Final disposition:
1. Release (or release to law enforcement, if the individual has been charged with a crime)
2. Release with a recommendation to seek outpatient care
3. Enter hospital on voluntary basis
4. Administrator of receiving facility files petition with court requesting involuntary treatment

II.   Involuntary treatment following 72-hour examination period

A.   Governed by section 467 of the Baker Act (Fla. Stat. ch. 394.467).

B.   Following petition filed with circuit court, a hearing is held to determine whether further hospitalization is appropriate. Hearing must be held within five days of when petition is filed.

C.   Standard for involuntary hospitalization:
1. Person is **mentally ill.**
2. Because of mental illness, individual has **refused** or is **unable to determine** whether hospitalization is necessary; *and*
   a.   Individual is **incapable of surviving alone or with help of others** and without treatment is likely to suffer harm from neglect which poses **real and substantial** threat of **present** harm; *or*
   b.   There is **substantial** likelihood that in the **near** future individual will inflict **serious bodily harm** on self or another, as evidenced by **recent** behavior; *and*
3. **No alternative less restrictive** than hospital available.

D.   Standard of proof is clear and convincing evidence. State bears burden of proof.

E.   Judicial review available. Section 459 of Baker Act also allows filing of writ of habeas corpus.

F.   Involuntary hospitalization lasts up to six months.

III.   Continued involuntary treatment

A.   May follow initial commitment of six months.

B.   Standard for continued involuntary treatment same as standard set out in section 467 of the Baker Act.

C.   Individual may be hospitalized involuntarily as long as he meets section 467 criteria.

43. How does a person receive *voluntary* psychiatric hospitalization and treatment?

Section 4625 of the Baker Act (Fl. Stat. ch. 394.4625) sets only minimal requirements for voluntary treatment. These requirements are designed to protect the patient rather than to limit admission. The reason is that the state wants to facilitate psychiatric treatment for those who need it. A facility may admit any person 18 years of age or older who makes application for admission (or, in the case of a minor, whose guardian makes the application) as long as the individual shows evidence of mental illness and is competent to provide informed consent (see question 26). A person age 17 or under who wants to admit himself to a psychiatric hospital may be admitted only after a hearing to verify the voluntariness of his consent.

A voluntary patient who requests discharge must be released within 24 hours or transferred to involuntary status. Clinicians should be aware that:

* According to section 394.4625 (Fla. Stat. ch. 394.4625[2][a]), the treatment facility may extend the discharge for three days, excluding weekends and holidays, to allow for discharge planning;
* The facility may transfer the individual to involuntary status following a voluntary request for discharge.

The requirements for voluntary admission and discharge are simple and nonrestrictive on purpose. The legislature wants to facilitate admission and treatment for those who need it, especially for those who seek treatment voluntarily. The preference for voluntary, rather than involuntary, hospitalizations is reflected in section 467 of the Baker Act (Fl. Stat. ch. 394.467), which authorizes the involuntary placement of competent patients only after they have been offered and have refused the possibility of voluntary placement.

44. When may a voluntary patient be held against his will?

Generally, a voluntary patient must be released upon request. A patient may be held involuntarily only when he meets the requirements for involuntary treatment *and* insists on leaving the treatment facility. According to section 4625 of the Baker Act (Fl. Stat. ch. 394.4625[5]), a facility that has received a request for a voluntary discharge must communicate the request as quickly as possible (and within a maximum of 12 hours) to a physician, clinical psychologist, or psychiatrist. If the examining mental health professional determines that the patient meets the criteria for involuntary placement, a petition seeking involuntary treatment must be filed with the court within two working days. If the petition is not filed within this period of time, the patient must be discharged. Between the time the request for discharge is made and the hearing actually occurs, the patient can be held and emergency treatment rendered in the least restrictive manner, provided a physician has determined that such treatment is necessary for the safety of the patient or others.

Although the distinction between involuntary and voluntary status may seem academic, it is significant. The six-month maximum time period applies only to *involuntary* patients. Thus, there is an advantage to remaining a voluntary patient, insofar as once a patient has become an involuntary patient, the hospital's authority over that individual increases substantially.

45. What rights does a psychiatric inpatient have?

Psychiatric patients retain the same rights that federal and state laws guarantee to all other citizens. Section 459 of the Baker Act (Fl. Stat. ch. 394.459[1]) provides that persons receiving treatment in psychiatric facilities cannot be deprived of any constitutional rights. In addition, section 459 of the Baker Act explicitly enumerates the rights of psychiatric inpatients. Under that section, patients have the right to dignity, the right to quality treatment that is the least restrictive under the patient's circumstances, the right to give informed consent before being treated, the right to communicate freely and privately with the outside world, the right to possess personal effects and clothing, and the right to vote. Section 394.4615 (Fla. Stat. ch. 394.4615) provides that patients have the right to see their records, and a right to have their records kept confidential. Regulations in the Florida Administrative Code—specifically Rules 65E-5.140, 65E-5.150, and 65E-5.160—make provisions to ensure that these rights are implemented.

46. Can any rights of a psychiatric inpatient ever be denied?

The law must sometimes balance the rights of the patient against competing state interests. When state interests are sufficiently compelling, the law may limit the patient's rights accordingly. For example, although section 459 of the Baker Act (Fla. Stat. ch. 394.459[5]) states that inpatients have the right to communicate freely and privately with persons outside the institution, staff could prevent a patient from speaking with a certain individual on the phone, if phone calls with that individual were extremely upsetting and determined by the treatment team to be harmful to the person or others.

47. Do psychiatric patients have the right to refuse antipsychotic medication?

Yes. According to section 459 of the Baker Act (Fla. Stat. ch. 394.459[3]) and rule 65E-5.170(d) in the Administrative Code, a patient must provide informed consent before antipsychotic medications can be administered. That is, before antipsychotic medication can be given the patient must *consent* to the medication. If a competent patient does not consent, antipsychotic medication cannot be administered.

This right is not, however, without limits. The right extends neither to emergency situations, nor to instances where the court has determined that the patient is not competent to make treatment decisions (see question 115). Under Rule 65E-5.1703, an emergency treatment order supersedes the individual's right to refuse psychotropic medication. To fall under Rule 65E-5.1703, the emergency order must be based upon a physician's determination that the individual is not capable of exercising voluntary control over his own behavior and that the uncontrolled behavior is an imminent danger to the patient or others in the facility.

48. The Baker Act gives a great deal of authority to psychiatrists, psychologists, psychiatric nurses, clinical social workers, and police officers. Could a patient who has been involuntarily hospitalized ever have cause to sue one of these individuals?

The Baker Act gives a great deal of authority to the individuals who play central roles in the care and treatment of psychiatric patients. At times, psychiatric care and treatment will involve involuntary confinement. An undue fear of litigation could seriously compromise the ability and willingness of a mental health professional or a police officer to carry out the responsibilities required of his or her job. Thus, the law does not want to invite litigation against these individuals for making innocent mistakes. At the same time, however, it is important that these individuals appreciate the seriousness of their responsibilities and know that a wrong decision may result in an inappropriate deprivation of a person's civil liberties. For this reason, the law has a "good faith" standard that governs the actions of individuals carrying out involuntary hospitalizations under the Baker Act. Any person who acts in good faith is immune from liability for actions in connection with the admission, diagnosis, treatment, or discharge of patients.

49. Does a mental health professional have a legal duty to hospitalize an outpatient who appears to meet the criteria for involuntary hospitalization?

According to Florida law, a mental health professional does *not* have a legal duty to hospitalize an outpatient who appears to meet criteria for involuntary hospitalization. The case that makes this point most clearly is *Paddock v. Chacko*, 522 So. 2d 410 (Fla. App. 5 Dist. 1988), which involved Linda Paddock, a 35-year-old woman who was temporarily residing with her parents in Orlando. Ms. Paddock had a history of suicide attempts and, shortly after arriving in Florida from North Carolina, had consulted a psychiatrist, Dr. Chacko, about certain symptoms she was experiencing. Shortly following her meeting with Dr. Chacko—later the same day—Ms. Paddock's symptoms began to intensify and she contacted Dr. Chacko about what to do. Dr. Chacko recommended hospitalization and arranged for a bed on an inpatient unit. Ms. Paddock said that she would need to speak with her father before going to the hospital; Ms. Paddock's father, however, would not consent to the hospitalization. Two days later Ms. Paddock ran into a wooded area near her parents' home, superficially slashed her wrists with a knife, and set her clothes on fire. Ms. Paddock then brought a lawsuit against Dr. Chacko, on the basis that Dr. Chacko had failed to take her into custodial care in a crisis situation.

The district court of appeals ruled that Dr. Chacko had no duty to take Ms. Paddock into his custody in order to prevent her from harming herself. The court reasoned that while mental health professionals have the *discretion* in certain instances to take a patient into custody, there is no *duty* to do so. In fact, explained the court, a patient can sue a mental health professional for malicious prosecution following an inappropriate hospitalization. To the court, it hardly seemed fair to place the mental health professional between a rock and a hard place—that is, between the prospect of a lawsuit for failing to hospitalize (should the patient harm herself, as Ms. Paddock had done) and for failing *not* to hospitalize (should the patient believe that the hospitalization was not warranted and so sue for malicious prosecution). The court concluded that:

> The principle underlying all these cases is the same. Where a patient has surrendered himself to the custody, care, and treatment of a psychiatric hospital and its staff, liability may be predicated upon the hospital's failure to take protective measures to prevent the patient from

injuring himself. We have found no case that has held a doctor liable
for the failure to take his patient into custody. Under the circumstances
and facts of this case, we are unwilling to extend the duty of custodial
supervision and care to the outpatient relationship between a psychiatrist and a patient. (*Paddock* at 417)

Following *Paddock,* a mental health professional does not have a duty to
take an outpatient into custody.

**50. Can alcohol or substance abuse (rather than mental illness) provide
the basis for involuntary hospitalization?**
Florida's Marchman Act, found in chapter 397 of the Florida Statutes
(beginning at section 301), governs treatment for substance abuse.
Section 675 of the Marchman Act (Fla. Stat. ch. 397.675) sets forth the
criteria for involuntary admission on the basis of substance abuse.
According to section 397.675, involuntary admission is appropriate
when there is a good faith reason to believe the person is substance-
abuse impaired and, because of such impairment:

• has lost the power of self-control with respect to substance use; and
  either
• has inflicted, or threatened or attempted to inflict, or unless admitted
  is likely to inflict, physical harm on himself or herself or another; *or*
• is in need of substance-abuse services and, by reason of substance-
  abuse impairment, his or her judgment has been so impaired that
  the person is incapable of appreciating his or her need for such
  services and of making a rational decision concerning substance-
  abuse treatment.

A person meeting the criteria who is brought to the attention of a law
enforcement officer or is in a public place can be placed in protective
custody (protective custody measures include, at the discretion of the
law enforcement officer, assisting the impaired person to his house, taking the person to a licensed detoxification or addiction treatment receiving facility, or bringing the person to jail). A person under protective
custody can be held against his will in a facility for a period no longer
than 72 hours unless he continues to meet involuntary admission criteria. When the person continues to meet involuntary admission criteria, a
court can order the person be held for assessment and stabilization for
up to five days. Should he continue to meet the criteria for involuntary

confinement after those five days, a court can order the person to be held for involuntary treatment for up to 60 days at a time. The Marchman Act demonstrates that while the legislature does not regard chronic alcohol or substance abuse as a mental illness, it does recognize that its effects can be equally debilitating. Thus, the Marchman Act attempts to provide for prompt evaluation and treatment of persons who are impaired by chronic alcoholism and substance abuse.

51. May seclusion and restraint be used for therapeutic purposes?

No. Whatever value seclusion and restraint have (their purpose and effect are often disputed; some argue a therapeutic value because they can help calm a patient or remove excess stimuli that might intensify agitation), the law sets clear guidelines regarding their use. Seclusion and/or restraint may only be used in treatment facilities that are authorized to use them. In addition, seclusion and/or restraint may only be used when a patient's behavior poses a serious threat of injury to self or others. As soon as the threat no longer exists, the patient must be released. Seclusion and/or restraint can never be used as a punishment or in place of a less restrictive alternative treatment, and they may only be used after receipt of a written order from a physician or in a legally defined emergency. Any use of seclusion and/or restraint must be accompanied by proper documentation.

Mental health professionals should note, however, that restraint refers to the unreasonable confinement of an individual's freedom to move. Restraint does not refer to orthopaedically prescribed appliances necessary for treatment, supportive body bands, protective helmets, or physical holding when necessary for surgical purposes, medical treatment, or to achieve functional bodily position or proper balance to protect a patient from falling out of bed.

52. If a client who clearly meets the criteria for involuntary hospitalization gets up to walk out of my office, should I attempt physically to restrain him?

The vast majority of mental health professionals are neither trained in the technique, nor legally authorized, to restrain a client. From a practical point of view, this lack of training *increases* the likelihood that someone will get injured if you attempt to restrain a client. From a legal point of view, you risk being sued for assault and battery should you attempt physically to restrain a client. *Do not attempt to do what you are neither trained nor legally authorized to do.*

If a client who appears to meet commitment criteria insists on leaving your office, call the people who are trained and authorized to handle this sort of situation: mental health workers at a community mental health center, security at a hospital, or the local police. Apprise the appropriate agency of the situation. Although it is difficult to watch such a client walk out of your office, it is best to use *your* expertise (in formulating a clinical assessment) to inform others so that they may use *their* expertise (in detaining a client for the purpose of assessment) to place your client in a safe setting.

53. Does Florida have a law providing for outpatient commitment?

Outpatient commitment requires an individual to comply with a treatment plan when *outside the walls of* a psychiatric unit. As an example, in certain states failure to comply with a treatment plan provides a sufficient reason for the authorities to take a person to the hospital against his will. That is, failure to comply with treatment, in and of itself, sets in motion a series of events that may lead to a person being taken to the hospital involuntarily.

There is only very limited outpatient commitment in Florida. The only direct statutory authority regarding outpatient placement deals with minors (section 394.4784) and mentally ill criminal defendants (see question 71). No Florida law allows for the involuntary detainment or hospitalization of an outpatient (other than a minor or a person convicted of a crime) solely because that person has failed to follow a treatment plan.

6

CRIMINAL LAW

Mental health professionals may be called upon to assess whether a criminal defendant is responsible for a crime he has committed, or whether he is competent to proceed. "Competence to proceed" is the term used in Florida for the defendant's ability to participate in any aspect of the criminal proceeding. Other jurisdictions use the term "competence to stand trial" or "fitness to stand trial" to denote the defendant's threshold ability to be placed on trial. The Florida term "competence to proceed" has a wider meaning, because it refers both to the defendant's competence to stand trial, as well as to his competence to participate in other stages of the trial process, such as sentencing.

Competence to proceed and criminal responsibility are often confused with one another. They are alike insofar as both require assessing a criminal defendant's state of mind. They differ insofar as competence to proceed focuses on the defendant's state of mind <u>at the time of the legal proceedings</u>, while criminal responsibility focuses on the defendant's state of mind <u>at the time of the crime</u>. An individual who is found not criminally responsible at the time of the crime is referred to as "criminally insane" or "not guilty by reason of insanity" (NGRI); insanity is thus a <u>legal</u> concept with <u>legal</u> consequences.

QUESTIONS DISCUSSED IN THIS CHAPTER

54. What is the Florida test for criminal insanity?
55. What happens to a person in Florida who is found criminally insane?
56. Is the "manifestly dangerous" standard for those who have been acquitted by reason of insanity different than the criteria for involuntary hospitalization under the Baker Act?
57. When is a person in Florida not competent to proceed (not competent to stand trial)?
58. What happens to a person in Florida who is found not competent to proceed?
59. What role do mental health professionals play in helping courts to decide whether a criminal defendant is criminally insane or not competent to proceed?
60. If it appears that the defendant is not competent to proceed, or that the defendant was insane at the time of the crime, who actually raises these issues in court, and when do the issues get addressed?
61. The prosecutor has the burden of proving all the elements of a crime beyond a reasonable doubt. Does the prosecutor also have to prove that a criminal defendant was sane at the time of the crime? If not, who has the burden of proof when the issue of insanity gets raised at trial?
62. What is the defense of "diminished capacity"?
63. How is a diminished capacity defense different from an insanity defense?
64. Does Florida have a defense based on diminished capacity?
65. Given that Florida does not have a defense based on diminished capacity, do mental health professionals have any role in providing expert testimony about mental illness or impairment when the defendant is not using an insanity defense?
66. Would a mental health professional be allowed to testify about psychological syndromes, such as battered-spouse syndrome or post-traumatic stress disorder, in a criminal trial?
67. Would a mental health professional be allowed to testify about a psychological autopsy in a criminal trial?
68. What happens if someone in a jail or prison becomes depressed, has a psychotic break, or otherwise needs mental health services?
69. Does an inmate have the right to refuse treatment that the jail or prison wants to provide?
70. What about someone who is committed because he is incompetent

to proceed—does that person have the right to refuse treatment, even though the purpose of the commitment is to return him to competence so the legal proceedings can move forward?

71. Can a court require a criminal defendant to receive mental health services as a condition of probation or parole?

72. If treatment is made a condition of probation or parole, what information should a mental health professional provide the probation or parole officer?

73. Some states have special laws regarding sexual predators or sex offenders. These laws allow for civil commitment immediately following the individual's prison sentence so that the person is never actually released from state custody. Does Florida have such a law?

74. Do mental health professionals have a role to play in death penalty cases?

DISCUSSION

54. What is the Florida test for criminal insanity?

When should society not blame an individual for his actions, even if those actions break the criminal law? If a person becomes psychotic and assaults a stranger, is he criminally insane? If a person steals a car while in a manic state, should he be sent to jail? If a person commits a murder while dissociating and later remembers nothing, is incarceration an appropriate response?

The test of legal insanity in Florida is taken from the M'Naghten rule, derived from England's M'Naghten case of 1843. To establish an insanity defense under the M'Naghten rule (also referred to as the "right-wrong" test), a defendant must prove that at the time of the criminal act, he was "laboring under such a defect of reason from mental illness as not to know the nature and quality of the act or not to know that the act was wrong." Florida has followed the heart of the M'Naghten rule since the Florida Supreme Court decided *Davis v. State,* 32 So. 822 (Fla. 1902), a century ago.

The substance of the M'Naghten rule is captured in the "Florida Standard Jury Instructions in Criminal Cases." These instructions are what the judge tells the jury when the evidence has been presented in a criminal trial and it is time for the jury to make its decision. Section 3.04(b) of the Jury Instructions states that "A person is considered to be insane when (1) he had a mental infirmity, disease or defect" and (2) because of this condition he did not know what he was doing or its consequences or, although he knew what he was doing and its consequences, he did not know it was wrong." This definition has three key ingredients:

- that **at the time of the crime** the defendant had a "mental infirmity, disease, or defect";
- that at the time of the crime the defendant had a **cognitive deficit**— he did not know what he was doing or the consequences of what he was doing, or he did not know that what he was doing was wrong;
- that there was a **causal link** between the defendant's mental infirmity, disease, or defect and his not knowing.

Unless each of these three elements is present, the defendant cannot be considered NGRI (not guilty by reason of insanity).

A question will inevitably arise about what degree of mental impairment or aberration is necessary to qualify for an insanity defense. The language of the Florida instruction suggests that almost any mental aberration will suffice. The jury instructions do make clear, however, that "[u]nrestrained passion or ungovernable temper" do not qualify as a mental illness even if they overcome the individual's normal judgment.

It is sometimes asked whether alcoholism or drug addiction constitutes a "mental infirmity, disease or defect" that will satisfy Florida's test for insanity. When chronic alcohol abuse produces organic brain pathology, (e.g., delirium tremens), and such pathology persists even after the effects of the intoxication have worn off, the pathology may serve as the basis for an insanity defense. For example, in *Cirack v. State*, 201 So. 2d 706 (Fla. 1967), the Supreme Court of Florida said that legal insanity may result from the "long and continued use of intoxicants so as to produce a 'fixed and settled frenzy of insanity either permanent or intermittent.'" As the Florida Supreme Court said in *Cirack*, to qualify for the insanity defense the "defect or disease" that results from the alcohol or drug use must rise to the level of being "fixed and settled," as opposed to merely temporary.

55. What happens to a person in Florida who is found criminally insane?
The answer to this question has generated vigorous debate in recent years. The debate is fueled by the belief that too many people are found not criminally responsible; simply put, that too many defendants are

judged criminally insane and therefore go free. This belief is not supported by fact. Only about 1% of criminal defendants plead insanity, and the plea is successful in only 25% of those cases. Thus, the insanity plea is relevant to only one quarter of one percent of criminal defendants. Moreover, defendants are not released after a court finds them criminally insane. On the contrary, criminal defendants found insane often receive lengthy commitments to maximum-security treatment facilities.

Following acquittal by reason of insanity in Florida, a hearing is held to determine what will happen to the defendant. The court has several choices. The defendant may be:

- committed to the Department of Children and Family Services (formerly the Department of Health and Rehabilitative Services, abbreviated as "HRS"); or
- given outpatient treatment; or
- discharged, according to Florida Rule of Criminal Procedure 3.217(b).

Chapter 916 of the Florida statutes deals with criminal laws that govern mentally deficient and mentally ill criminal defendants. Sections 15 and 17 of chapter 916 (Fla. Stat. chs. 916.15[1] and 916.17) set forth the criteria under which the defendant's disposition will be determined following an acquittal by reason of insanity. A defendant will be involuntarily committed to the Department of Children and Family Services if the court finds that "the person is mentally ill and, because of the person's illness, he is manifestly dangerous to himself or herself or others." Commitment to the Department of Children and Family Services may entail either inpatient treatment or outpatient care. If the person is not mentally ill and "manifestly dangerous," he must be released from the court's jurisdiction.

56. Is the "manifestly dangerous" standard for those who have been acquitted by reason of insanity different than the criteria for involuntary hospitalization under the Baker Act?

Laws that govern mental illness and dangerousness apply to two different sets, or classes, of individuals. One class is made up of those individuals who have been acquitted of a crime by reason of insanity. Chapter 916 of the Florida statutes governs this class of individuals. Another class is made up of individuals who have not been found to commit a crime. The Baker Act governs this class of individuals.

The Baker Act authorizes commitment if a person is mentally ill and, because of his or her mental illness, "[t] here is a substantial likelihood that in the near future he or she will inflict serious bodily harm on himself or herself or another person . . ." (see chapter 5). By contrast, the "manifestly dangerous" standard in section 15 of chapter 916 (Fla. Stat. ch. 916.15) does *not* contain language that requires an imminent risk of serious bodily harm. As a result, the requirements of section 916.15 are easier to satisfy than the Baker Act—that is to say, an individual may more readily be committed under section 916.15 than under the Baker Act. Moreover, while the Baker Act requires bodily harm, section 916.15 has been read to justify commitment when the danger is to property alone. In *Hill v. State*, 358 So. 2d 190 (1st DCA 1978), for example, the court construed the "manifestly dangerous" language to include "threatened injury to property and other societal interests."

Note, however, that "commitment" of the acquitted by reason of insanity under section 916.15 means commitment to the Department of Children and Family Services, and may entail either inpatient *or* outpatient treatment. Commitment under the Baker Act is to a locked psychiatric facility only. Why does section 916.15 give the judge wider options than the Baker Act does? In Florida, unlike in some jurisdictions, the state's civil commitment statute (the Baker Act) authorizes inpatient commitment only. Outpatient commitment is not allowed. The judge or hearing officer in a Baker Act proceeding must either order the total deprivation of liberty (inpatient commitment) or set the individual free. By contrast, a judge dealing with a defendant acquitted by reason of insanity who meets the "mentally ill" and "manifestly dangerous" standard of section 916.15 has broader options of ordering either inpatient or outpatient treatment. The legislature has given the judge these broader options because individuals acquitted by reason of insanity may significantly vary in their need for treatment. When such an individual's risk of dangerousness can be reasonably contained through outpatient treatment alone, the judge has that option. Thus, good reason stands behind section 916.15's broader scope.

Once a defendant has been committed to the Department of Children and Families following an acquittal by reason of insanity, section 17 in chapter 916 (Fla. Stat. ch. 916.17) thereafter authorizes "conditional release . . . based on an approved plan for providing appropriate outpatient care and treatment." If at any time it appears that the defendant has failed to comply with the conditions of release or has deteriorated to the point of necessitating inpatient treatment again, section

916.17(2) authorizes the court to modify the release conditions or order inpatient treatment.

57. When is a person in Florida not competent to proceed (not competent to stand trial)?

To be competent to proceed, a person must be able to assume the role of a criminal defendant. According to section 916.12(1), a person is not able to assume the role of a criminal defendant "if the defendant does not have sufficient present ability to consult with his or her lawyer with a reasonable degree of rational understanding or if the defendant has no rational, as well as factual, understanding of the proceedings against him or her" (see Fla. Stat. ch. 916.12[1] and Fla. R. Crim. P. 3.211[a][1]). In other words, if a person is not able to understand what's going on around him or to help his attorney put on a defense, the trial isn't a fair trial and therefore should not go forward. In such a case the defendant is not competent to proceed.

The above test is taken directly from the United States Supreme Court case *Dusky v. United States*, 362 U.S. 402 (1960), where the U.S. Supreme Court held that, in determining whether a criminal defendant is competent to stand trial, a court should ask:

> whether [the defendant] has sufficient present ability to consult with his lawyer with a reasonable degree of rational understanding and whether he has a rational as well as factual understanding of the proceedings against him. (402)

Examples of questions that would help to assess competence to proceed would therefore be: Is the defendant able to understand that the prosecutor thinks he has done something wrong? Is the defendant able to understand that his attorney is there to help him? Is the defendant able to understand the nature of the charges against him? Is the defendant able to understand that he may be put in jail or told to pay a fine if he is found guilty? Is the defendant able to sit in court and comprehend what other people say about him, or about what people claim he did? Is the defendant able to answer questions his attorney may need to ask in order to put on a defense? Notice how the first four questions begin with "Is the defendant able to understand . . ." rather than "Does the defendant know that . . ." The reason for beginning the questions in this manner is that competence to stand trial is based on what the individual is *able* to understand about the judicial process, not on what he *actually* understands. If a person does not actually understand something about the trial, but is able to understand this information, one can educate him.

The inquiry regarding whether the defendant is competent to proceed at the trial stage is narrow. A diagnosis of "mentally ill," in and of itself, will not justify a finding of incompetence. Also, note that according to the standard described above a defendant can be found incompetent to proceed *without* being mentally ill. As an example, a physical impairment that substantially interferes with comprehension or ability to communicate effectively with counsel—such as deaf-muteness—may justify a finding of incompetence to proceed (see *Holmes v. State*, 494 So. 2d 230 [Fla. 3d DCA 1986]).

58. What happens to a person in Florida who is found not competent to proceed?

Under rule 3.210(a) of the Florida Rules of Criminal Procedure, a defendant found incompetent to proceed "shall not be proceeded against while he is incompetent." In other words, as long as the defendant remains incompetent to proceed, the case will not go forward. If the court determines that the defendant is indeed incompetent, rule 3.212(c) requires that the court consider what treatment is necessary to restore the defendant to competence. Under sections 916.13 and 916.17, and rule 3.212(c)(1), the court may order the defendant to undergo treatment, either on an inpatient or outpatient basis, if it finds the defendant to be mentally ill or retarded, in need of treatment, and appropriate treatment is available (that is, treatment that holds the possibility of returning the individual to competence). The court will order periodic evaluations to determine whether the defendant has regained his competence. If the court finds that the defendant has returned to competence, the court will enter an order with its finding and the legal proceeding will move forward.

In certain cases, a court will need to determine whether a defendant who is incompetent to proceed should be placed in a hospital involuntarily. The criteria that guide a court in making this decision are found in section 916.13 (Fla. Stat. ch. 916.13[1]), and in rule 3.212(c)(3) of the rules of criminal procedure (Fla. R. Crim. P. 3.212[c][3]). According to section 916.13(1), involuntary hospitalization is appropriate

- if the defendant cannot care for himself alone or with the help of family or friends; *and*

- without treatment, is likely to suffer substantial harm from neglect or refusal to take care of himself; *or*
- in the near future he is likely to harm himself or someone else.

Section 916.13(1) also requires that no less restrictive treatment alternative be available. In addition to the conditions for involuntary hospitalization set forth in section 916.13(1), rule 3.212 (c)(3) further requires that there be a substantial probability that the mental illness or mental retardation causing the defendant's incompetence will respond to treatment, and that the defendant will regain competence to proceed in the reasonably foreseeable future.

Note how section 916.13(1) and rule 3.212 (c)(3) work together. Defendants deemed incompetent to proceed may be placed in a hospital against their will on the basis of their incompetence only when:

- harm will result if they are not hospitalized; *and*
- no less restrictive alternative is available; *and*
- hospitalization offers a reasonable prospect that they will regain their competence to proceed.

All three conditions must be met before involuntary hospitalization is appropriate. According to the law, treatment for a criminal defendant found not competent to proceed is designed primarily to restore the defendant to competence—not to cure his mental illness. When the defendant regains his competence to proceed, he goes back to court and the case moves forward.

A defendant cannot remain designated incompetent to proceed for an indefinite period of time. Rule 3.213(a) of the Rules of Criminal Procedure states that the court must conduct a hearing after one year (if the charge was a misdemeanor), or after five years (if the charge was a felony) for any criminal defendant who was found incompetent to proceed. If the court determines at this hearing that there is no substantial probability that the defendant will be restored to competence in the foreseeable future, the court must dismiss the charges. When the defendant's incompetence to proceed is due to mental retardation rather than mental illness, the charges may be dismissed after two years. If the charges are dismissed and the defendant continues to meet commitment criteria, the court will order that the defendant be hospitalized or provided residential services under the Baker Act or the Developmental Disabilities Prevention and Community Services Act. The court may also order appropriate out-patient treatment.

COMPETENCE TO PROCEED AND CRIMINAL RESPONSIBILITY IN FLORIDA

I. Involve **criminal** proceedings (person has been charged with a crime)

II. Involve assessment of person's mental state at a given point in time:
    A. At **time of criminal conduct** (criminal responsibility)
    B. At **time of legal proceedings** (competence to proceed)

III. Involve assessment of **mental capacity**
    A. Person not criminally responsible (insane) if, **at the time of the criminal conduct**
        1. Has a mental infirmity, disease, or defect
        2. Because of mental infirmity, disease, or defect:
            a. did not know what he was doing or its consequences *or*
            b. although he knew what he was doing and its consequences, did not know what he was doing was wrong
    B. Person not competent to proceed if, **at the time of legal proceedings**:
        1. Does not have sufficient present ability to consult with his lawyer with a reasonable degree of rational understanding *or*
        2. Has no rational, as well as factual, understanding of the proceedings

---

59. What role do mental health professionals play in helping courts to decide whether a criminal defendant is criminally insane or not competent to proceed?

Mental health professionals are frequently called upon to evaluate criminal defendants and to serve as expert witnesses at criminal trials. In this capacity, they play an enormously important role in the judicial system. Mental health professionals may be asked to assist the judge or jury to answer questions having to do with the defendant's mental state at particular points in time. In the case of competence to proceed, the questions concern the defendant's mental state at the time of the legal proceedings: Is the defendant able to understand the nature of the proceedings? Can he communicate effectively with counsel? In the case of the insanity defense the questions concern the defendant's mental state at the time of the crime: Was the defendant suffering from a mental illness that prevented him from understanding the wrongfulness of his conduct, for example because he was suffering from a paranoid delusion at the time he killed the victim?

It is important to note that mental health professionals do not make the final determination about any *legal* question. It is up to the judge to determine whether the defendant is incompetent to proceed, and it is up to the jury (unless the defendant has waived his right to a trial by jury) to determine whether the defendant was insane at the time of the crime. These are legal, not clinical questions. The mental health professional's role is to inform the court by providing data and to help the court understand that data. The legal conclusions to be drawn are up to the judge and jury.

60. If it appears that the defendant is not competent to proceed, or that the defendant was insane at the time of the crime, who actually raises these issues in court, and when do the issues get addressed?
Either party—prosecutor or defense—and even the judge can raise the question of competence to proceed at any time. That makes sense—any individual with a role central to the trial can raise a question about the trial's fundamental fairness. Any one of these individuals can say, "This is not a fair trial," and ask that the defendant be examined to ensure that the proceedings move forward in a fair manner. The issue of insanity, on the other hand, can be raised only by the defense and must be raised *before* trial, at the time the defendant pleads guilty or not guilty to the charges. This rule makes sense as well. Insanity is a defense that will exonerate the defendant from the charges against him, and so it is up to the defense to raise this issue.

61. The prosecutor has the burden of proving all the elements of a crime beyond a reasonable doubt. Does the prosecutor also have to prove that a criminal defendant was sane at the time of the crime? If not, who has the burden of proof when the issue of insanity gets raised at trial?
The prosecutor has the burden of proving all the elements of a crime beyond a reasonable doubt. There is, however, a presumption that the defendant was sane at the time of the crime, and in order to raise a suc-

cessful insanity defense the defendant must present some evidence to rebut the presumption of sanity. Once the defendant has done so, the prosecutor then has the burden of proving beyond a reasonable doubt that the defendant was sane. The Second District Court of Appeal made this point clear in *Matevia v. State*, 564 So. 2d 585 (Fla. 2nd DCA 1990), where it stated that a jury should be instructed as follows, "All persons are presumed to be sane. However, if the evidence causes you to have a reasonable doubt concerning the defendant's sanity, then the presumption of sanity vanishes and the State must prove beyond a reasonable doubt that the defendant was sane" (at 586). Thus, the trial begins with a presumption of sanity, but when the defense raises a reasonable doubt about this presumption, the burden shifts to the prosecutor to prove beyond a reasonable doubt that the defendant was sane at the time of the crime.

62. What is the defense of "diminished capacity"?
When a criminal case comes to trial, an individual—the defendant—has been charged with a crime. To win a criminal case, the prosecutor, who bears the burden of proof, must show beyond a reasonable doubt that the defendant is guilty of the crime with which he has been charged. Every crime consists of two elements: an actus reus (a guilty act) and a mens rea (a guilty mind). If either an actus reus or a mens rea is missing, no crime has been committed and the defendant must be found not guilty. To win, the prosecutor must therefore show that the defendant both did something wrong (actus reus) and had the necessary criminal state of mind (mens rea) while he was acting.

Certain crimes require a specific state of mind (specific intent). Assault with intent to kill, for example, requires that the defendant placed a victim in fear of bodily harm (assault) and intended to kill the victim (assault with intent to kill). To convict a defendant of this crime, the prosecutor must therefore show beyond a reasonable doubt that the defendant both performed certain acts and, while doing so, had the necessary mental state (mens rea): the intent to kill.

Evidence of diminished mental capacity (sometimes referred to as "diminished responsibility") may be used to defeat the prosecutor's attempt to prove the mens rea element of the offense. The defense would argue that the defendant lacked the capacity to form the necessary mens rea—mental state—at the time of the crime. For example, the defense attorney may introduce psychiatric testimony showing that the defendant lacked the capacity to form an intent to kill. Perhaps the defendant was of exceedingly limited intelligence or suffered from a delusion affecting his capacity to understand and appreciate the significance of someone dying. This testimony would then be used to argue that the defendant was not guilty of the crime of assault with intent to kill. Why? Because a necessary element of this crime, the requisite mens rea—intent to kill—could not have been present, since the defendant was not capable of forming that intent. Note that the defendant may still be found guilty of a lesser offense, that of assault, because he may very well have intended to place the victim in fear of bodily harm.

63. How is a diminished capacity defense different from an insanity defense?

Diminished capacity addresses whether a specific criminal intent is present. It says, "Look, to find this defendant guilty, you have to show that he had this specific criminal intent at the time of the crime. But *he didn't have the capacity to form that intent*—so he can't be found guilty of that crime." Note, however, that this argument does not preclude the defendant being found guilty of another crime with which he has been charged—perhaps the intent necessary for another crime, one that required a less severe intent, was indeed present. If so, the defendant can be found guilty of an alternative charge, such as second rather than first degree murder. Thus, diminished capacity generally acts as a *partial* defense to criminal guilt. The insanity defense, on the other hand, acts as a *complete* defense to criminal guilt. When using an insanity defense, an individual claims that he lacked *any* criminal responsibility at the time of the crime. The implication of a successful insanity plea is that the defendant does not belong in the criminal justice system at all.

The final disposition may therefore be very different for defendants who use an insanity defense and for those who rely on the defense of diminished capacity. An individual found not guilty by reason of insanity could be placed in a hospital for an indefinite period of time. Or, such a defendant could be released to outpatient care. Whichever the case, a defendant acquitted by reason of insanity is no longer subject to the criminal justice system; he leaves that system's purview. Individuals who successfully argue diminished capacity, on the other hand, may be able to reduce the offense, but may still be guilty of something, and so may remain in the criminal justice system. It sometimes happens that an individual relies on diminished capacity and there is no lesser offense of which he could be held guilty. In such a case, a successful diminished capacity defense acts as a complete defense and will result in acquittal and release.

64. Does Florida have a defense based on diminished capacity?

Unlike some other states, Florida does not recognize a defense of diminished capacity. In *Chestnut v. State,* 538 So. 2d 820 (Fla. 1989), the Florida Supreme Court rejected the contention that mental health testimony could be used to reduce the defendant's criminal responsibility other than when the insanity defense has been raised. In making its ruling, the court expressed a concern about what implications allowing a defense based on diminished capacity would have for the criminal justice system and for society as a whole:

> It could be said that many, if not most, crimes are committed by persons with mental aberrations. If such mental deficiencies are sufficient to meet the definition of insanity, these persons should be acquitted on that ground and treated for their disease. Persons with less serious mental deficiencies should be held accountable for their crimes just as everyone else is. If mitigation is appropriate, it may be accomplished through sentencing, but to adopt a rule which creates an opportunity for such persons to obtain immediate freedom to prey on the public once again is unwise. (*Chestnut* at 825)

Even when the defendant is not raising an insanity defense, however, his mental state may still be relevant to the criminal proceeding in certain, very limited circumstances (see the next question). When such circumstances are present, mental health professionals may be called upon to provide expert testimony.

65. Given that Florida does not have a defense based on diminished capacity, do mental health professionals have any role in providing expert testimony about mental illness or impairment when the defendant is not using an insanity defense?

When a defendant is charged with certain crimes and his defense is that he was not able to form the necessary mens rea (mental state) because of age, intoxicants, intoxicants coupled with mental illness (see *Bias v. Florida,* 634 So. 2d 1120 [Fla. 2d DCA 1994]), or a neurological condition (e.g., epilepsy; see *Bunney v. State,* 603 So. 2d 1270 [Fla.1992]), mental health professionals may be permitted to testify to the existence of these conditions and to their impact on the defendant's ability to form the requisite intent (see *Boswell v. State*, 610 So. 2d 670 [Fla. 4th DCA 1992]). In these very specific situations, mental health professionals may be called upon to give expert testimony even though the defendant has not raised the insanity defense.

66. Would a mental health professional be allowed to testify about psychological syndromes, such as battered-spouse syndrome or posttraumatic stress disorder, in a criminal trial?

At times, mental health professionals are asked to testify about specific psychological syndromes. As examples, a child may exhibit signs of having been sexually abused, but may be too young to provide sufficient testimony about what occurred to satisfy the rigors of a legal proceeding. Or an abused woman may kill a spouse or partner, and claim insanity or self-defense. In each case, psychological testimony may aid in understanding behavior that would be outside a jury's experience. Mental health professionals may be asked to explain the relevant psychological dynamics.

The Supreme Court of Florida has permitted experts to testify about both battered-spouse syndrome and about posttraumatic stress disorder. In *State v. Hickson*, 630 So. 2d 172 (Fla. 1993), the court held concerning battered-spouse syndrome that "an expert can generally describe the syndrome and the characteristics of a person suffering from the syndrome and can express an opinion in response to hypothetical questions predicated on facts in evidence" (at 173). Thus, the court's posture toward testimony regarding battered-spouse syndrome was positive—such testimony may be admitted, so that an expert can discuss the syndrome in a general manner and answer hypothetical questions based on evidence that has been presented in the case. The court went on to say, however, that if the expert talks about whether the woman on trial actually suffers from the syndrome, the prosecution must then be given the opportunity to interview and examine her.

In *Kruse v. State*, 483 So. 2d 1383 (Fla. App. 4 Dist. 1986), the Fourth District Court of Appeals examined the admissibility of expert testimony concerning posttraumatic stress disorder. The *Kruse* case involved a child who had allegedly been sexually assaulted at the age of seven. At the criminal trial, an expert testified that a psychiatric examination, coupled with the child's behavior before and after the alleged assault, led to the conclusion that the child had indeed suffered a sexual trauma. The district court ruled that the expert's testimony—that the child suffered from posttraumatic stress disorder—was admissible into evidence. The court cautioned, however, that the expert's testimony must be limited to a medical conclusion. While the expert, explained the court, could testify that the child suffered from posttraumatic stress disorder and that the syndrome resulted from a sexual assault, the expert could not testify that a criminal act had occurred or that the defendant was the perpetrator.

Florida has asked mental health professionals to use their expertise in educating the courts and juries about specific psychological syndromes relevant to a legal proceeding. At the same time, courts have been careful to make sure that expert testimony is admitted or not admitted into evidence consistent with the rules of evidence and other court procedures.

67. Would a mental health professional be allowed to testify about a psychological autopsy in a criminal trial?

In *Jackson v. Florida*, 553 So. 2d 719 (Fla. 4th DCA 1989), the Fourth District Court of Appeals ruled that a psychological autopsy, "a retrospective look at an individual's suicide to try to determine what led that person to choose death over life," was appropriate to admit into evidence at a criminal trial. The court reasoned that psychological autopsy is "accepted in the field of psychiatry as a method of evaluation for use in cases involving suicide" (*Jackson* at 720); psychological autopsy thus meets the *Frye* test for admissibility (see question 13.) Second, the court likened the process of a psychological autopsy—a retrospective evaluation of a person's psychological state at a given point in time—to what experts do as a matter of routine when they evaluate a defendant's mental state at the time of a crime to assess criminal responsibility.

68. What happens if someone in a jail or prison becomes depressed, has a psychotic break, or otherwise needs mental health services?

It is estimated that about 11% of inmates in the Florida Correctional System, the nation's fourth largest, suffer from a mental disorder. Many inmates have mental or emotional disabilities that are not sufficient to relieve them of criminal responsibility, yet these inmates nevertheless require some form of mental health care. Section 916.107 (Fla. Stat. ch. 916.107) requires that in every case in which a mentally ill or mentally retarded person is held in a jail, some mental health services shall be provided in the jail until the person is transferred to the custody of the Department of Children and Family Services. Penal institutions differ, however, in their requirements and ability to treat mentally disturbed inmates.

Although the terms "jail" and "prison" are sometimes used inter-changeably, the two institutions serve some distinct purposes. County jails typically house pretrial detainees (individuals waiting for their trial) and inmates who are incarcerated for up to one year. There are 67 jails in Florida with varying degrees of treatment resources. In jails that employ full-time or part-time mental health professionals, the jail can provide services within the facility when the patient consents. When the patient is unable or unwilling to consent to services, or when the jail lacks suffi-cient treatment resources, the jail may initiate proceedings to commit the inmate to a psychiatric hospital pursuant to the Baker Act (see chapter 5).

State prisons hold prisoners for much longer sentences and therefore need more substantial medical and mental health treatment facilities. The Florida Corrections Mental Health Act (sections 40 through 49 of chapter 945 in the Florida Statutes) provides for evaluation and treat-ment of mentally ill inmates through a continuum of services. The Department of Corrections may provide services within its correctional facilities or contract with persons or agencies qualified to provide such services. Section 42 in chapter 945 (Fla. Stat. ch. 945.42) provides that inmates who have a mental illness that poses a "real and present threat of substantial harm to the inmate's well being or to the safety of others" may be transferred to a mental health treatment facility. Such a facility may be either within the prison itself or in an outside institution. When the harm is immediate, real, and present, the inmate may be transferred to the mental health facility immediately (with a hearing to follow).

69. Does an inmate have the right to refuse treatment that the jail or prison wants to provide?

If an inmate refuses mental health treatment, the jail may not go ahead and provide involuntary treatment even if it believes that the treatment is nec-essary. The jail does, however, have two options in such a case. First, the jail may initiate proceedings under the Baker Act and transfer the inmate to a local receiving facility (if the facility possesses security capabilities), to a state hospital, or to a Baker Act receiving facility. Second, if an inmate will not consent to treatment that a facility deems necessary for the inmate's care and safety, or for the safety of others, the facility may petition the court for an order authorizing involuntary treatment. The court will then conduct a hearing. If the court finds by clear and convincing evi-dence (see question 4) that the inmate is mentally ill, that the treatment is essential to the inmate's care, and that the treatment is not experimental or does not present an unreasonable risk of serious, hazardous, or irreversible side effects, the court may authorize that the inmate be treated. Thus, when an inmate refuses treatment the jail may either initiate proceedings under the Baker Act or seek a court order authorizing treatment. The jail may not, however, simply proceed to treat the inmate.

A special case arises when an inmate presents an *immediate* danger to himself or others. In this case, section 945.48 (Fla. Stat. ch. 945.48[a]) allows a physician to write an order that authorizes treatment for up to 48 hours. If the inmate continues to refuse treatment after two days, the administrator of the facility must petition the court for an order authorizing continued treatment. The facility may provide treatment while it waits for a court to issue the order, provided a physician certifies that the situation continues to be an emergency. This procedure for petitioning the court to authorize involuntary treatment relates to treatment needed on an emergency basis when safety is at issue, and does not relate to the situation when the state's sole reason for involuntary treatment is to restore the defendant to competence to proceed.

70. What about someone who is committed because he is incompetent to proceed—does that person have the right to refuse treatment, even though the purpose of the commitment is to return him to competence so the legal proceedings can move forward?

If the facility's reason for insisting upon involuntary treatment is to restore the defendant to competence to proceed, the trial court will usually have already authorized such treatment. Sections 916.13, 916.17, and rule 3.212(c)(1) allow a court that has found a defendant incompetent to proceed to order the defendant to undergo treatment on either an inpatient or outpatient basis. The defendant must be mentally ill or retarded and in need of treatment, and treatment that promises to restore him to competence must be available. The defendant does not have the right to refuse such treatment when it has been ordered by the court.

71. Can a court require a criminal defendant to receive mental health services as a condition of probation or parole?

Yes. A prisoner may be released on parole before his prison sentence is completely up. A court may also order probation or community control as an alternative to confinement in prison. In both cases, a court may order that the individual receive treatment, and not doing so may mean that the person goes (or goes back) to jail or prison. To impose a conditional treatment, the court must first order that the individual be evaluated to determine the need for treatment. Treatment as a condition of parole will usually be imposed when the offender was already receiving services within the prison.

72. If treatment is made a condition of probation or parole, what information should a mental health professional provide the probation or parole officer?

Because a court may make treatment a condition of probation or parole, mental health professionals are sometimes placed in the position of working with individuals whose activities are supervised by a probation or parole officer. (It is quite helpful for a treater to know *which* of her patients fall into this category.) Most probation and parole officers are extremely busy and are more interested in knowing that the treatment is proceeding than what's actually going on in sessions. That said, probation and parole officers differ in what they want to know about a court-mandated treatment. A treater should therefore make an effort to schedule a meeting (in person or on the phone) before the treatment begins, for two reasons. First, the treater, patient, and probation or parole officer should discuss the frame of the treatment (e.g., frequency and length of sessions, consequences for missed sessions, period over which the treatment will continue). Second, it is absolutely essential that the treater, the parole or probation officer, and the patient all be clear about what information the treater will disclose (see chapter 3 for a discussion of the Law of No Surprises), and in what form the disclosure will take place (e.g., monthly telephone conversations, quarterly reports, a simple confirmation that the patient shows up for sessions). It can be clinically useful to review with the patient what information is shared with the probation or parole officer, either by providing the patient a copy of written reports or by indicating what was said in telephone conversations. *Clarity* is the watchword—clarity about whether the treatment is mandated, about the treatment's frame, and about whether and in what form confidential information will be disclosed to a probation or parole officer.

73. Some states have special laws regarding sexual predators or sex offenders. These laws allow for civil commitment immediately following the individual's prison sentence, so that the person is never actually released from state custody. Does Florida have such a law?

Yes. The Jimmy Ryce Involuntary Civil Commitment for Sexually Violent

Predators Treatment and Care Act (Fla. Stat. ch. 916.37), Florida's sexually violent predator commitment law, provides that individuals classified as sexually violent predators may be held against their will after their prison term has expired. To be committed under this statute, the court must determine by clear and convincing evidence (see question 4) that the offender "has been convicted of a sexually violent offense and suffers from a mental abnormality or personality disorder that makes the person likely to engage in acts of sexual violence if not confined in a secure facility for long term control, care, and treatment." If an individual is determined to be a sexually violent predator under this standard, the statute requires that the offender be committed to the custody of the Department of Children and Family Services for control, care, and treatment and held in a secure facility until it is safe for him to be back in the community. Following commitment under the statute, the offender must be reevaluated at least once each year (more frequently at the court's discretion). The offender may petition the court for release, in which case the court must hold a hearing. Mental health professionals may serve as expert witnesses and evaluators in the proceedings to determine whether a sexual offender should be committed and retained as a sexually violent predator.

74. Do mental health professionals have a role to play in death penalty cases?
Yes. Once a defendant is found guilty of a crime for which the death penalty can be given, Florida law requires a second trial to determine whether the defendant shall receive life imprisonment or the death penalty. Chapter 921 (Fla. Stat. ch. 921.141 and ch. 921.142) leaves the ultimate decision about the death penalty to the judge, but requires that the jury render an advisory recommendation. In formulating its advisory recommendation, the jury must consider whether there are circumstances that speak in favor of or against imposing the death penalty ("aggravating and mitigating circumstances") and then must balance those circumstances against one another to determine whether the death penalty is appropriate.

Two mitigating circumstances named in section 921.141 involve issues that relate to the defendant's psychological condition. Section 921.141(6)(b) says that the jury should consider whether, at the time of the crime, the defendant was under the influence of extreme mental or emotional disturbance. Section 921.141(6)(f) tells the jury to consider whether the defendant's capacity to appreciate the criminality of his conduct or to conform his conduct to the requirements of the law was substantially impaired. In addition to these statutorily identified mitigating circumstances, Florida courts (consistent with the United States Supreme Court) have held that a jury may consider other factors that speak against giving the defendant the death penalty. In *Campbell v. State*, 571 So. 2d 415 (Fla. 1990), for example, the Florida Supreme Court said that

> valid nonstatutory mitigating circumstances include but are not limited to: (1) Abused or deprived childhood. (2) Contribution to community or society as evidenced by exemplary work, military, family, or other record. (3) Remorse and potential for rehabilitation. (at 419)

Mental health professionals can assist the court and jury in determining whether any of these—or any other—mitigating factors are present.

If the defendant chooses to have an evaluation for the purpose of identifying factors that speak against his receiving the death penalty, the defendant must tell the prosecutor that he intends to do so. The prosecutor then has the opportunity for its own expert clinician to examine the defendant, in order to rebut the defendant's claim of mitigating circumstances.

7

SUBPOENAS AND
COURT ORDERS

*As you read these questions, recall (from chapter 3) the close relation-
ship between confidentiality and testimonial privilege. To say that a
communication is "confidential" means that the mental health professional cannot disclose the communication without the client's consent.
To say that a communication is "protected by testimonial privilege"
means that the mental health professional cannot disclose the communication <u>in a legal proceeding</u> without the client's consent. When a client
allows a mental health professional to disclose communications that are
protected by testimonial privilege, the client is said to "waive privilege."
If a client instead "invokes privilege," the mental health professional
may not reveal the communication unless ordered to do so by a court.*

QUESTIONS DISCUSSED IN THIS CHAPTER

75. What is a subpoena?
76. If an individual comes to my office to deliver a subpoena, or a sub-
    poena arrives through the mail, should I simply accept it?
77. Once the subpoena is in my possession, should I do whatever it
    says?

78. What is the first thing I *should* do if I receive a subpoena?
79. Is there any legal action I can take to avoid complying with the subpoena?
80. What if I don't think my client is competent to waive privilege?
81. What if I cannot locate my client?
82. What if the subpoena asks for the records of a client who has died?
83. Once my client has invoked privilege or I have invoked privilege on my client's behalf, do I need to do anything else?
84. Please clarify—do I appear in court and *then* claim privilege, or do I refuse to appear in court at all?
85. Is a client's consent necessary for me to appear at a legal proceeding, or is a client's consent necessary only in order for me to testify or to release records?
86. If my client waives privilege, how do I actually go ahead and comply with the subpoena?
87. What if a patient decides to waive privilege for only *part* of the record?
88. Having received a subpoena duces tecum, may I refuse to provide parts of the record that have nothing whatsoever to do with the matter under investigation and that contain sensitive and possibly embarrassing information?
89. What if the client waives privilege, thereby allowing me to comply with the subpoena, yet at the legal proceeding I am asked questions that have nothing to do with the matter at hand?
90. Is a court order different than a subpoena?
91. Is a court order like a subpoena insofar as either the entire record or none of the record at all will be released?
92. I work as the custodian of records at a busy mental health center. What are my legal responsibilities when I receive a subpoena in my official capacity?
93. I work as the medical director of a community mental health center. How should we respond when a subpoena arrives for a mental health professional who no longer works here?
94. I do not believe judges fully understand the importance of confidentiality to the therapeutic relationship and believe strongly that mental health professionals should always refuse to release confidential information, even if ordered by a court to do so. What power does a judge have if a mental health professional refuses to testify or release records?

DISCUSSION

75. What is a subpoena?

The word "subpoena" comes from the Latin words "sub" and "poena" which, taken together, mean "under a penalty." A subpoena is a legal instrument authorized for lawyers to use in discovery (see question 8) or to require a witness to appear at a legal proceeding. An individual who does not comply with a subpoena may be placed under a penalty, which may be a fine, arrest, and even jail. A special kind of subpoena, a subpoena *duces tecum*, requires that an individual bring certain materials to the proceeding. It is important to note that a subpoena is a requirement: that you appear at a given place at a given time (subpoena) or that you appear at such place and time with specified materials (subpoena duces tecum).

A sample subpoena duces tecum is included in appendix B.

76. If an individual comes to my office to deliver a subpoena, or a subpoena arrives through the mail, should I simply accept it?

To be valid and effective, a subpoena must be served on the individual whose appearance is desired. The law requires that you accept service. If you are not present when the subpoena is served, anyone who works on your behalf (such as a secretary) may accept a subpoena for you. One problem with attempting to avoid service is that the attorney who issued the subpoena has the authority to adjust the time when you are legally required to appear. An attorney may even be willing to keep you on "standby," requiring an appearance in court or at a deposition only if you are notified (either by phone or by page). So keep in mind that by making service of the subpoena difficult you may be aggravating someone who has the power to make the whole process significantly less burdensome for you.

77. Once the subpoena is in my possession, should I do whatever it says?

No—you need to worry about your client's confidentiality! A subpoena is a demand for your *appearance*; once you have *appeared* you have complied with the subpoena. Although a subpoena is a very scary looking piece of paper, a subpoena *neither requires nor allows you to reply to questions or to produce materials that are protected by testimonial privilege*. You may only answer questions or produce materials if your client grants you permission (waives privilege), if a court orders you to do so, or if a statute requires you to. If your client decides to waive privilege, you will ask him to do so in writing (see question 86).

Lawyers who do not understand or who choose to ignore the concept of testimonial privilege may insist (rant and rave, jump up and down, threaten you with contempt) that you provide the information they want. Simply explain that you are not able to do so without your client's consent or a court order, and ask the lawyer to contact your or your patient's attorney with any further questions.

78. What is the first thing I *should* do if I receive a subpoena?

Inform your client that you have received the subpoena and indicate what the subpoena demands. Next, determine if your records and testimony are protected by testimonial privilege (see chapter 3). If your client is willing to waive privilege, that is, to allow you to disclose information protected by testimonial privilege, you may then go ahead and do what the subpoena asks. Make sure your client waives privilege in writing (see question 86). If your client invokes privilege, that is, does *not* allow you to testify or to release records, have your client's lawyer contact you and proceed as directed. If your client does not have a lawyer, contact your own lawyer.

79. Is there any legal action I can take to avoid complying with the subpoena?

There are two possibilities. First, you can ask a judge to "quash" the subpoena. When a judge "quashes" a subpoena, the subpoena is rendered void. Second, when your client invokes privilege, you may contact the attorney who issued the subpoena in order to ask that you be released from the subpoena until a judge sorts out whether the materials are protected by privilege or whether an exception to privilege applies.

One final note. According to rule 1.410(e)(1) of the Florida Rules of Civil Procedure, a person may object in writing to a subpoena to produce materials (a subpoena duces tecum) for a deposition. If a person does make a written objection within 10 days after the subpoena was served, or before the materials have to be produced, if that period is less than 10 days after the subpoena was served, an order from the court is required before the materials must be produced.

80. What if I don't think my client is competent to waive privilege?

Section 90.503 (Fla. Stat. ch. 90.503[2]) makes clear that the patient is the "holder" of the privilege. The patient therefore has the right to decide whether you may testify or release records. This rule holds unless the patient has a guardian, or is deceased, in which case the guardian or personal representative of the estate holds the privilege. If the patient or the person who holds the privilege is unavailable, you may not release records or testify in court (see the following question), unless a judge orders you to do so.

In the absence of evidence to the contrary, the law generally assumes that individuals are competent—that they appreciate the consequences of what they do and can act accordingly. A strong argument can be made, however, that a mental health professional is in a good position to determine whether a client is indeed competent, and that when evidence to the contrary arises the mental health professional should consider the client "unavailable" to waive privilege. Our advice is therefore the following: If, in your professional judgment, you determine that your client is unable to understand the implications of waiving privilege, do not release any information. Bring the matter to the attention of the court. The court will then determine whether the individual is competent and, based on this determination, will decide whether to appoint a guardian (see question 99) to determine whether to assert privilege on behalf of the individual.

81. What if I cannot locate my client?
Remember that privilege belongs to the client (in legal parlance, your client holds the privilege). You therefore cannot waive privilege for your client. Only your client may give you permission to testify or to release records. If you cannot find your client (perhaps because the treatment has terminated and your client has moved), you should invoke privilege on your client's behalf. In this case you do not testify or release records until a court orders you to do so.

82. What if the subpoena asks for the records of a client who has died?
Confidentiality and testimonial privilege survive death. A client's death does not in any manner lessen a mental health professional's obligation to keep that client's communications confidential. A mental health professional needs to be every bit as careful about releasing information after a client has died as she does about releasing information while the client is living.

The circumstances in which the records of a deceased client may be released are similar to those in which the records of an incompetent client may be released. These circumstances arise when an individual with the appropriate authority allows the mental health professional to release records or when a court orders the mental health professional to release records. In the case of a deceased client, the individual with the appropriate authority is the executor of the estate or the deceased client's personal representative; this individual may waive privilege and may consent to the release of records. A mental health professional should always confirm the appointment of the individual as executor or personal representative before disclosing any information about the client, and should get the consent or waiver in writing. If the mental health professional does not have the appropriate consent or waiver or, even with this individual's consent or waiver, does not believe the records should be released, perhaps because of ethical concerns (see question 128), the mental health professional should claim privilege and let the matter go before a court. A judge will make a ruling and issue an order that says what, if any, material to disclose.

83. Once my client has invoked privilege or I have invoked privilege on my client's behalf, do I need to do anything else?

Even though your client has invoked privilege or you have invoked privilege on your client's behalf, the subpoena remains valid insofar as a subpoena's demand is for your *appearance*. Once privilege is invoked, you may contact the attorney who issued the subpoena and request that you be "released" from the subpoena. If you are able, get the release in writing; if you are not able to get the release in writing, make a note of the day and the time of the release in your records. Most lawyers will not force you to appear at a deposition or trial until it has been determined what materials will be disclosed.

84. Please clarify—do I appear in court and *then* claim privilege, or do I refuse to appear in court at all?

The law requires that you respond to a subpoena. The response required is that you *appear* at a given place, at a given time (with records, if the subpoena is a subpoena duces tecum). Separate from your legal obligation to respond to the subpoena are matters that pertain to testimonial privilege. Put another way, once you have fulfilled your obligation under the subpoena through your *appearance* at the legal proceeding, it remains to be determined whether you will then testify and what records you will release. Thus, from the law's point of view, your legal obligation to respond to a subpoena and your client's testimonial privilege are separate and distinct matters, and you must treat them as separate and distinct. Bottom line: You respond to the subpoena by appearing as directed. Once you have fulfilled your obligation to respond to the subpoena by appearing at the appropriate place and time, you then claim privilege.

85. Is a client's consent necessary for me to appear at a legal proceeding, or is a client's consent necessary only in order for me to testify or to release records?

Because your legal obligation to respond to a subpoena and your client's testimonial privilege are separate and distinct legal issues (see the question above), you do *not* need your client's consent to appear at a legal proceeding. You *do* need your client's written consent to disclose information protected by testimonial privilege. Put simply, you don't need your client's permission to show up at court, because the subpoena says you have to. You do need your client's written permission to talk or to release records once you get there.

86. If my client waives privilege, how do I actually go ahead and comply with the subpoena?

When your client says that he intends to waive privilege, tell him that you would like a letter to that effect, and that you will provide a copy of the subpoena to review and attach to the letter. The letter need not be long. Essential ingredients of the letter are the date, a statement that your client waives privilege and thereby allows you to comply with the attached subpoena, and your client's signature. It is important to remember that unless your client is under guardianship, only he can waive privilege, so that only *his* signature on the letter will suffice.

87. What if a patient decides to waive privilege for only *part* of the record?

Section 90.507 (Fla. Stat. ch. 90.507) makes clear that privilege cannot be waived in part. This point is important and separates privilege from confidentiality. A patient may ask that a treater only discuss certain confidential information with, for example, an employer or a family member. Testimonial privilege is different. A patient either waives privilege or she does not. If a patient voluntarily testifies to a privileged matter, then the matter may be opened to a full inquiry, testimonial privilege notwithstanding, For this reason, patients must be extremely careful when they speak in any sort of legal proceeding. Once the floodgates have opened, it may be impossible to close them. (See also the following question.)

88. Having received a subpoena duces tecum, may I refuse to provide parts of the record that have nothing whatsoever to do with the matter under investigation and that contain sensitive and possibly embarrassing information?

This question provides an excellent illustration of why matters involving testimonial privilege must be handled with care. Remember that a subpoena, in and of itself, does not grant the authority to disclose information. Rather, a client's consent is necessary. Once a client waives privilege, thereby allowing the mental health professional to disclose confidential information, the client may be prevented from "picking and choosing" which information gets released. For this reason, clients must be *very* thoughtful when choosing to waive privilege.

Our advice is the following: If client does not want certain information in the record disclosed, he should not waive privilege. Rather, the client's lawyer should go to a judge and ask that the court issue an order that specifies which parts of the record will be released. The judge, who has the authority to give access to specific parts of the record, will then make a decision about what information will be disclosed (see question 91). It is *not* within the mental health professional's discretion to decide which aspects of the record to release and which to withhold.

89. What if the client waives privilege, thereby allowing me to comply with the subpoena, yet at the legal proceeding I am asked questions that have nothing to do with the matter at hand?

Unfortunately, it is neither your role nor your prerogative as a witness to determine what information is relevant to the proceeding and what questions you should answer. The judge and the attorneys decide what will be discussed in the courtroom or at a deposition. That said, it is good practice when testifying to pause before you respond to a question. A pause allows your client's attorney time to object before you answer. If the attorney's attention seems elsewhere and the questioning turns to matters patently irrelevant to the matter before the court, say, "I'm not sure what that has to do with what we are here for," and then stare intently in the attorney's direction. At that point the attorney should object, and the judge will tell you whether you have to answer the question.

90. Is a court order different than a subpoena?
Yes—while an *attorney* may issue a subpoena, a *judge* issues a court order. The judge will hold a hearing to determine whether the communication under review is protected by testimonial privilege. To make this determination, the judge may ask: Is the mental health professional licensed? Did the communication take place in the context of a professional relationship? Does the mental health professional belong to a discipline named by one of the privilege statutes? If the answer to any of these questions is "no," the judge may decide that the communication is *not* protected by privilege, which means that it may be introduced into the legal proceeding. If the judge determines that the communication *is* protected by privilege, she will then determine whether any exception to privilege applies that would allow disclosure (see chapter 3).

If the judge determines that the communication is not privileged or that the communication falls under an exception to privilege, she will order the mental health professional to produce all or part of the record. Section 394.459 (Fla. Stat. ch. 394.459[9]) makes clear that a mental health professional must follow an order of the court to release records. If the judge determines that the communication *is* protected by testimonial privilege and that no exception to privilege applies, she will "quash" (invalidate) the subpoena and you need not do anything else.

Bottom line: The judge will either order you to produce all or part of the record, or she will "quash" the subpoena.

91. Is a court order like a subpoena insofar as either the entire record or none of the record at all will be released?
No, and this difference is extremely important. A court order will specify what material from the record is to be released. *You only release material specified in the court order.* Whenever you receive an order from a court, you must read the order carefully and follow its instructions exactly.

92. I work as the custodian of records at a busy mental health center. What are my legal responsibilities when I receive a subpoena in my official capacity?
A custodian of business records (including mental health records) should release records only when the subpoena is accompanied by the patient's signed authorization to release the records. If the patient has not signed an authorization, the attorney who sent the subpoena can seek a court

order for the records. If the patient has signed an authorization or if the court has issued an order for the records, the custodian should submit copies of the records in envelopes marked "confidential." Note that, under rule 1.410 of the Florida rules of Civil Procedure (Fla. R. Civ. P. 1.410), unless the subpoena duces tecum explicitly says so, the custodian of records does not need to deliver the records in person, so that she need not "appear" anywhere.

93. I work as the medical director of a community mental health center. How should we respond when a subpoena arrives for a mental health professional who no longer works here?

If a subpoena is delivered to a mental health center, intended for a mental health professional who no longer works at the center, the person delivering the subpoena should be so informed. The reason is that rule 1.410 of the rules of civil procedure (Fla. R. Civ. P. 1.410) says that the subpoena cannot be enforced unless it is served "in the manner provided by law" on the individual or entity named in the subpoena. Section 48.031 (Fla. Stat. ch. 48.031) states that a subpoena must be served on the individual *in person*. Thus, if the individual whose name appears on the subpoena no longer works at the mental health center, the service is not valid, and the individual delivering the subpoena will need to be told that.

If the name on the subpoena is the mental health center itself—for records of a mental health professional who no longer works there—the center should assert privilege on behalf of the patient. Because the patient holds the privilege (see chapter 3 and question 80), it does not matter where the professional is. The center should handle the subpoena in the same manner as would any mental health professional who receives a subpoena, by attempting to contact the patient to see whether he wants to invoke or waive privilege.

94. I do not believe judges fully understand the importance of confidentiality to the therapeutic relationship and believe strongly that mental health professionals should always refuse to release confidential information, even if ordered by a court to do so. What power does a judge have if a mental health professional refuses to testify or release records?

Some mental health professionals believe that a client's confidentiality should be protected and preserved at all costs. The strength of their con-

WHEN YOU RECEIVE A SUBPOENA

I.   What **not** to do:
   A.   Do not attempt to avoid service (that is, avoid receiving the subpoena itself).
   B.   Do not disclose **any** information (or release **any** records) protected by testimonial privilege.
   C.   Do not contact the attorney who issued the subpoena (except to ask that you be released from the subpoena).

II. What to do:
   A.   Contact your client and indicate that you have received a subpoena.
   B.   Find out whether your client wishes to **waive** or **invoke** privilege.
      1.   If client **waives** privilege
         a.   Get waiver in writing.
         b.   You may now disclose client information in the legal proceeding.
      2.   If client **invokes** privilege
         a.   Ask to be released from the subpoena.
         b.   If not released from the subpoena, you must comply with the subpoena by appearing at the specified time and place.
         c.   If the subpoena is a subpoena duces tecum, you will take the physical documents requested with you to the legal proceeding.
         d.   At the proceeding you will state that your client has invoked privilege. You will not say anything else, and you will not give the physical documents to anyone unless ordered to do so by the court.
         e.   The judge will determine whether you must disclose client information. The judge will issue an order telling you what to do.

III. If you are unsure of what to do (e.g., because you cannot find your client), invoke privilege.
   A.   The question of whether you must testify or release records will go before a judge.
   B.   The judge will determine whether the material is "protected by privilege."
   C.   If the judge decides that the material is protected by privilege, she will "quash" the subpoena.
   D.   If the judge decides that the material is not protected by privilege or that the material falls under an exception to privilege, she will issue an order.
   E.   Follow the judge's order exactly.

victions is rarely tested, but may well be when they are faced with a court order to testify or to release records. A court order has the force of law. Section 394.459 (Fla. Stat. ch. 394.459[9]) directs individuals to follow a court order to release records. A mental health professional who refuses to follow the order of a court may be found in contempt of court and may be given a fine or even placed in jail. When you refuse to follow the order of a court because you believe a greater value is at stake, you are—by definition—engaging in civil disobedience. Like all who engage in civil disobedience, you may be required to pay a price for your convictions.

8

GUARDIANS AND SUBSTITUTE DECISION-MAKING

A fundamental value upon which our society is built is <u>individual autonomy</u>. Individuals are allowed great leeway in the choices they may make: how to worship, what to read, where to live, whom to marry. In our society these and many, many other choices belong to the individual. Because of the value we place on individual autonomy, we presume that individuals are competent to make choices about how to live their lives in whatever fashion they reasonably choose.

The presumption of competence holds until we have evidence to the contrary. When such evidence comes to light and we have reason to believe that an individual is not competent to make important decisions, the state looks to its <u>parens patriae</u> power, its authority to take care of individuals who are not capable of caring for themselves. Under the parens patriae power the state may appoint a substitute decision-maker, such as a guardian. Also, through such instruments as a durable power of attorney and a health care surrogate, the law allows an individual to anticipate and plan for his own incapacity to make decisions.

QUESTIONS DISCUSSED IN THIS CHAPTER

DISCUSSION

95. Where does one find the laws that govern guardianships?

Florida laws that govern guardianships are found in chapter 744 of the Florida Statutes, titled, fittingly enough, "Florida Guardianship Law." Chapter 744 discusses the various types of guardians, as well as the rules that govern how guardians get appointed and do their job. In addition, three Florida statutes provide for the appointment of a guardian advocate (see question 109) under certain circumstances. The Florida Mental Health Act (Fla. Stat. ch. 394.4598) provides for the appointment of a guardian advocate when a mentally ill person who is incompetent to consent to treatment is committed to a psychiatric hospital. Section 393.12 (Fla. Stat. ch. 393.12) allows the court to appoint a guardian advocate for a person with developmental disabilities. Finally, section 39.825 (Fla. Stat. ch. 39.825) provides for the appointment of a guardian advocate for drug dependent newborns. (For the difference between a guardian and a guardian advocate, see question 108.)

96. What is the purpose of a guardian?

A court appoints a guardian for an individual who does not have the capacity to make certain important decisions. The guardian makes those decisions on behalf of the individual, who is referred to as the "ward." A guardian is thus a substitute decision-maker; substitute because the guardian stands in the shoes of the individual who needs help in making decisions. The court gives the guardian both the power and the responsibility to make appropriate decisions on the ward's behalf. In making decisions for the ward, the guardian should attempt to ascertain what the ward would choose were she capable of making decisions for herself. If the guardian is not able to ascertain the ward's preference, the guardian considers what decision would be in the ward's best interest. Part of a guardian's responsibilities is to file a report each year with the court, indicating whether the ward still needs a guardian, or whether the ward has regained any of his capacities (see the following questions).

97. What kind of decisions does a guardian make on behalf of a ward?

Section 744.3215 (Fla. Stat. 744.3215) identifies the rights that a court may delegate to a guardian. These rights, which the guardian will exercise on behalf of the ward, include the right:

- to consent to medical and mental health treatment
- to file a lawsuit
- to apply for benefits from the government
- to manage property
- to make a contract
- to determine where the ward will live

When the court appoints a guardian, it must specify which of these rights the ward is unable to exercise for him- or herself. A guardian will have the authority to exercise *only* those rights that a court has determined the ward is incapable of exercising. There are times when an individual is not able to exercise any of the rights named above. In those cases, the guardian is referred to as a "plenary" guardian. A plenary guardian is appointed when the court finds the ward incapable of performing all tasks necessary to care for his person and his property. Otherwise, the guardian is a "limited" guardian. A limited guardian has the authority to perform only those tasks the court has determined the ward is not capable of performing.

Section 744.3215 (Fla. Stat. ch. 744.3215[4]) sets out a group of rights that are special. A guardian has the authority to exercise the rights named in section 744.3215(4) only after the court has given the guardian special permission to do so. These rights include the right:

- to commit the ward to a facility (such as a psychiatric hospital) without a formal placement proceeding
- to consent to any experimental procedure, or to consent to the ward's participation in an experiment
- to end the ward's marriage
- to consent to terminate the ward's rights as a parent
- to consent to an abortion or to be sterilized

Again, a court will specify precisely which of these rights a ward is incapable of exercising. The guardian will have authority to exercise only those rights.

98. Once a guardian is appointed, does the ward retain the right to make any decisions for himself, or any rights at all?

A ward retains those rights not specifically delegated to the guardian. Thus, unless the guardian is a plenary guardian, the ward will still have the right to make certain kinds of decisions for him or herself. In addition, regardless of whether the court has appointed a limited or plenary guardian, rights the ward will retain include, among others, the right to have the guardian's plan reviewed on an annual basis; to be treated with dignity and respect; to be protected against abuse, neglect, and exploitation; to remain as independent as possible; to be properly educated; to be free from discrimination because of his or her incapacity; and the right to privacy. The ward will retain these rights, as well as the right to make any decisions the court has not explicitly delegated to the guardian.

99. How is a guardian appointed?

An individual may ask that a guardian be appointed for himself. Such a guardianship is referred to as a "voluntary" guardianship (See question 121). In other cases, a guardian is appointed when a court finds that an individual is "incapacitated" to perform some or all of the tasks needed to care for himself or his property. When a person exhibits signs of physical or mental inability to handle his affairs, any concerned adult may petition (submit a written request to) the circuit court for a determination of incapacity and for the appointment of a guardian.

Within five days of when the petition is filed, the court will appoint a three-person committee, which must include a psychiatrist and two other mental health practitioners, or a gerontology specialist, to examine the individual on behalf of whom the guardianship is proposed. The report of the three-person committee must include a physical examination, a mental health evaluation, and an assessment of the individual's functioning. If the committee finds that the person is *not* incapacitated, the court will dismiss the petition. If, on the other hand, the court finds that there is clear and convincing evidence (see question 4) that the individual *is* incapacitated, the court will write an order that indicates whether the individual is incapacitated in all respects (in which case the court will appoint a plenary guardian), or in certain, specified respects (in which case the court will appoint a limited guardian). As an example of how a limited guardianship works, a person found incompetent to manage his property could still exercise his right to vote and to marry.

It is extremely important to note that, according to section 744.331 (Fla. Stat. ch. 744.331), the court will make specific findings concerning the "exact nature and scope" of the individual's incapacities; the "exact areas" where the person is unable to make decisions regarding care and treatment; the individual's "specific legal disabilities"; and the "specific rights" the person is unable to exercise. Rather than viewing incapacity as an "all or nothing" sort of thing, the law focuses in on the ward's specific disabilities and hands decision-making authority over to the guardian in only those areas. In this way, the law seeks to foster as much of the ward's capacity to make independent decisions as possible.

100. Who may ask that a guardian be appointed?
According to section 744.3201 (Fla. Stat. ch. 744.3201), any concerned adult can ask a court to appoint a guardian over an individual who appears to be incapacitated. The individual does so by filing a petition (a written request) with basic information about the person believed to be incapacitated (such as name and address), and the reasons why the individual filing the petition believes the person is incapacitated.

101. How does Florida law define "incapacitation"?
Chapter 744 says that a person is incapacitated when he is unable to meet at least some of the requirements essential to his health and safety. Section 744.102 (Fla. Stat. ch. 744.102[10][b]) defines such requirements as "those actions necessary to provide the health care, food, shelter, clothing, personal hygiene, or other care without which serious and imminent physical injury or illness is more likely than not to occur." An individual is also considered incapacitated if he is unable to manage at least some of his property or financial interests (for example, to obtain, administer, or dispose of income such as social security benefits).

102. Are guardians appointed only for incapacitated persons?
No. Sometimes a person is mentally competent but unable to manage his or her property or financial affairs because of age or physical infirmity. In such a case, section 744.341 (Fla. Stat. 744.341) allows the individual to petition the court to create a voluntary guardianship. The ward can terminate this voluntary guardianship by filing a notice of termination with the court.

103. Who may serve as a guardian?
Any Florida resident 18 years of age or older may serve as a guardian. If the proposed guardian is not a resident of the state, section 744.309 (Fla. Stat. ch. 744.309 [2][a–d]) requires that the guardian be a family member of the ward, or the spouse of a family member. Corporations can also be appointed as guardians. Under section 744.309 (Florida Stat. ch.

744.309[4] and [5]), corporations such as state banks, trust companies, or federal saving and loan associations may serve as guardians of the property of the ward. In addition, any nonprofit corporation organized for religious or charitable purposes may serve as a guardian.

If a person or corporation receives compensation for services rendered to two or more wards, then that person or corporation is called a "professional guardian." Section 744.1085 (Fla. Stat. ch. 744.1085) regulates professional guardians. Section 744.1085 requires that professional guardians post a bond with the circuit court and receive at least 40 hours of training and 16 hours of continuing education thereafter. A family member who serves as a guardian for a single ward, on the other hand, does not need to post a bond but, at the discretion of the court, may be required to complete 8 hours of training provided by a court-approved organization.

The court has the final say in who is appointed as a guardian. Courts prefer to appoint someone who knows the ward and will know what the ward wants. Section 744.312 (Fla. Stat. ch. 744.312[2][d]) establishes an order of preference. First, the court will consider any person who is related to the proposed ward by blood or marriage. If a relative is not available or is deemed not suitable to be a guardian, the court will give preference to a person who has the necessary educational, professional, or business experience to deal with the specific needs of the ward, or a person who has the capacity to manage the financial resources of the ward. The court must also consider the ward's wishes about whom to appoint as a guardian.

104. What happens when an incapacitated person has no funds to pay a private guardian and no family or friends are willing to serve as a guardian?

According to Florida law, any guardian (including a family member) is entitled to reasonable reimbursement and compensation for costs incurred on behalf of the ward. Such costs are to be paid out of the ward's property. When an incapacitated person does not have adequate assets and no family member or corporation is willing to provide services without appropriate compensation or reimbursement, the Public Guardianship Act, (Fla. Stat. ch. 744.701), provides a mechanism to appoint a public guardian. To fall under the Public Guardianship Act, an individual's assets must be no greater than those for Medicaid eligibility and the individual must have an income of less than $4,000 per year. The public guardian has the same powers and duties as a guardian who is a family member, a friend, or a corporation.

105. What medical treatment may a guardian authorize?

When a court is deciding whether to appoint a guardian, it will ask what specific decisions the individual is not able to make for him- or herself. If the court determines that the individual does not have the capacity to consent to medical or mental health treatment, the court may then give that authority over to the guardian. Again, however, the court will do so only after having specifically found that the ward is not capable of making those decisions.

Even should this authority be granted to the guardian, certain situations require extra protection. According to section 744.3215(4), a guardian must have "specific authority" from the court:

- to commit the ward to a psychiatric hospital or receiving facility without a formal placement proceeding
- to consent to experimental treatment, sterilization, or abortion
- to have the ward participate in research

To grant a guardian the authority to do any of the above, a court must follow special procedures set forth in section 744.3725 (Fla. Stat. ch. 744.3725), which addresses situations in which guardians are given "extraordinary authority." Section 744.3725 says that before granting extraordinary authority to a guardian, a judge must appoint an attorney to represent the individual, and the judge him- or herself must meet with the incapacitated person to allow that individual to express his views to the judge directly. The judge will grant the guardian extraordinary authority only if doing so is in the ward's best interests.

106. May a guardian authorize treatment with antipsychotic medication?

A guardian may authorize treatment with antipsychotic medication only if the court gives the guardian the authority to make health care decisions at the time the guardian is appointed. A guardian does not, however, need to receive "extraordinary authority" from the court (see the question above) to consent to treatment with antipsychotic medication. The permission to make health care decisions will suffice.

107. May a guardian authorize ECT or psychosurgery?

Section 458.325 (Fla. Stat. ch. 458.325) says that ECT or psychosurgery cannot be performed unless the patient, or the patient's guardian, gives written consent. Nothing in section 458.325 or in chapter 744 suggests that such consent falls under the provisions for "extraordinary authority," so a guardian given the authority to make medical and mental health decisions could consent to ECT and psychosurgery. Note, however, that a guardian advocate (see question 108) may *not* consent to ECT or psychosurgery without the court's explicit approval.

108. What is the difference between a guardian and a guardian advocate for a mentally ill person?

The appointment of a guardian advocate for a mentally ill person is intended to expedite treatment—perhaps needed by the person only on a temporary basis—by obviating the necessity of going through formal guardianship procedures at the time of commitment. For example, when a patient in need of hospitalization and treatment is found to be incompetent to provide informed consent as a result of his symptoms—as examples, delusions, paranoid ideations, confusion—section 394.467 (Fla. Stat. ch. 394.467[6][d]) allows the court to appoint a guardian advocate to consent to hospitalization and treatment. As treatment progresses, the patient may regain his ability to understand and to provide consent for treatment. At that time, the guardian advocate should be discharged from his duties.

109. When is a guardian advocate for a mentally ill person appointed?

A guardian advocate for a mentally ill person is appointed when a patient is involuntarily committed to a mental health facility and it appears that the individual is incompetent to consent to treatment. Under section 394.4598 (Fla. Stat. ch. 394.4598), a guardian advocate makes decisions about mental health treatment as long as the ward remains incompetent and involuntarily committed to the facility. Thus, a guardian advocate's duties will end when the individual regains competence or is discharged from the hospital. Note that not all individuals committed to a psychiatric facility will have a guardian advocate—only those who have been found incompetent to consent to treatment at the commitment hearing.

In selecting a guardian advocate, the court gives preference to an individual whom the patient has previously designated as a health care surrogate. If the patient has never designated a health care surrogate, section 394.4598 directs the court to select from the following individuals (in order of preference): (a) the patient's spouse, (b) an adult child of the patient, (c) a parent of the patient, (d) an adult next of kin, (e) an adult friend of the patient, or (f) an adult trained and willing to serve as a guardian advocate.

110. What happens when a person who already has a plenary guardian is involuntarily committed to a psychiatric facility?

A guardian advocate is not necessary when the patient (the ward) already has a plenary guardian.

111. Who can ask to have a guardianship reviewed?

Section 744.464 (Fla. Stat. ch. 744.464[2][a]) says that any person, including the ward, can go before a court and ask that a guardianship be reviewed. After the request is filed, the court will appoint a physician who will evaluate the ward and file his report with the court within 20 days. The purpose of the evaluation is to determine whether the ward has regained all, or some, of his capacities. The court will then make a ruling based on the physician's evaluation. In addition, section 744.3715 (Fla. Stat. ch. 744.3715) allows any individual to go before a court at any time and claim that the guardian is not fulfilling his duties or is not acting in the bests interests of the ward.

112. When does a guardianship end?

According to section 744.521 (Fla. Stat. ch. 744.521), a guardianship ends when the ward returns to competence—that is, when the ward is again capable of making decisions for himself. In addition, a guardianship ends when the guardian cannot find the ward, after a reasonable search, or when the ward dies. Also, if the guardian was appointed solely to look after aspects of the ward's property, the guardianship ends when these aspects are sold or otherwise disposed of.

Under section 744.3675 (Fla. Stat. ch. 744.3675) each guardian must file an annual guardianship plan with the court. The guardianship plan must include a medical report that gives a recent evaluation of the ward's condition and indicates the ward's current level of capacity. The plan must also say what steps have been taken to restore the ward to competence. For example, the plan must include a list of activities designed to increase the ward's capacity, and a statement concerning whether the guardian will ask the court to restore any of the ward's rights. In this sense, one purpose of the guardianship plan is to get the ward to a place where he no longer needs a guardian.

113. Can a guardian be removed for any reason?
Section 744.474 (Fla. Stat. ch. 744.474) says that a guardian may be removed for a number of reasons. These reasons include:

- fraud in obtaining his or her appointment as guardian
- failure to discharge the duties of a guardian
- abuse of his or her powers
- incapacity or illness, including substance abuse, which renders the guardian incapable of discharging his or her duties
- conflict of interest with the ward
- failure to file annual guardianship reports

The court may remove a guardian for any of these reasons (among others), and may then appoint someone else who the court believes will serve the ward's best interests.

114. How can medical treatment be provided to a person who lacks the capacity to provide informed consent but does not have a guardian?
A clinician may legally treat without informed consent (see question 26) only in emergency situations. When a patient who requires treatment for an existing or continuing *nonemergent* medical condition is unable to give informed consent, a clinician who provides that treatment exposes herself to legal liability. Florida law provides a mechanism to address this problem through a health care surrogate or a health care proxy.

115. What is a health care surrogate?
A health care surrogate makes health care decisions on behalf of an individual when that person is incompetent to make such decisions himself. The advantage of a health care surrogate is that it allows an individual (called the "principal") to identify a trusted family member or friend as a health care surrogate who will then step in and make health care decisions when the principal cannot. A health care surrogate can be designated in writing at any time the principal wishes to do so. Often people will tell their doctors whom they have designated, and will give their doctor a copy of the official designation. Section 765.110 (Fla. Stat. ch. 765.110) requires that health care facilities provide their patients with written information concerning advance directives (advance directives include: designation of health care surrogate, living wills, and orders not

to resuscitate) and document in the patient's record whether the person has executed an advance directive or not.

The principal can designate any competent adult whom he chooses to be a health care surrogate. Clearly the decision to designate a health care surrogate is important, because the surrogate will be the one making health care decisions in the event the principal becomes incapacitated. These decisions must be based on the surrogate's best guess about what the principal would have wanted, so it makes sense for the principal to designate as a surrogate someone whom he knows well.

116. If a competent individual designates a health care surrogate, what happens if that individual becomes incompetent and needs a guardian?

A competent individual may designate a health care surrogate. If that individual then becomes incompetent, he may need a guardian (remember that a guardian may have far wider powers than will a health care surrogate—a plenary guardian will have the authority to make a host of decisions on the ward's behalf). Because a plenary guardian may be asked to make decisions that involve health care matters, the court that creates the guardianship should indicate what relationship the guardian will have to the health care surrogate—that is, whose decisions take precedence. Unless the court modifies or revokes the authority of the health care surrogate, the guardian should defer in matters that the ward has explicitly delegated to the health care surrogate (see section 744.3115 [Fla. Stat. ch. 744.3115]).

117. What is a health care proxy?

A health care proxy is appointed for an individual who has become incapacitated but who has never designated a health care surrogate. Section 765.401 (Fla. Stat. ch. 765.401) provides for the appointment of a health care proxy in the following order of priority: (a) a previously appointed guardian; (b) the patient's spouse; (c) an adult child of the patient or the majority of the adult children available for consultation; (d) a parent of the patient; (e) any adult sibling; (f) an adult relative; or (g) a close friend. Like the decisions of a health care surrogate, the decisions of a health care proxy must be based on what the proxy believes the patient would have wanted. The proxy has the same powers as a health care surrogate. The only difference between a health care surrogate and a health care proxy is the manner in which the appointment takes place: The principal designates a health care surrogate, while a medical facility designates a health care proxy (because the principal had not done so before incapacitation).

118. What is an emergency temporary guardian?
In Florida, a guardianship often takes several months to obtain. The reason is that appointing a guardian means taking decision-making authority away from the ward, and so is a serious matter. As a consequence, numerous procedural requirements must be met along the way. When a guardian must be appointed immediately, the court may appoint an emergency temporary guardian under section 744.3031 (Fla. Stat. ch. 744.3031). A temporary guardianship is focused and limited, insofar as its purpose is to address a specific harm. For example, if the health or safety of the incapacitated person is at risk, the temporary guardian could make emergency health care decisions, or take over the management of the person's property if it is in danger of being wasted, misappropriated, or lost. The authority of the emergency temporary guardian will expire 60 days after its appointment or when a guardian is appointed. In case a permanent guardian is not yet in place at the end of the 60 days, the authority of the temporary guardian can be extended for an additional 30 days.

119. What is a natural guardian?
Parents are the natural guardians of their children and any adopted children.

120. What is a standby guardian?
A guardian who is concerned about his own ability to continue serving in that role may ask the court to appoint a "standby" guardian. A standby guardian steps into the shoes of the guardian if the guardian dies, resigns, or is removed from his duties. As an example, a guardian may chose to resign if the demands of his duties are too much to handle. In such case, the standby guardian immediately assumes the responsibilities of the guardian, considerably alleviating the disruption caused by the resignation, death, or removal of the original guardian.

121. What is a preneed guardian?
A competent person can make provisions to have a guardian appointed *prior* to becoming incapacitated. An individual can do so by making a written statement to that effect, having the statement witnessed by two

individuals, and filing the statement with the court. The individual designated in this manner to serve as a guardian is called a "preneed" guardian. The preneed guardian will assume the duties of a guardian when a court judges that the individual seeking to have the guardian appointed is no longer competent. Section 744.3046 (Fla. Stat. ch. 744.3046) also provides for the designation of a preneed guardian for minors. This statute allows parents to nominate a person to take care of the property or person of their children, or both, in the event the last surviving parent becomes incapacitated or dies.

122. What is a guardian ad litem?

A guardian ad litem is a guardian for the purposes of a legal proceeding. A guardian ad litem may be appointed for any person by the court in which the legal matter is being heard, if the court determines that the person's interests would otherwise not be adequately represented. The court may even choose to appoint a guardian ad litem for individuals who already have a guardian. The point of a guardian ad litem (often referred to as a "GAL") is for the court to make sure that the individual's legal rights and interests are adequately protected during the course of a legal proceeding.

The GAL is not considered a party to the legal proceeding. In other words, a GAL is not someone, like the plaintiff or defendant, whose interests are directly at issue. Rather, the GAL is considered the *personal representative* of a party—it is as if the guardian ad litem were standing in the party's shoes. Because the GAL represents a party in this manner, she has the authority to make important decisions affecting the outcome of the case, such as whether to settle. Note that attorneys are not allowed to make decisions of this sort; an attorney must have a client's approval first. The power of a GAL is, however, limited in that she cannot waive fundamental rights of the ward. A GAL cannot, for example, waive a party's right to trial by jury.

123. What is a power of attorney?

A power of attorney is a document by which one individual (the "principal") authorizes another individual (the "agent") to perform acts having to do with the principal's person, property, or both. Examples of the sorts of things a principal may authorize an agent to do include writing checks, selling property, or making health care decisions. The principal is bound by what the agent does, in the same way the principal would be bound if she herself had performed the acts. The power of attorney will specify precisely what the agent is allowed to do on behalf of the principal.

124. What is a durable power of attorney?
A *durable* power of attorney is a power of attorney that continues to be valid when the principal becomes incompetent, for example, because of mental illness or dementia. A durable power of attorney may commence *upon* or may remain valid *despite* the principal's incompetence. Whichever the case, the agent is authorized to act on the principal's behalf during a period of the principal's incompetence. As with a power of attorney, the principal is bound by what the agent does, in the same way as the principal would be bound if she herself had performed the acts.

125. What is a representative payee?
A representative payee is a person or an agency who accepts payment from an entitlement program on behalf of a recipient. An individual need not have a guardian or be incompetent to have a representative payee. Rather, the standard is whether having a representative payee is in the person's interest. According to the Social Security Act, a representative payee is automatically judged to be in the interest of an individual whose disability includes drug or alcohol addiction.

9

Confidentiality, Testimonial Privilege, and Mandatory Reporting

That we have both an entire chapter and a set of questions on the subject of confidentiality emphasizes the importance of this topic to mental health professionals. As you read, recall that confidentiality involves the obligation of a mental health professional to keep patient communications within the bounds of the professional relationship. Testimonial privilege, or simply "privilege," refers to a patient's right to prevent the mental health professional from disclosing confidential information in a legal proceeding. Mandatory reporting statutes require a mental health professional to disclose confidential information in certain well-defined situations; this disclosure must take place regardless of whether the client consents.

The number of questions that can arise when a clinician is attempting to treat difficult or severely compromised patients is staggering; even the most routine work will inevitably raise dilemmas about when to release clinical material. The questions below are presented as much for their content as for their demonstration of the process that should govern a treater's thinking when she is faced with the possibility of disclosing confidential information.

QUESTIONS DISCUSSED IN THIS CHAPTER

126. Is there a duty to breach confidentiality if a patient talks about having committed a crime in the past?

127. Is there a duty to breach confidentiality if a patient talks about intending to commit a crime in the future?

128. In certain circumstances following a patient's death, the personal representative of the estate may waive privilege. What happens when the personal representative of an estate wants clinical records?

129. What is a mandated reporter?

130. Does the mandatory reporting statute for child abuse require a clinician to report child abuse that is not inflicted by a parent or caretaker? What if the abuser is another child?

131. An extremely religious set of parents forbade me to breach confidentiality when their 12-year-old child talked about having been sexually touched by a member of their church's clergy. The parents were adamant that this information was to go *nowhere,* or else I would never see the child again and I would face a lawsuit for breach of confidentiality. What is the best way to handle this situation?

132. If I make a report under the mandatory reporting statute for children, can the child's parent—or the alleged perpetrator—find out that I was the one who reported?

133. What should I do if a patient tells me that another treater has harmed her?

134. Must a client be given notice before a psychological evaluation can be introduced into a legal proceeding?

135. What are the rules of confidentiality regarding consultations?

136. Treaters often keep notes of their own countertransference fantasies separate from the record. These are neither progress nor process notes; their purpose is to help the treater gauge the nature and intensity of her own psychic processes as they relate to the clinical work. Could a lawyer ever obtain them?

DISCUSSION

126. Is there a duty to breach confidentiality if a patient talks about having committed a crime in the past?

Florida law (as well as federal law) recognizes that the psychotherapist-patient relationship requires complete trust and open communication.

Without safeguards protecting the confidentiality of patient communications, many people would simply forego psychotherapy. For this reason, both state and federal law provide that what a patient communicates to a mental health professional should remain within the treater-patient relationship.

The decision regarding when confidential information will be revealed belongs to the patient—"privilege belongs to the patient," as the saying goes. Section 503(2) of the Florida Evidence Code (Fla. Stat. ch. 90.503[2]) states, "a patient has a privilege to refuse to disclose, and to *prevent any other person from disclosing,* confidential communications . . . between the patient and the psychotherapist." The only exceptions to section 503 are found in the Florida statutes dealing with elderly and disabled person abuse, neglect, or exploitation (Fla. Stat. ch. 415.109), and child abuse, neglect, or abandonment (Fla. Stat. ch. 39.201). The conditions set forth in these mandatory reporting statutes (see chapter 3) are not protected by testimonial privilege, which means that a patient no longer has the right to prevent a mental health professional from disclosing this information when it comes to light.

A single exception to confidentiality or privilege allows a mental health professional to disclose client communications about a past crime (other than a crime involving child, elderly, or disabled person abuse or neglect, which must always be reported). Section 397.501(7) (Florida Stat. ch. 397.501[7]) allows a provider to disclose to law enforcement officers information about a client who has committed or threatened to commit a crime on the provider's premises or against a provider's employee. Section 397.501(7) limits the information that may be disclosed to the circumstances of the incident, the client status of the individual, his name and address, and his last known whereabouts. Material concerning past crimes—other than crimes set forth in the mandatory reporting statutes and section 397.501(7)—should be treated in the same manner as any other material disclosed within the therapeutic context—it remains between treater and patient.

127. Is there a duty to breach confidentiality if a patient talks about intending to commit a crime in the future?

The issue of future crimes—the contemplation of a crime—is complicated. While there is no duty to report a client's intent to commit a future crime, the following points nevertheless merit consideration.

First, there is no duty to warn in Florida (see chapter 2). While both the common law and statutes say that a mental health professional may disclose a patient's intent to injure a third party, there is no legal obligation to do so. Future crimes are therefore within the realm of permissive and discretionary, rather than mandatory, reporting.

Second, virtually all crimes entail the possibility of harm either to a third party or to the perpetrator. Breaking into a home or apartment, for example, can place both the inhabitants and the individual entering at great risk. Stealing a car brings with it the possibility of a police chase, which could kill or injure the individual who stole the car, a police officer, or innocent bystanders. Whenever a client talks about committing a crime in the future, the treater should assess the degree to which harm is foreseeable. If the crime is against an identifiable third party, the treater should assess whether the situation falls under section 455.671 (Fla. Stat. ch. 455.671), and then rely on her clinical judgment in deciding whether to disclose information to protect the intended victim.

Third, a question arises whenever a treater listens to a client talk about a future crime: To what extent is the treater subtlety encouraging— if only by failing to *discourage*—the client? Any action by a treater— before or after a crime—which could reasonably be viewed as encouraging, aiding, or harboring a criminal could be considered actionable by the police. When such material arises during the course of a therapy, the treater should be keenly aware of what posture she adopts. A consultation could prove invaluable.

128. In certain circumstances following a patient's death, the personal representative of the estate may waive privilege. What happens when the personal representative of an estate wants clinical records?

A well-known psychiatrist, Martin Orne, perhaps unwittingly brought the issue of confidentiality following a patient's death to the forefront of public attention when he released audiotapes of his treatment sessions with Anne Sexton. Sexton, who won a Pulitzer Prize for her poetry following several years of therapy with Orne, had complained that she was frequently unable to remember what was said during their hours, a complaint Orne addressed by suggesting they tape-record their sessions. Following Sexton's suicide in 1974, Orne provided over 300 of these audiotapes to Diane Middlebrook, an English professor at Stanford University and Sexton's biographer. Orne's decision to release the tapes without Sexton's written permission or express consent was met by a firestorm of controversy; the sum total of what Sexton had to say on the subject appears to have been a comment she made to Orne in 1964, when the treatment ended because Orne moved from Massachusetts (where Sexton lived) to Philadelphia. According to Orne, Sexton told him to keep the tapes to help others as he saw fit. When Orne gave the tapes to biographer Diane Middlebrook, he did so with the permission of Sexton's literary executor, who was also her daughter, Linda Grey Sexton. Despite that permission, Orne soon became the target of vehement condemnations. (*The New York Times* opined that Orne had "dishonored" his profession.)

Given that mental health professionals must not reveal confidential communications even after a patient has died, how could Orne have found his decision to release the tapes defensible?

In certain, very limited circumstances, an individual other than your patient may have the legal authority to consent to the release of your patient's records. Usually this individual is a parent or guardian; parents and guardians are entrusted with protecting the interests of a minor or someone who has been deemed unable to care for himself, and are therefore presumed to be acting in the best interest of their child or ward when they allow confidential treatment information to be shared with a third party. The personal representative of a patient's estate fills a similar role: Charged with protecting the interests of the estate, the personal representative may consent to the release of a deceased patient's treatment records. Given Linda Grey Sexton's authority as personal representative of her mother's estate, why was Orne so severely criticized?

A distinction arises between what is legally permissible and what is ethically permissible. Whatever a mental health professional is *legally* permitted to do, the *ethical* mandate to keep patient communications confidential remains. (Keep in mind the distinction between what mental health professionals are legally permitted to do and what they are legally required to do; disclosures of information pursuant to a mandatory reporting statute or a court order are legal *requirements*.) To assess the *ethical* acceptability of releasing the records of a deceased patient when you have *legal* permission to do so from the personal representative of the patient's estate, ask the following four questions: (1) Will this release serve a specific and legitimate purpose? (2) Is this release the only reasonable, or clearly best, way to achieve that purpose? (3) Is this release consistent with what the patient would have wanted, insofar as those wants can be ascertained? (4) Is there a clear and substantial reason why the patient did not provide an explicit consent for this release while alive? Unless your answer to each of these four questions is "yes," our recommendation is not to release the records. The party making the request can issue a subpoena and a judge will then determine what materials will be released (see chapter 7, Subpoenas and Court Orders). When in doubt, consult a colleague; doing so will help demonstrate that you were attempting to act in an ethically responsible manner.

Consider the following three examples. First, a patient commits suicide and her family, perhaps a bit guilty because of an estrangement, asks if they could speak to you about your patient's treatment and even look at some of your notes. The family member who makes the request is the personal representative of the estate and that individual, also a lawyer, cites the law that gives him the authority to consent to a release of records. In this case you would explain that you are under an ethical obligation to protect your patient's confidentiality and so are not free to release her records or to discuss details of her treatment. While you are free to meet with the family and to discuss their feelings of sadness, loss, and even anger over the death (doing so may be enormously helpful to them), there is no "specific and legitimate" reason to release any information. The family may pursue legal means to obtain the records, in which case a judge will make a determination and indicate what you should do.

Second, an elderly patient who had been suffering from a dementia sold a valuable painting of great sentimental value shortly before her death, for a fraction of its actual worth. The personal representative of her estate approaches you and asks for records that might show the patient was incompetent at the time of the sale, a showing that would allow the personal representative to reclaim the painting for the estate and return it to the family. You, yourself, had serious questions about the patient's competence, and feel that she would want her family, with whom she was very close, to have this painting. In this case you would confirm the family member's appointment as personal representative of the estate; ask the personal representative to provide you with a written consent to release records; review the record and pick out material related to your patient's competence at the time of the sale; and release only those entries you have selected. The release in this case is ethically acceptable, because (1) it serves a specific and legitimate purpose; (2) the release is the only reasonable, or clearly best, way to achieve that purpose; (3) the release is consistent with the patient's wishes as best you can ascertain them; and (4) since the patient was incompetent, there is a clear and substantial reason why she did not provide explicit permission while alive for the release of this information.

In the third example, the personal representative returns for additional material after you release the records of your elderly patient, material that you do not feel speaks to your patient's competence and that you feel could result in hurt feelings and perhaps affect the family's memory of your patient. Although you have legal permission, the release has no specific and legitimate purpose. You cite your ethical obligation to keep the material confidential and do not comply with the request.

Requests for records following the death of a patient highlight the distinction between what is legally permissible and what is ethically acceptable. The intensity of the reaction to Martin Orne's release of the therapy tapes may find at least a partial explanation in this distinction. Orne may well have stood on sound *legal* footing when he gave the therapy tapes to Diane Middlebrook. The ethical dimensions of what he did are more complicated. However legitimate a purpose the release was intended to achieve, Anne Sexton had hardly left explicit permission for Orne to provide the tapes to a biographer, and Orne certainly had the option of citing his ethical obligation of confidentiality had he chosen to do so. A judge would then have decided how the matter would be handled. Far from refusing the request, it was Orne who apprised Middlebrook of the tapes' existence and then offered them to her; subsequently he wrote an introduction to the biography and provided a photograph of himself to be included in the book. In defending his release of Anne Sexton's therapy tapes, Martin Orne remarked, "I was often more concerned about her privacy than she was." Ethics demand that mental health professionals remain concerned with their patients' privacy in perpetuity.

129. What is a mandated reporter?

A mandated reporter is any individual for whom a mandatory reporting statute creates a duty to report. Each mandatory reporting statute (see chapter 3) lists a series of individuals who are required to report to a designated state agency under certain circumstances. These individuals are mandated reporters. A mandated reporter's failure to make a required report may result in criminal and civil liability and/or professional disciplinary action. Bottom line: If you're mandated to report and do not, you can be charged with a crime, sued by someone who suffers an injury because of your failure to report, and brought before your discipline's licensing board.

130. Does the mandatory reporting statute for child abuse require a clinician to report child abuse that is not inflicted by a parent or caretaker? What if the abuser is another child?

In Florida, two statutes specifically address and define child abuse: section 827.03 (Fla. Stat. ch. 827.03) and section 39.201 (Fla. Stat. ch. 39.201). Section 827.03, the criminal statute, defines child abuse as:

- intentional infliction of physical or mental injury upon a child;
- an intentional act that could reasonably be expected to result in physical or mental injury to a child; or
- active encouragement of any person to commit an act that results or could reasonably be expected to result in physical or mental injury to a child.

Section 827.03(1) does not limit the identity of the perpetrator. As a consequence, whether an adult is a parent or caretaker is not relevant to a clinician's duty to report—in fact, Florida law makes special provision for when the adult suspected of abuse is not a caretaker. In such a case, the civil statute, section 39.201(2)(a), requires that the report be transferred "immediately" from the hotline to the county sheriff's office.

Incidents involving physical, sexual, or emotional abuse between children can be more complicated. Mental health practitioners need to exercise judgment about when an incident is best understood as typical for what goes on between children, and when the incident is more serious and merits adult intervention. If a mental health professional is unsure about whether to make a report, we recommend the following. Whenever, in your capacity as a mental health professional, you reasonably suspect child abuse, call the statewide central abuse line. Explain the situation and let the agency decide whether a report is necessary. If the agency decides a report is required, defer to their judgment. You will have made your report in good faith and so are protected from liability. If the agency feels that a report is unnecessary, document your call by recording the time, date, name of the individual with whom you spoke, and the facts you provided. You have then attempted to comply with the statute and may rely on the agency's judgment that no report is necessary. Remember that the individual with whom you speak will make a determination based on the facts you provide; if you are incomplete in explaining the situation—even though you may be attempting to protect your client—you will defeat the purpose of your call and so cannot rely on the advice given.

Mental health professionals should be aware that a specific statute, section 39.201(2)(d)(1–3) (Fla. Stat. ch. 39.201(2)(d)(1–3), identifies and describes specific procedures to follow after a report of child-on-child abuse. Section 39.201 states that any incident involving a known or suspected juvenile offender must be reported. The central registry will then determine the appropriateness of the report and follow the procedures set forth in the statute.

Recall (from chapter 3) that neglect is also a reportable condition under the mandatory reporting statute for children. Thus, if an older child is physically injuring a younger child, the adult caretaker may not be providing adequate supervision. In this case, you may be mandated to report because the caretaker has been neglectful.

131. An extremely religious set of parents forbade me to breach confidentiality when their 12-year-old child talked about having been sexually touched by a member of their church's clergy. The parents were adamant that this information was to go *nowhere*, or else I would never see the child again and I would face a lawsuit for breach of confidentiality. What is the best way to handle this situation?

Cases in which a disclosure of confidential information may end a therapy are especially difficult. Most poignant is that the victim—a child, and your patient—is made to suffer a second betrayal. Nevertheless, the law allows no room for discretion in this instance. Section 39.201 (Fla. Stat. ch. 39.201) mandates that you report. You need not worry about a lawsuit; section 39.203 (Fla. Stat. ch. 39.203) grants immunity to any mandated reporter who makes a report in good faith. The intensity of the parents' feelings may be tempered somewhat if, in the first session, you reviewed the exceptions to confidentiality (see the discussion of the Law of No Surprises in chapter 3). In this case the parents would already have been apprised of your obligation to disclose.

132. If I make a report under the mandatory reporting statute for children, can the child's parent—or the alleged perpetrator—find out that I was the one who reported?

Florida wants to encourage mental health professionals to protect abused and neglected children. For this reason, section 39.202 (Fla. Stat. ch. 39.202) requires that the identities of all persons who report under mandatory reporting statutes remain confidential. While certain exceptions do arise—the name of the person making the report may be disclosed between child protective agencies, to an attorney representing a child protective agency, to the district attorney in a criminal prosecution, or to an attorney representing the parties in dependency court—none of the exceptions allow the alleged perpetrator or the child's parents to discover who reported the incident.

133. What should I do if a patient tells me that another treater has harmed her?

Mental health professionals frequently ask this question, usually about a female patient who has been sexually involved with a male therapist. To answer the question, you must determine whether any mandatory reporting statute applies (see chapter 3). If, for example, your patient is under 18, you may be a mandated reporter because of your obligation to report child sexual abuse. If you are not mandated to report by virtue of any reporting statute, you must have your client's consent before disclosing anything she tells you.

134. Must a client be given notice before a psychological evaluation can be introduced into a legal proceeding?

Always be clear whether your client is *the court* or *the individual with whom you are speaking*. The difference is extremely important. Section 503 of the Evidence Code (Fla. Stat. ch. 90.503[4]) states, "there is no privilege . . . for communications made in the course of a court-ordered examination of the mental or emotional condition of the patient." When you have been hired by a court for the purposes of assessment or diagnosis, the court is your client. Testimonial privilege does not apply. The purpose of your work is to garner information for the legal proceeding and you will disclose what you learn. It is your ethical obligation to inform the evaluee, before the evaluee discusses any clinical information, that what he says will be shared with the court. If the individual begins speaking before you have had a chance to explain that what he says will be shared in court, stop him and explain the limits of confidentiality before proceeding. Section 503 creates one exception to this rule: When a defense lawyer asks a court to appoint a psychotherapist to help determine whether an insanity defense is appropriate, the interview remains confidential and need not be disclosed. Bottom line: Psychotherapists appointed by a court order to conduct an assessment must inform the patient of the limits to confidentiality at the very outset of the interview.

If your client is the individual with whom you are speaking—that is, you are not working for the court—you are bound by confidentiality and cannot testify unless your client waives privilege. The regular rules of confidentiality and testimonial privilege apply.

135. What are the rules of confidentiality regarding consultations?

As with many areas of mental health law, there is no crystal clear guideline that governs the confidentiality of patient information that treaters may share in consultations and supervisions. The lack of clarity stems from two realities that occasionally conflict. The first is that information and records obtained in the course of providing mental health services are confidential (see chapter 3); the second is that in order to provide appropriate care psychotherapists sometimes need to consult with and seek professional advice from their colleagues. Often these realities can be molded to fit one another. Many times, for example, therapists are able to ask for and receive enormously helpful consultations that do not require disclosing any information that could reasonably lead to a client's identification. When a therapist is able to obtain a consultation without revealing identifying information, both the need to maintain confidentiality and the need to seek professional advice and assistance are met.

Section 455.667 (Fla. Stat. ch. 455.667), which governs confidentiality of records, makes an explicit exception to confidentiality that is relevant to consultations and supervisions. According to section 455.667, the patient's records may not be furnished to, and the medical condition of a patient may not be discussed with, any person other than the patient or the patient's legal representative or *other health care practitioners and providers involved in the care or treatment of the patient,* except when the patient grants permission to do so in writing. A strong argument could be made that section 455.667 would allow a treater to share information with another mental health professional for the purpose of aiding in a patient's care or treatment. It is important to note that testimonial privilege and a duty of confidentiality would then extend to those who are consulted.

It is helpful if, during your first session, you follow the Law of No Surprises by informing your client about how you handle consultations. (See appendix B for a sample informed consent letter.) When you get the actual consultation, follow the Parsimony Principle: Be as precise as you can about what questions you would like the consultant to answer and then provide only the information necessary for the consultant to answer that question. Make every effort to avoid sharing any information that could identify your patient, and do so only when such information is absolutely necessary for the consultant to answer your clinical question.

136. Treaters often keep notes of their own countertransference fantasies separate from the record. These are neither progress nor process notes; their purpose is to help the treater gauge the nature and intensity of her own psychic processes as they relate to the clinical work. Could a lawyer ever obtain them?

When it comes to records or notes arising out of a treatment, the rule is: If the records exist, a lawyer may be able to obtain them. While the records may not actually be introduced as evidence into a legal proceeding, at the very least they will be made available to a judge who will review them.

The records described in this question are the treater's personal notes. As such, they are not part of the record. The treater is not required to keep them and may dispose of them whenever she wishes *prior to receiving a subpoena*. Once the treater receives a subpoena—which will almost certainly call for "any and all" records—she is then obligated to ensure that *all* of her records remain intact until a decision is made about what material will be released. Many treaters believe that keeping a set of notes separate from the official record will insulate their notes from a subpoena. Not so. Whatever written materials arise out of a treatment may be requested—and possibly obtained—by a lawyer.

10

RECORDS AND RECORD-KEEPING

Keeping records is an integral part of every mental health professional's work. Records provide an archive for what happened during an assessment or therapy and are thus indispensable should care be transferred from one clinician to another. A record review is often an excellent way to help a therapy that has become "stuck" move forward. And a worthwhile consultation depends upon a reliable record. The law comes into play in a limited number of areas as, for example, in a lawsuit or action before a professional board, when an accurate record of what happened is essential, or when a patient wishes to see her records and the treater does not believe such a review will be in the patient's best interests. Below are questions that address situations in which the law touches upon this area of clinical practice.

Mental health professionals should note that the laws governing records and record-keeping in Florida are complex and represent the result of a complicated interplay between state and federal law (see chapter 3). To make things even more complicated, public debates over privacy will inevitably lead to changes in these laws. When a legal matter involving records arises, mental health professionals should consult with an attorney to ensure that decisions are made on the basis of current statutes and regulations.

QUESTIONS DISCUSSED IN THIS CHAPTER

137. **Must a mental health professional keep records?**
138. **Who owns a therapist's records?**
139. **What happens if a patient asks to see his records?**
140. **When a patient asks for a copy of his records, can a mental health professional provide a summary of the record, rather than the complete file?**
141. **Please clarify—if I am allowed to provide a summary of the record, rather than a copy of the entire record, does that mean the patient no longer has a right to see the entire record?**
142. **Under what circumstances, if any, may a treater deny a patient access to his records?**
143. **What if a patient believes part of the record is inaccurate and asks to have it changed?**
144. **How long should a mental health professional retain her records?**
145. **What should a treater do with her records after retirement?**
146. **Can a mental health professional withhold records from a patient who has not paid his bill?**

DISCUSSION

137. Must a mental health professional keep records?

Yes. Records serve a variety of enormously important functions, and keeping records is considered standard practice for mental health professionals. In addition, Florida Statutes and regulations make record-keeping a legal requirement for mental health professionals. As examples, section 490.0148 (Fla. Stat. ch. 490.0148) states that psychologists must maintain records, section 491.0148 (Fla. Stat. ch. 491.0148) states that psychotherapists must maintain records, and section 458.331 (Fla. Stat. ch. 458.331[m]) makes clear that psychiatrists must keep records. Section 458.331 (Fla. Stat. ch. 458.331) has an additional requirement for psychiatrists—the records must be legible.

Statutes and regulations provide detailed descriptions about what information the record must contain. As examples, section 458.331 (Fla. Stat. ch. 458.331[m]) states that psychiatrists' records must include "patient histories; examination results; test results; records of drugs prescribed, dispensed, or administered, and reports of consultations and hospitalizations." The regulation governing the practice of psychology (Fla. Admin. Code

Ann. r.64B19-10.0025[1]) states that a psychologist's records must include basic identification data, presenting symptoms or request for services, dates and types of services rendered, fees billed for and collected and, as applicable, test data, a history, a description of what transpired during sessions, notes concerning conversations with people significant in the patient's life, progress notes, and significant actions taken by the psychologist during the course of the work. The regulation concerning social workers, marriage and family therapists, and mental health counselors (Fla. Admin. Code Ann. r.64B4-9.002[2]) states that a psychotherapy record must include "basic information about the client, including name, address, and telephone number, dates of therapy sessions, treatment plan and results achieved, diagnosis if applicable, and financial transactions between therapist and client including fees assessed and collected."

Note that section 455.667 (Fla. Stat. ch. 455.667[9]) states, "All records owners shall develop and implement policies, standards, and procedures to protect the confidentiality and security of the medical records." Section 455.667 makes the owner of the records responsible for training his or her employees in these policies, standards, and procedures.

138. Who owns a therapist's records?

The best way to answer this question is to think of the patient as owning the *contents* of the record and the therapist as owning the *physical document*. To explain, while the therapist owns the physical document, the laws of confidentiality, privilege, and mandatory reporting determine how that ownership is exercised. Thus, unless directed otherwise by statute or court order, the therapist can only do with the record what the patient authorizes.

Mental health professionals should note that section 455.667 (Fla. Stat. ch. 455.667[1]) includes in the definition of a records owner "any health care practitioner's employer" provided, the section goes on to say, "the employment contract or agreement between the employer and the health care practitioner designates the employer as the records owner." It is therefore possible that an employer (such as a clinic or hospital) will actually own the records, if such a clause is found in the mental health professional's contract.

139. What happens if a patient asks to see his records?

Florida statutes and regulations give patients a general right of access to their records. As an example, section 455.667 (Fla. Stat. ch. 455.667[4]) states that when a patient requests his records, the health care practitioner must "furnish, in a timely manner, without delays for legal review, copies of all reports and records" relating to examinations, assessments, and treatment. Section 455.667 states that the request may be made either by the patient or the patient's legal representative. Section 394.4615 (Fla. Stat. ch. 394.4615[9]), referring to patients who have been in a psychiatric facility, states that "patients shall have reasonable access to their clinical records." Note that the right is to *access*; the physical records themselves continue to belong to the provider. Regulations that govern specific mental health professions also speak to this question. The regulation governing psychologists (Fla. Admin. Code Ann. r.64B19-19.005[1]), for example, states that a psychologist must provide records or a summary of records within 30 days of the request (see questions below for exceptions).

Mental health professionals should note that disciplines take a patient's right to access records seriously. Section 490.009 (Fl. Stat. ch. 490.009[n]) states that a psychologist may be disciplined for "failing to make available to the patient or client, upon written request, copies of test results, reports, or documents in the possession or under the control [of the psychologist]." In addition, both the regulation governing psychologists (Fla. Admin. Code Ann. r.64B19-17.002[n]) and the regulation governing social workers, marriage and family therapists, and mental health counselors (Fla. Admin. Code Ann. r.64B4-5.001[n]) impose fines for not making a patient's records available after the patient has made a written request for the records.

For both clinical and risk management reasons, you should insist that you and your client review the record together. From a clinical perspective, the patient may encounter material that is unclear or troubling and your presence will be important to address questions or concerns. From a risk management perspective, clients sometimes walk away with the record tucked under their arm. You are then deprived of your most important defense should the client make a claim against you. Under no circumstances should a client ever be left alone with the original record.

140. When a patient asks for a copy of his records, can a mental health professional provide a summary of the record, rather than the complete file?

According to section 455.667 (Fla. Stat. ch. 455.667[4]), a mental health practitioner may respond to a patient's request for records by providing a summary (a "report," in the words of the statute), of the examination and treatment, rather than a copy of the complete file. A mental health professional is required, however, to send a copy of the entire record to a subsequent treating psychiatrist, if the patient makes such a request in writing.

141. Please clarify—if I am allowed to provide a summary of the record, rather than a copy of the entire record, does that mean the patient no longer has a right to see the entire record?

Florida laws provide patients with complete access to their records except under specific and well-defined circumstances (see question 142). A treater is free to ask a patient what specific records he would like, and to clarify with a patient the purpose of the patient's request for records. If a treater and a patient agree that only certain records, or certain aspects of a record, are to be released, doing so is perfectly acceptable. Such agreements notwithstanding, a patient retains the right to have a treater forward his entire record to a psychiatrist and to seek access to the records himself.

142. Under what circumstances, if any, may a treater deny a patient access to his records?

Section 394.4615 (Fla. Stat. ch. 394.4615[9]) creates the sole exception to an adult patient's right of access to mental health records. According to this statute, when the patient's physician determines that a patient's access to records would be "harmful to the patient," the physician may refuse to allow the patient to inspect all or any part of his records. Rule 65E-5.250 of the Florida Administrative Code (Fla. Admin. Code Ann. r.65E-5.250[5]) imposes on each receiving facility the responsibility to develop policies and procedures governing the release of psychiatric records and criteria for determining what type of information could be considered "harmful." The rule further states that a decision to restrict or deny a patient access to his records, as well as the reasons for the denial or the restriction, must be documented in the patient's clinical chart. Written notice of the restriction must be given to the patient and the patient's guardian, guardian advocate, and attorney (if the patient has one). The restriction or denial is good for seven days, and can be renewed upon review. In addition, the mental health professional is not required to provide a summary or copy of the record.

143. What if a patient believes part of the record is inaccurate and asks to have it changed?

A mental health record is considered a legal document. As such, section

394.4615 (Fla. Stat. ch. 394.4615[10]) prohibits a treater from "fraudu-lently alter[ing]" the record. "Altering" consists of making any change to what has been written; as examples, whiting out, blacking out, and crossing out all constitute altering the record.

It sometimes happens that you or your client discover inaccuracies or mistakes in the record. While you cannot alter the record, you also do not want to perpetuate inaccurate clinical information. If you become aware of a mistake in the record, you may make an additional entry. In the entry, note the date of the mistaken information, explain that previously recorded information is inaccurate, provide the accurate information, and then date the entry according to when it is written. You may make a notation next to the entry with the mistaken information, such as "See note of December 18, 1999, for correction." Initial and date this notation. In this manner you are adding correct information to, rather than altering, the record.

It may happen that a patient brings to your attention mistaken infor-mation that has been released to a third party. (The best preventative medicine is to review the material with your patient *before* disclosure.) If material is released, perhaps in the form of a letter, and your patient wants a part of the letter corrected, you may send a second letter explaining that incorrect information was contained in the initial missive and that the purpose of the second letter is to provide a correction.

144. How long should a mental health professional retain her records?
Regulations governing major mental health professional disciplines pro-vide time periods to retain records. The regulation for social workers, marriage and family therapists, and mental health counselors (Fla. Admin. Code Ann. r.64B4-9.001[2]), for example, states, "A full record of services shall be maintained for 7 years after the date of the last con-tact with the client or user." The regulation for psychologists (Fla. Admin. Code Ann. r.64B19-19.004[3]) states that "complete psychological records shall be retained by the licensed psychologist for a minimum of 3 years after (a) the completion of planned services or (b) the date of the last contact with the user, which occurs later in time." The regulation then states that after this three-year period, "either the complete psycho-logical records or a summary of those psychological records shall be retained for an additional 4 years." Thus, psychologists must keep a record for at least three years; they may then retain a summary of the record for the next four. The regulation for psychiatrists (Fla. Admin. Code Ann. r.64B8-10.003) states that "a licensed physician shall keep

adequate written medical records . . . for a period of at least five years from the last patient contact."

It is advantageous to retain records as long as possible, for a variety of reasons: patients sometimes wish to begin a second treatment long after finishing a first therapy, in which case records from the prior treatment can be enormously helpful; patients may need to document a claim for certain benefits such as SSI, in which case records showing the history of a disability could prove invaluable; a treater may wish to review the child records of an adult patient, for many reasons; and patients may bring a claim against the treater, in which case records will be important to defend against an allegation of negligence or wrongdoing. That said, maintaining records can become expensive, and takes up a lot of space.

Our recommendation is to keep records as long as is reasonably possible. Keeping records for a period of 10 years after the last clinical contact, and 10 years after a minor-patient has turned 21, should place you beyond the reach of any statute of limitations. If it is reasonable for you to keep the records longer, do so; if not, the records may be destroyed or, as an alternative, you may reduce the record to a brief (1 to 3) page summary.

145. What should a treater do with her records after retirement?
Records are important after a treater retires, in at least two ways. First, patients may continue to need mental health services, in which case the treater's records may assist the transition to another clinician. Also, a treater's retirement does not bar a patient from bringing a complaint or an action in malpractice. Notes may be crucial to the treater's defense. After a treater retires, records should be retained in a safe, accessible location, so that patients who wish to continue with another treater may obtain copies.

Section 455.667 (Fla. Stat. ch. 455.667) states that when a record owner retires, he must place an advertisement in the local newspaper, or notify patients in writing, that he intends to retire and that offers patients the opportunity to obtain a copy of their medical records. Section 455.667 also states that a retiring record owner must notify the appropriate licensure board to specify who the new records owner is and where the records will be located. Regulations are more specific about the duties of a retiring mental health professional. The regulation for psychiatrists (Fla. Admin. Code Ann. r.64B8-10.001) states that a retiring psychiatrist must place a notice "in the newspaper of greatest general circulation in each county in which the physician practices or practiced and in a local newspaper that serves the immediate practice area, a notice which shall contain the date of termination . . . and an address at which the records may be obtained." The regulation for social workers, marriage and family therapists, and mental health counselors (Fla. Admin. Code Ann. r.64B4-9.001[3]) has a similar requirement, and adds that the records must be kept for two years after that mental health professional has retired. The regulation for psychologists (Fla. Admin. Code Ann. r.64B19-9.004[1]) states that the notice must be published for four consecutive weeks.

146. Can a mental health professional withhold records from a patient who has not paid his bill?

No. A mental health professional may not withhold a patient's record or a summary of the patient's record because the patient has not paid his bill. To do so would be unprofessional conduct, and could lead to the mental health professional being suspended from practice or having her license revoked, as made clear by section 455.667 (Fla. Stat. ch. 455.667[4]), "The furnishing of such report or copies [following a patient's request] shall not be conditioned upon payment of a fee for services rendered."

Note, however, that mental health professionals may charge a fee for copying records, including the time taken to do the actual copying. The mental health professional may refuse to provide the records until this fee is received. As an example, the regulation governing the practice of psychology (Fla. Admin. Code Ann. r.64B19-19.005) states that the psychologist "may charge a reasonable fee for the preparation of the report and may condition the issuance of the report upon payment of the reasonable fee," while the regulation that governs psychiatrists (Fla. Admin. Code Ann. r.64B8-10.003[2]) states, "Any person . . . required to release copies of patient medical records may condition such release upon payment by the requesting party of the reasonable costs of reproducing the records." The regulation for psychiatrists goes on to say that "reasonable costs for copying" means not more than $1 per page for the first 25 pages, and 25 cents per page after the first 25 pages.

11

PROFESSIONAL LIABILITY

Questions about professional liability are like fingerprints—no two are exactly alike. Change the facts, however slightly, and the answer will change as well. No wonder lawyers love the phrase "It depends."

The responses below are best understood as providing ways to think about problems mental health professionals often face. They are not intended as definitive answers or legal advice. When faced with your own dilemma, we have three recommendations: First, think carefully through your problem and consider alternative ways of responding as they present themselves; second, get a consultation; third, document your thinking and the consultation. Pay every bit as much attention to the process by which you come to your decision, and your documentation of that process, as you do to the decision itself.

QUESTIONS DISCUSSED IN THIS CHAPTER

tion when not appropriate, my patient could then sue me. Does the statute protect a therapist against a claim that she wrongfully disclosed confidential information?

149. What if an employee of mine inadvertently discloses confidential information—could I be held liable for a breach of confidentiality?

150. Recently my car was broken into and my briefcase stolen. In the briefcase were two patient files—that identified the patients by name—I had taken home to review. Is it necessary to tell my patients what happened?

151. Is it a crime for a psychotherapist to become sexually involved with a patient?

152. Is it unethical to become sexually involved with a former patient?

153. A colleague, also a psychotherapist, confessed to me that he had slept with a patient. He seemed quite fully to appreciate the possible consequences of becoming sexually involved with a client, but I was dumbstruck when he said he'd "do his best" to make sure it didn't happen again. While I consider this person a friend, I also want to know whether I have any legal or ethical obligation to report his behavior.

154. Should I continue to see a patient who is suing me?

155. What material should I be sure to cover during a first session?

156. Some clinicians give their clients an "informed consent" letter at a first session. Is this a good idea?

157. I meet with a supervisor to discuss my cases. Often, I share enough about a client that the supervisor could identify this person. Should I obtain my clients' written consent to share this much clinical material?

158. Can you offer any guidelines as to when it is okay to accept a gift from a client and when it is not?

159. From a professional liability standpoint, what are the implications of therapist self-disclosure?

160. I have a policy not to conduct a session with a patient who is under the influence of drugs or alcohol. Recently a client arrived at my office visibly intoxicated. When I said that we would not be having a session, he got back in his car and drove away, still clearly under the influence of alcohol. What should I do in this situation to minimize my liability?

161. Can I bill for a session that I have refused to hold because the patient arrived at my office under the influence of drugs or alcohol?

162. What is my liability if a patient commits suicide?

163. I'm semiretired and volunteer as a supervisor at a local mental health clinic. Given that I only do a few hours of supervision each week, need I worry about getting malpractice insurance?

164. Will my malpractice insurance pay for a lawyer to represent me before a licensing board?

165. If I receive a letter of complaint from my licensing board, may I go ahead and respond?

166. What should I do when I receive a request for records from an insurance company?

167. If I'm sued, should I hire a personal attorney, in addition to the attorney the insurance company will provide?

168. What legal and ethical steps can I take to terminate with a harassing or threatening patient?

169. I know that I am obligated to notify my insurance company if anything ever happens that might give rise to a malpractice lawsuit. Under what circumstances should I notify the company, and what is the best way to do the actual notification?

170. I've just received a managed care contract. Should I have a lawyer read it over?

171. Can a treater be held liable for not providing services that a managed care company has denied?

172. What obligations does a researcher have when, during a research interview, a subject reveals information that would require a treater to act, for example that a child is being abused or neglected?

173. What are the concrete steps I can ethically and legally take to collect an unpaid fee?

174. Do you advise meeting with the family after a patient commits suicide?

175. I am a psychiatrist who works for several nursing homes. Often I prescribe a low dose of an antipsychotic medication to settle a patient. Is this an acceptable practice?

176. What should I do if a patient who is HIV positive reveals to me that he is sexually active with unsuspecting partners?

177. From a professional liability perspective, what is the difference between a consultation and supervision?

178. Is a trainee required to tell a patient that the treatment is being supervised?

179. What is negligent supervision? What would be an example of negligent supervision?

DISCUSSION

147. What is the risk management value of a consultation?

From a risk management perspective, the value of a consultation cannot be overemphasized. Every mental health professional has a legal duty to provide care that is reasonable. If a mental health professional's care falls below that which is reasonable, she may then be held responsible for any damages that result from her negligence. How do we determine whether a clinician's care is "reasonable"? By looking to the professional community. The standard set by the community of mental health professionals will determine what care is reasonable and any individual clinician's care will be judged against that standard. Consultations are valuable because they provide a link between an individual clinician and the community. In short, *consultations bring a clinician into the professional fold.*

Consultations are particularly helpful in difficult treatments or when there is a transference or countertransference problem. Consultations show that the treater was working in a thoughtful manner, that she made an effort to reach out to her professional community, and that she was aware enough to know that a difficult aspect of the treatment—perhaps a countertransference issue—needed to be looked at from a perspective other than her own. A consultation is also powerful evidence against a claim that a mental health professional was exploiting a patient or using the transference for personal gain. Exploitation is usually shrouded in secret; consultations provide a way of bringing a treatment into the open, thus serving to refute a suggestion or innuendo that the mental health professional was behaving unethically.

148. Florida confidentiality statutes allow me to disclose confidential information when a patient threatens to harm a third party. I worry that if I make a mistake and disclose confidential information when not appropriate, my patient could then sue me. Does the statute protect a therapist against a claim that she wrongfully disclosed confidential information?
Section 455.671 (Fla. Stat. ch. 455.671) allows a psychiatrist to breach confidentiality when a patient threatens to harm a third party (see chapter 2). Section 455.671 also provides that "no civil or criminal action shall be instituted, and there shall be no liability on account of disclosure of otherwise confidential communications by a psychiatrist in disclosing a threat pursuant to this section." The confidentiality statutes that apply to psychologists (section 490.0147) and social workers, marriage and family therapists, and mental health counselors (section 491.0147) also state that confidentiality is "waived" when there is a "clear and immediate probability of physical harm" to others. Finally, section 394.4615 (Fla. Stat. ch.

394.4615[7]) states, "Any facility or private mental health practitioner who acts in good faith in releasing information [according to the requirements of this section] is not subject to civil or criminal liability for such release." (See appendix A for the full texts of these statutes.)

For a professional malpractice claim to succeed against a mental health professional who discloses confidential information, the client or patient will have to prove that the therapist was negligent, that is, that the therapist was not reasonable in breaching his duty to keep communications confidential and that the breach caused harm to the patient. The therapist should therefore ask what a reasonable therapist of his or her particular discipline would do. A consultation could prove invaluable. If, following a consultation, the mental health professional decides that a reasonable therapist would break confidentiality, that person will be protected from liability.

149. What if an employee of mine inadvertently discloses confidential information—could I be held liable for a breach of confidentiality?
Yes. Under the law, you will be held responsible for the negligent acts of your employees. It is important that you both impress upon your employees the importance of maintaining confidentiality and have clear rules that govern how confidential material is to be kept confidential. Note also that the regulation governing the practice of psychology (Fla. Admin. Code Ann. r.64B19-19.006[5]) states, "The licensed psychologist shall also ensure that no person working for the psychologist, whether as an employee, an independent contractor, or a volunteer violates the confidentiality of the service user."

150. Recently my car was broken into and my briefcase stolen. In the briefcase were two patient files—that identified the patients by name— I had taken home to review. Is it necessary to tell my patients what happened?
Yes. First and foremost, the therapeutic relationship is a fiduciary relationship—it is a relationship built upon trust. Few things will destroy that trust faster than hiding from a client a mistake you have made—however unwittingly or unintentionally—that could have an impact on the client's life. Clinicians in this position will sometimes use the transference implications of what has occurred as a reason for not being up front with the client; rarely, however, are the *counter*transference implications of hiding such an event given as a reason to *tell* the client about lost records.

Consider that you will have a secret from your client—that something has happened, possibly to his detriment—and that you will be hiding the secret for the duration of the therapy. Moreover, whatever fears you have about telling your client will pale in comparison to what will happen if your client finds out *without* your having discussed the matter. If you lose a patient record or it is stolen, tell the client in a direct and forthright manner as soon as is reasonably practical after you have been able to confirm the loss or theft. In our experience, clients have demonstrated an enormous amount of understanding (and empathy for the clinician!) in such circumstances. Obviously, a better scenario is to keep records in a safe place that minimizes the chance they will be lost or stolen. And it always pays to think twice about whether you *really* need to take those records home before placing them in the front seat of your car.

151. Is it a crime for a psychotherapist to become sexually involved with a patient?

Florida laws makes having sex with a patient a crime. Sex with a former patient is also a crime, if the relationship was terminated primarily for the purpose of engaging in sexual conduct. Each of these crimes is considered a felony in the second degree, which is punishable by many years in prison and a fine of many thousands of dollars. The statute that criminalizes this behavior, section 491.0112 (Fla. Stat. ch. 491.0112), makes it a felony in the second degree—a more serious crime—to use "therapeutic deception" to entice the patient to engage in sex. Therapeutic deception occurs when the therapist tells the patient that sex is part of the treatment.

152. Is it unethical to become sexually involved with a former patient?

Ethical codes speak to this issue. The *Ethical Principles of Psychologists and Code of Conduct* (American Psychological Association, 1992), for example, states, "Psychologists do not engage in sexual intimacies with a former therapy patient or client for at least two years after cessation or termination of professional services" (Standard 4.07). *The Principles of Medical Ethics, with Annotations Especially Applicable to Psychiatry* (American Psychiatric Association, 1995), states, "Sexual activity with a current or former patient is unethical."

Florida regulations also speak to the issue of becoming sexually involved with a former patient or client. The regulation governing psychologists, (Fla. Admin. Code Ann. r.64B19-16[1–5]) is more stringent than the American Psychological Association. That regulation states that "sexual misconduct is herein prohibited . . . the Board finds that the effects of the psychologist-client relationship endure after psychological services cease to be rendered. Therefore, the client shall be presumed incapable of giving valid, informed, free consent to sexual activity. . . ." The regulation then states that "the psychologist-client relationship is deemed to continue in perpetuity." The regulation governing social workers, marriage and family therapists, and mental health counselors (Fla. Admin. Code Ann. r.64B4-10) states that sexual misconduct is prohibited during the psychotherapist-client relationship, and that the psychotherapist-client relationship is "deemed to continue for a minimum of two years" after the last professional contact.

Psychiatrists and psychologists, then, are prohibited from becoming sexually involved with a current or former patient or client. Social workers, marriage and family therapists, and mental health counselors must refrain from sexual involvements for "a minimum of two years" after the professional relationship has ended.

153. A colleague, also a psychotherapist, confessed to me that he had slept with a patient. He seemed quite fully to appreciate the possible consequences of becoming sexually involved with a client, but I was dumbstruck when he said he'd "do his best" to make sure it didn't happen again. While I consider this person a friend, I also want to know whether I have any legal or ethical obligation to report his behavior.
What is a mental health professional's responsibility when a colleague confesses unprofessional conduct—and a crime—that has the potential to seriously harm a patient? In answering this question we first note that such a communication is not confidential. We are not dealing with patient confidentiality because the information came directly from the offending therapist. As a consequence, you must be guided by your professional ethics. Specific ethical codes can assist in this balancing.

If a patient, rather than your therapist-colleague, had brought the sexual relation to your attention, the information would be confidential (see question 133 for possible exceptions to this rule). In that case, you may wish to advise your client that he or she can contact the Florida Agency for Health Care Administration (phone number 1-888-419-3456) to obtain information about the rights and remedies for patients who have been sexually exploited by a previous therapist. Your client's options include filing a complaint with the licensing board, filing a criminal complaint, or filing a lawsuit. Without your patient's consent, however, you may not disclose the confidential information.

154. Should I continue to see a patient who is suing me?

When a patient initiates an action against you—whether by submitting an ethics complaint or filing a lawsuit—the nature of your relationship with that patient has fundamentally changed. The frame of the therapy has shifted from words into action. While the change in your relationship will have clinical implications, the potential effects of the change extend far beyond the treatment. Your reputation, your income, and even your professional practice may be jeopardized. Your personal life cannot remain unaffected. Even the most extraordinary mental health professional would be severely challenged to control the countertransference under such circumstances and we recommend that you not try.

First, the complaint or lawsuit will have to be discussed in the therapy; to do otherwise would constitute a major resistance for both you and your patient. Talking about a pending lawsuit or complaint will inevitably evoke an intense reaction because your patient is attacking you—not with words, but with *actions*. No treater should place him or herself under such a burden. Second, adding to this burden, any interpretation, recommendation, or suggestion you make to your patient immediately becomes suspect as flowing out of a countertransference reaction. You therefore have a higher standard to meet in explaining the reasons behind your work. Third, your legal bills are likely to accrue much faster than any fee your client is paying. You will thus be losing money while treating the client who is suing you. Doesn't sound like much fun to us.

You have no ethical obligation to continue treating a patient who has brought an action against you. You should arrange for an appropriate termination and ask for a consultation as the termination takes place. If you do decide to go ahead and treat a patient who has filed a complaint or lawsuit against you, it is essential that the treatment be supervised.

155. What material should I be sure to cover during a first session?

In the first session you should cover all the matters that speak to the "frame" of the therapy. The frame consists of those aspects of your work that create the context in which the therapy takes place. The frame therefore includes the length of sessions, your per-session fee, whether you charge for missed sessions, whether you treat client vacations as missed sessions, whether you provide legal testimony, how you handle consultations and supervisions, whether you are available on an emergency basis, whether you accept phone calls at home, how often you bill, how you handle missed payments, what rules govern confidentiality, and the like.

What's important is to convey to the client a clear sense of how you work. The Law of No Surprises is relevant: A client should never be in a position of ignorance about the frame of the therapy. What will create problems in a treatment is not so much that a client doesn't *like* your policies as that a client doesn't *know* your policies.

156. Some clinicians give their clients an "informed consent" letter at a first session. Is this a good idea?

An informed consent letter has a number of advantages. First, such a letter makes clear the frame of the therapy. Second, an informed consent letter provides the client with a *physical* reminder of that frame, available whenever the client wishes to look at it. Third, it can be used to fulfill the ethical and legal obligation of mental health professionals to apprise clients at the beginning of the relationship of the rules concerning confidential information. Fourth, an informed consent letter can provide an excellent reference when, during the therapy, you must disclose information for the purposes of a consultation or because a mandatory reporting statute requires you to do so: The possibility of disclosing information has already been addressed.

These advantages notwithstanding, many clinicians have very strong feelings that providing such a letter is *not* the way to begin a therapy, primarily because of what they see as the implications for the transference. Our recommendation is to think through the advantages and disadvantages of an informed consent letter for your own practice, and proceed accordingly. One alternative to a letter would be a form, which many clinics and hospitals use, given to a client before, during, or immediately following the first session. Another alternative is to convey the information orally. In considering what will work best for you, keep in mind three things. First, you will be conveying a significant amount of information, more than most people can probably absorb in one sitting, especially when they may be feeling some anxiety, as is likely at a first therapy session. Second, you are ethically obligated to convey information about exceptions to confidentiality at the beginning of the relationship. Third, problems that arise in the course of a therapy often arise because a client had not been fully informed about some aspect of the frame.

If you decide to provide your client with an informed consent letter, we suggest you make a time, no later than the second session, to discuss any questions she may have about what is in the letter. Document that you have done so. From a professional liability point of view, it makes good sense to record in your notes at least one question the client has asked. Doing so illustrates that your client read the letter, and that you took the time to clarify questions she may have had. Even if the patient does not have any questions, record that you set aside time to review the contents of the letter. A sample informed consent letter is included in appendix B.

157. I meet with a supervisor to discuss my cases. Often, I share enough about a client that the supervisor could identify this person. Should I obtain my clients' written consent to share this much clinical material?

Many mental health professionals meet with a supervisor to discuss their cases and doing so is an excellent way to improve the general quality of mental health care provided. It is best, if possible, not to reveal information that could allow your client to be identified—certainly there is rarely, if ever, a reason to give your client's last name, address, or anything nearly so specific. That said, it does sometimes happen that the amount of confidential information shared in a supervision is such that a great deal about the client is being revealed. In such a case, it makes good sense to obtain your client's consent. The regulation for psychologists (Fla. Admin. Code Ann. r.64B19-19.006[1]) makes obtaining your client's written consent a requirement, "In that situation [where the supervised individual will be sharing confidential information with the supervising psychologist], it is incumbent upon the licensed psychologist to secure the written acknowledgment of the service user regarding that breach of confidentiality."

158. Can you offer any guidelines as to when it is okay to accept a gift from a client and when it is not?

Unfortunately, there are virtually no hard and fast rules that govern the exchange of gifts between a mental health professional and a client. Most often, the issue of gift-giving arises in an ethics complaint; once the issue is raised, the burden shifts to the treater to show what therapeutic role the gift played. If the treater can show none, the exchange will almost certainly be seen as contrary to good treatment and therefore unethical. Accepting (or giving) gifts of high monetary value (a piece of jewelry, a car) or of an intimate nature (a negligee, a card with clear sexual content) is always looked upon as unethical.

The most important principle to keep in mind is that for the vast majority of mental health professionals, words are the tools of the trade. Because the exchange of a gift is a communication, the mental health professional must ask herself what is being communicated and why the communication is not taking place in the currency of the profession, that is, with *words*. If you are faced with the dilemma of accepting or giving a gift, ask yourself the following three questions: First, does the gift comport with social convention? That is to say, is the gift of small or reasonable value, is the gift appropriate to a professional relationship, and does the exchange take place on an occasion that, in your patient's culture, calls for an exchange of gifts? Second, can the intrapsychic meaning of the gift be talked about in a manner appropriate to your patient's treatment? That is to say, can the communication be put into words and used to enhance or further your work, or at the very least to maintain the therapeutic alliance? Third, do you document the exchange? That is to say, do you record the fact of the exchange itself, as well as your clinical assessment of what the exchange means to the patient and what effect it will have on the treatment? If an exchange of gifts takes place and your response to any of these questions is "no," get a consult. You're headed for troubled waters.

Finally, what you do with the gift is important. Placing cards and letters in the file shows that you are treating them as part of the therapy. Do not place birthday cake in the file. If the gift is a perishable item, there still may be a card that can be made part of the record. If the item is expensive or of an intimate nature the only prudent path is not to accept the gift. The burden of explaining why you accepted the gift, should you be called by an ethics board to do so, will be virtually insurmountable.

159. From a professional liability standpoint, what are the implications of therapist self-disclosure?

This question is somewhat complicated, insofar as *everything* a therapist does is, in some manner, self-disclosing. The cars we drive, the clothes we wear, what we choose to place on our desks, whether we wear wedding rings, how we greet our patients each day—all are enormously, and inevitably, disclosing of who we are. The question, then, can perhaps be reframed to ask what liability implications follow from a considered decision to disclose something about ourselves to a client.

Therapists from a wide range of backgrounds engage in self-disclosure for a variety of reasons. Substance abuse counselors often disclose their own histories of abuse on the theory that doing so will aid an individual's recovery; cognitive-behavioral therapists may self-disclose for the purposes of modeling effective behavior; feminist therapists have considered self-disclosure important for addressing a power-difference in the therapy relationship; other therapists use self-disclosure as a manner to temper an idealizing transference or to address a patient's intense experience of shame by normalizing an experience. Psychoanalytically oriented psychotherapists, and psychoanalysts, have tended to engage in less self-disclosure, but recent years have shown a burgeoning literature on the role of self-disclosure in psychoanalytic work as well.

From a professional liability standpoint, self-disclosure can be thought about in the same manner as the exchange of a gift: It is important to clarify what role the disclosure plays in the therapy. While a carefully considered self-disclosure can have enormous clinical benefit, inappropriate disclosures about a therapist's personal life have been associated with involvements hugely harmful to patients, and indeed often seem to be the precursors of such involvements. If self-disclosure is an essential and ongoing aspect of your work, it would be wise to indicate as much in your treatment plans. If you self-disclose in a manner other than what you normally do, or if you choose to self-disclose when you normally would not, document the fact of the disclosure, and your assessment of how the disclosure fits into the therapy. As with gifts, if you're unwilling both to consider and document the fact of a self-disclosure and its role in the therapy, get a consultation—it's an excellent way to prevent exposing yourself to liability.

160. I have a policy not to conduct a session with a patient who is under the influence of drugs or alcohol. Recently a client arrived at my office visibly intoxicated. When I said that we would not be having a session, he got back in his car and drove away, still clearly under the influence of alcohol. What should I do in this situation to minimize my liability?

This question provides an excellent example of when *the process by which you come to a decision* and the *documentation* of that process are every bit as important as the decision itself. Our response will therefore focus on the decision-making process.

First, consider whether the confidentiality statutes (see above) are relevant. The statutes give you discretion only if your patient has communicated a serious threat of physical violence toward a reasonably identifiable victim as discussed above. Although the statutes are probably not relevant to the situation you describe, pay attention to whether your patient has named any individual as the object of his anger as he walks away.

Next, consider the possibility of involuntary hospitalization under Florida's Marchman Act (chapter 397 of the Florida Statutes). Under section 397.675 (Fla. Stat. ch. 397.675), if a person, by virtue of being impaired because of substance abuse:

- has lost the power of self-control with respect to substance use; and *either*
- has inflicted, or threatened or attempted to inflict harm, or unless admitted is likely to inflict, physical harm on himself or herself or another; *or*
- by reason of substance abuse impairment, his or her judgment has been so impaired that the person is incapable of appreciating the need for, or making a rational decision about, substance abuse treatment,

the person can be taken into protective custody for up to 72 hours for treatment and evaluation. Special facilities have been designated by the county for individuals who suffer from alcohol abuse. Unfortunately, many counties do not have these facilities; if no such facility is available, consider involuntary hospitalization under chapter 394 of the Florida Statutes (the Baker Act), which provides for involuntary placement and examination when a person is a danger to himself or others as a result of mental illness. The complication with involuntary hospitalization under chapter 394 is that mental illness—and not inebriation—provides the basis for the hospitalization. Do not, however, simply assume that the diagnosis of alcohol abuse precludes another diagnosis such as depression. A mental disorder would provide the basis for an involuntary hospitalization under chapter 394.

At this point in your decision-making process, you have legal principles that are in conflict: first, the principle of respect for your patient's autonomy and privacy, which counsels confidentiality, and second, the principle of safety, which permits you to release confidential information if a patient presents a danger to self or others. We place these two conflicting principles in the context of the Law of No Surprises—to the extent that is practical and appropriate, you should discuss with your client at the beginning of the relationship the general parameters that might lead to disclosure of confidential information, and the Parsimony Principle—disclosure of information is kept to the absolute minimum needed to achieve your goal.

How is our balancing act put into practice? Begin by raising the dilemma directly with your patient, "We won't be meeting, but you're in no shape to drive. What other arrangements can we make?" Other arrangements may be for your client to sit in your waiting room with a cup of coffee, contact a friend or relative for a ride, take a bus or other public transportation, or call a cab. Each of these alternatives represents a way to work with your client that entails a minimum of intrusion. By considering and raising these possibilities, you are demonstrating to anyone who reads the record that you are approaching a difficult situation in a thoughtful, clinically appropriate manner.

If your client refuses your suggestions and insists on getting in his car, you then indicate that given the dangerousness of the situation, you may need to contact some authority. What allows you to take this next step is that all your suggestions for a *less* intrusive intervention have been rejected. If you now decide to contact the police, and indicate that an intoxicated individual is driving down U.S. 1, you have protected yourself from a claim that your disclosure was premature, unwarranted, or more than necessary. Note that even this release of information is minimal—your "disclosure" is limited to a description of the client's car and perhaps a license plate number. You have acted because your client's substance abuse is creating a likelihood of serious harm and no intervention short of disclosing this information to the police is sufficient to attenuate the danger.

Keep in mind that every bit as important as what you eventually decide to do is the process by which you make your decision and your documentation of that process.

161. Can I bill for a session that I have refused to hold because the patient arrived at my office under the influence of drugs or alcohol?

If you're asking this question when it comes time to write your bills, you're asking too late. You may bill for the session, not bill for the session, or reschedule the session, without concern for unwanted repercussions, *provided you made your policy clear at the beginning of your work*. Trouble will arise not from what you decide to do, but rather from failing to have a treatment agreement that tells your client what you will do under these circumstances. If you intend to work with patients who struggle with substance abuse, it is wise to include your policy in an informed consent letter (see appendix B).

162. What is my liability if a patient commits suicide?

No behavior can be predicted with absolute certainty. Suicide is a behavior. Suicide cannot be predicted with absolute certainty.

The task a mental health professional faces with a suicidal patient is not to predict whether the patient will commit suicide. Rather, the task is *to assess the likelihood* that the patient will commit suicide. In assessing the likelihood that a patient will commit suicide, the clinician examines factors in the individual's life associated with a *greater* risk of suicide, factors in the individual's life associated with a *lesser* risk of suicide, and how the factors compare with one another. Lest this analysis seem overwhelming, consider that you do the same sort of thing each time you debate whether to carry your umbrella out the front door. You identify factors associated with a greater risk of rain (rain is predicted; it's windy; it's raining to the west) and factors associated with a lesser risk of rain (the sun is out). You then balance the factors against one another and decide whether to take your umbrella.

The crucial part of a suicide assessment is identifying those factors that are relevant to the likelihood your patient will commit suicide. Examples of factors associated with a greater risk of suicide are a history of suicide attempts, the intent to commit suicide, a plan to commit suicide, the means to carry out the plan, feelings of hopelessness, a panic disorder, a delusion that suicide is a way to join a loved one who has died, social isolation, current or chronic substance abuse, a history of suicide in the family, and a belief that suicide is "fated." Examples of factors associated with a lesser risk of suicide are plans for the future, religious convictions that prohibit suicide, living with another person or persons, a sense that someone or something still endows life with meaning, and a belief that feelings of sadness, loss, or hopelessness are temporary and will pass.

In assessing the likelihood that an individual will commit suicide, you will therefore explore factors associated with greater and lesser risks of suicide, examine how the factors you have identified compare with one another, decide what to do based upon the comparison, and document the reasons behind your decision. What protects you from liability is *not* that you have made the "right" decision, but that you have documented a process—the process by which you have assessed and responded to the likelihood that your patient would commit suicide. Your documentation should answer three basic questions: What did I do, why did I do it, and on what basis did I reject alternative ways of responding?

163. I'm semiretired and volunteer as a supervisor at a local mental health clinic. Given that I only do a few hours of supervision each week, need I worry about getting malpractice insurance?
The need for malpractice insurance depends neither upon the number of

hours you work nor upon how much you are paid. Once you establish a professional relationship with a supervisee you are held to a standard of care. If you fall below that standard, you can be held negligent, and thus responsible for any damages that result from your negligence.

By volunteering as you do, you are establishing a professional relationship with your supervisees. Don't be fooled—the word "professional" in this context refers neither to a salary, nor to a full-time position. "Professional" refers to a relationship based upon your experience and expertise as a trained clinician. You therefore need malpractice insurance as much as any other supervisor.

164. Will my malpractice insurance pay for a lawyer to represent me before a licensing board?

Some malpractice carriers will insure you for up to a specified amount in legal expenses for representation before administrative agencies, such as boards of registration and professional societies. You should review your general malpractice policy to determine whether this coverage is included.

If a complaint is filed against you before a licensing board, be sure to find a lawyer who has experience before regulatory boards. The reason is that, in a great many cases, a complaint will be dismissed at the initial stage if your response is well-written.

165. If I receive a letter of complaint from my licensing board, may I go ahead and respond?

You need to exercise a good deal of caution when answering a letter from a licensing board. The board may ask you to produce certain materials, along with a letter responding to the allegations. Your response may require you to disclose confidential material. A complaint to a licensing board or professional association by a patient does not, in and of itself, grant the authority to discuss the patient's case or to release the patient's records. The patient must first sign a release. *If you disclose confidential information to the board without a release, you risk another complaint against you—for breach of confidentiality.*

A sample reply letter to a licensing board is contained in appendix B. It is best to send the letter by certified mail, return receipt requested, thus obtaining written confirmation that the board has received your letter. If you subsequently do receive a release from the patient, it makes good sense to contact your malpractice carrier, whose claims representative should help you draft a letter in response to the allegations. The reason contacting the carrier is a good idea is that your response to the board is subject to discovery, which means that the other side in a lawsuit can obtain your response if the case goes to trial. For this reason, what you say in the letter can be extremely important, both in the matter before the board as well as in a future lawsuit.

166. What should I do when I receive a request for records from an insurance company?

Whenever a treater receives a request for records from an insurance company, the treater should discuss the request with the patient. *Do not simply rely on the fact that the insurance policy contains a clause allowing for a release of records—the request must be discussed with the patient before you do anything.* It is well within a patient's prerogative to forego insurance benefits by refusing the request.

In terms of what records to release, an insurance company is entitled to as much of the record as is necessary to determine whether the treatment is consistent with the diagnosis. This information would include, for example, diagnosis, prognosis, dates of treatment, and length of treatment sessions. An insurance company is not entitled to process notes, which should be released only when your patient gives specific permission to do so. Certain third party payors may require additional information.

167. If I'm sued, should I hire a personal attorney, in addition to the attorney the insurance company will provide?

A personal attorney is an attorney of your own choosing, whom you will pay out of your own pocket. There are three ways in which a personal attorney could be helpful if you are sued. First, litigation is enormously stressful. A lawsuit has the potential to invade all areas of your life, personal as well as professional, and involves people, places, and events that will feel foreign and hostile. A personal lawyer can be helpful in shepherding you through the process, explaining how things will work, and calming your anxieties. The attorney assigned by the insurance company may fill this role, but not necessarily.

The second way in which a personal attorney can be helpful is to be mindful of how your interests may diverge from the interests of the insurance company. The attorney assigned by the insurance company has the duty to pursue your interests at all times. It is the carrier, however, who pays him, and you may worry that he will pursue the company's interests. Most often, but not always, these will coincide with yours. Examples of times when the insurance company's interests may differ include when the insurance company would prefer to settle and you want the case to go forward, or when the insurance company is representing more than one defendant in a single lawsuit. In the latter case, the company will want to minimize its *total* losses, which will not necessarily entail minimizing *your* losses. A personal lawyer can be helpful in watching for these and other situations where the interests of the insurance company differ from your own.

The third way in which a personal attorney can be helpful is that, unbeknownst to many clinicians, a malpractice policy may include a "consent to settle" clause. Such a clause requires the carrier to obtain your written consent before settling the case. Your own attorney can review your policy for such a clause, discuss the pros and cons of settlement if the issue arises, and deal with the carrier should there be any difference of opinion.

For these three reasons, it may well be worth the expense to hire a personal attorney as a consultant during a malpractice suit. You will want an attorney who is experienced in malpractice litigation, particularly on the defendant's side. Keep in mind that the attorney from the insurance company, not your personal attorney, is managing the case, and work to avoid any conflicts between them. That said, your own personal attorney, with whom you can "check in" as you feel the need, and who will have only your interests at heart, can be an important asset during the often long and always tumultuous experience of a lawsuit.

168. What legal and ethical steps can I take to terminate with a harassing or threatening patient?

When facing the need to terminate with a difficult patient, a treater should keep two points in mind. First, a therapist is not required to treat every patient. Choice about whom to treat belongs to the treater. Second, termination is *not* the same as abandonment. The second point bears elaboration.

Abandonment can be described as an inappropriate termination. Examples of abandonment occur when a treater terminates a treatment without notice, without regard for the patient's condition at the time of termination, without an adequate plan for follow-up treatment, or in order to retaliate against a patient. *A treater may not abandon a patient.*

Termination is a process that the circumstances of a treatment may demand. Termination may be appropriate because a therapy is no longer in a patient's best interest. Perhaps, for example, the patient is treatment resistant, has continuously missed sessions, or often comes to appointments under the influence of drugs or alcohol. Termination may also be appropriate because the patient has intruded upon the therapist's private life, has violated a professional boundary such as by breaking into the therapist's office, or has threatened the therapist. *While a treater may not abandon a patient, a treater may terminate with a patient.*

When termination with a difficult patient is appropriate, what becomes important is the *process* by which the termination takes place. We find it helpful to break this process down into five parts, which may occur sequentially or simultaneously, depending upon the circumstances. First, discuss the difficulty with the patient and explain that, if change does not occur, termination will result. Be clear about what changes must occur, in a way that can be measured and documented. Second, if termination is or becomes the only alternative, explain to the patient why you are terminating and offer termination sessions (between one and three), unless precluded by the patient's behavior. Third, obtain a consultation to maintain your objectivity and to review whether you are proceeding appropriately. Fourth, to the extent possible, provide the patient with the names and telephone numbers of other treaters in the area. If your patient refuses the referrals, inquire why and then document both the refusal and your patient's reasons. (If your patient is in crisis, the responsibility will be yours to ensure that another treater is immediately available and to consider whether a hospitalization is appropriate. If other treaters are not immediately available, you will need to delay the termination until the crisis has abated.) Fifth, document your reasons for termination and your plan for referral. Send a letter to your patient with this information, either by registered or certified mail or by first class, depending upon what you believe is clinically indicated.

Not all terminations go smoothly. Some patients will resist, and then claim abandonment and threaten to sue or file a complaint with your licensing board. The more difficult you expect the termination to be, the more attention you should give to outside consultations and proper documentation. A sample letter of termination is included in appendix B.

169. I know that I am obligated to notify my insurance company if anything ever happens that might give rise to a malpractice lawsuit. Under what circumstances should I notify the company, and what is the best way to do the actual notification?

Insurance companies require notice from treaters whenever a threat of a lawsuit arises, for several reasons. First, the insurance company will want to review the problem, decide whether something must be done, and assign the matter to an attorney for further action if called for.

Second, if the insurance company decides the matter does warrant action, the company's attorney will be in touch with the treater to make sure that the treater does not make any statements that could negatively affect the lawsuit. Third, certain legal papers require a response within a defined period of time. The insurance company will want to make sure that responses are timely.

In regard to the actual notification, a treater should contact the insurance company whenever there is a reasonable basis to believe that a lawsuit is a possibility. The following circumstances would therefore warrant notification: The treater receives a summons and complaint for a lawsuit; a treater receives a letter from a lawyer representing a present or former patient that states the patient intends to bring a lawsuit; a treater receives a letter from a present or former patient or a lawyer representing a present or former patient that requests a copy of the treatment record, and something has happened in the treatment that might give rise to a complaint or lawsuit; some event occurs during the course of a treatment that a reasonable person would assume could lead to a complaint or lawsuit. Examples of such an occurrence would be a suicide, a homicide committed by a patient, or a patient complaint that the treater breached confidentiality.

There is no "right" way to notify the insurance company. The best way to begin is to call the carrier, ask to speak with a claims representative, and explain the situation. If the claims representative says that the matter is not something the company would address at present, make a note of the date, the time, and the name of the representative. If the claims representative says that the company will want to deal with the situation, send the company any documents you have received, along with a cover letter that makes note of the date and time you initially made contact with the company.

In providing information to the insurance company, you may describe the incident. *You may not send treatment records to the insurance company without a release from your patient.* Do not, however, fear that a patient may prevent you from disclosing records necessary to your defense; if the case goes to trial, you will be allowed to use whatever records necessary to defend yourself (see chapter 3).

170. I've just received a managed care contract. Should I have a lawyer read it over?

When most therapists receive a manage care contract they sign it, return it to the managed care company (MCC), and file their copy away for future reference. The next time they look at the contract is to read it—usually for the first time—when a problem arises. At that point they discover that the "one-year contract" may be canceled with 60 days notice for no reason at all. This is just one of several reasons why you should never sign a managed care contract without carefully reading it through with an experienced attorney. The following are four additional examples of why it is good to be familiar with a managed care contract before you sign.

Most contracts contain some sort of *indemnification clause*. An indemnification clause requires a therapist to reimburse the MCC for losses or expenses that arise from a claim or lawsuit, if the loss or claim results from the therapist's participation in the contract. The therapist's malpractice insurance will probably not cover the cost of the reimbursement. The reason is that most malpractice insurance covers only actions in negligence, not actions based in contract, which is what an action arising from an indemnification clause will be. The wording of an indemnification clause is important, and most MCCs will work with a treater to alter the wording. The advice of an attorney as you work with the MCC is worthwhile.

Most contracts stipulate *duties that the therapist owes to the MCC and that are for the benefit of the patient*. MCCs will usually require that a therapist be available to see patients at specific times for emergencies. MCCs may also require the therapist to be available 24 hours a day, both by beeper and by "live" telephone coverage. Almost always the therapist will be required to cover for other therapists. All such contractual agreements with the MCC are for the "benefit" of the patient. If you fail to fulfill one of these requirements, and a patient comes to harm as a result of your failure, a lawsuit may ensue. It is therefore essential that you become familiar with the clinical responsibilities required by the contract.

Most contracts require a therapist *both to maintain patient confidentiality and to provide the MCC with access to and copies of all treatment records*. These two requirements often conflict and it is important to have some resolution before beginning work under the contract. The reason a resolution is important is that your agreement with the MCC is not binding on the patient. Confidentiality belongs to your patient, who must consent before you release records to the MCC. Make this clear with the MCC before beginning to treat patients.

A therapist has *a duty to appeal a decision to deny services when the therapist believes the services are medically necessary*. When an MCC denies a service because, in the opinion of the MCC, the service is not medically necessary, a therapist has a duty to appeal the MCC's denial.

Such an appeal may create an uncomfortable situation for the therapist, insofar as she will be appealing a decision of the company that is paying her. The therapist's failure to appeal, however, could lead to a claim of abandonment, especially if the therapist believes that a denied service is medically necessary. Regardless of the MCC's decision not to fund, the therapist must be careful not to stop treatment if she believes stopping would be harmful to the patient. If the therapist does decide to stop treatment, she may do so only when the patient is stabilized, and only after she has referred the patient to other treaters.

These four examples—many more could be provided—illustrate the value of having an attorney read over a managed care contract with you before you sign.

171. Can a treater be held liable for not providing services that a managed care company has denied?

A managed care company's (MCC) decision to deny services will not in any way protect a therapist from a claim of negligent treatment or abandonment. A therapist must provide care that is "reasonable." Care that falls below what is reasonable, regardless of an MCC's decision to deny services, may be considered negligent and may give rise to an action in malpractice.

A treater's obligation to provide reasonable care and an MCC's decisions about what treatment to fund are entirely separate. The two should not be linked. If a treater believes that an MCC will not fund care that is reasonable, and the treater wishes to stop treatment, the termination must be handled in the same manner as any other termination (see question 168).

172. What obligations does a researcher have when, during a research interview, a subject reveals information that would require a treater to act, for example that a child is being abused or neglected?

Perhaps the best advice we could give in this situation would be to follow the Law of No Surprises: When conducting research that is likely to uncover information that would create a duty to act were you a treater and your subject a patient, state explicitly how this situation will be handled in your informed consent form. Use your clinical judgment about what material your survey, interview, or questionnaire is likely to pull for. Once you've made that judgment, be up front about what you will do if such a situation arises. You may have concerns about whether your subject will be as forthcoming for your research; being up front at the outset, however, will save you much angst and spare your subject the feeling that you have betrayed a confidence that you promised you'd keep.

Consider the example in the question. The mandatory reporting statute for child abuse makes no mention of the relationship between the individuals involved. If the researcher is listed as a mandatory reporter, and she is acting in her professional capacity—which she will be, when conducting research—she is mandated to report if she "has reasonable cause to suspect" child abuse or neglect (see chapter 3).

173. What are the concrete steps I can ethically and legally take to collect an unpaid fee?

You have no ethical duty to treat a patient who does not pay you, and you may terminate in an appropriate manner as you initiate proceedings to collect your fee. Attempting to pursue legal means to collect a fee, however, will likely cause you more trouble than it's worth. Your legal bills for collecting the fee will almost certainly surpass—perhaps substantially so—the fee itself, and your attempts to collect the fee may generate a countersuit or an ethics complaint, the only basis for which may be the patient's rage at what you're doing.

Our recommendation is that you bring the matter up with your client. Assess the client's ability to pay; virtually all clients will be able to pay *something*. Then determine what sort of free-care component your practice can allow. If you are able to accommodate your client's financial situation, work out a payment schedule and offer the client a reduced fee. If you are not able to accommodate your client's financial situation, arrange for an appropriate transfer of care to a low-fee clinic. Give serious thought to forgiving a debt that your client says she cannot, or refuses, to pay. In no case may you refuse to comply with a client's request for records in order to get the client to pay an unpaid bill (see question 146).

The best way to avoid this problem is to make clear to your client your policy about late or missed payments. *Payment for your services is as much a part of therapy as therapy itself; late or missed payments, if not addressed in a clear, direct manner, will inevitably be disruptive to your work.* (See the sample informed consent letter in appendix B.)

174. Do you advise meeting with the family after a patient commits suicide?

Meeting with a family after a patient commits suicide is like sailing between the Scylla of family grief and the Charybdis of confidentiality.

Many clinicians feel an instinct to avoid any contact whatsoever with the family; most often these clinicians use confidentiality as a reason for not doing so. For the reasons explained below, we recommend that you accommodate the family's wishes in this regard.

First, meeting with the treater may be part of the family's process of grieving. In many instances, the treater is the individual who knows most about what was going on in the patient's life and merely sitting with that individual can provide comfort to many families. Second, a meeting affords the opportunity for the treater personally to express her grief to the family and to tell the family how sorry she is about their loss. Hearing the treater speak these words in their presence can be an enormous service to many families. Third, while confidentiality must be maintained, confidentiality places no constraint on the treater listening to what the family has to say about their own feelings of loss, anger, and confusion. Although a treater may not reveal what was said during sessions, she may paint with broad brushstrokes issues salient in the patient's life: "We know he had been struggling with depression for many years," "Feelings of anxiety made it difficult for him to enjoy things he had enjoyed in the past." Fourth, more from a risk management point of view, suspicions or paranoia about whether a treater is responsible for a patient's death will only be enhanced by a refusal to meet.

You need to be clear that, while you will not be free to discuss details about your work, you are very interested in hearing what the family is experiencing. You should also feel free to tell the family that you are very sorry for their loss; such a statement is an expression of sympathy. (Take care, however, not to say that you are very sorry because your screw-up *caused* their loss; such a comment is called a "statement against interest," and may be used against you at trial.)

175. I am a psychiatrist who works for several nursing homes. Often I prescribe a low dose of an antipsychotic medication to settle a patient. Is this an acceptable practice?

Many psychiatrists follow this practice. When doing so, however, it is essential that you obtain informed consent from your patient. After being appropriately informed about a treatment, alternatives to the treatment, and the consequences of no treatment at all, competent patients have the right to refuse antipsychotic medication.

Exceptions to the right to refuse antipsychotic medication arise when the situation is a recognized statutory emergency or when the patient has been legally found incompetent to make treatment decisions. If the patient has a guardian, the guardian can give consent for the medication. If there is no guardian and the patient is unable to give informed consent, then you must follow the procedures for obtaining consent (see chapter 8). What's important is that you be sure to obtain informed consent from competent patients, and to follow appropriate guardianship procedures when your patients are not competent to give consent.

176. What should I do if a patient who is HIV positive reveals to me that he is sexually active with unsuspecting partners?

This question (once again) raises the issue of balancing the confidentiality of patient information against the safety and protection of other individuals. Florida law generally protects the confidentiality of information related to HIV status and testing. Section 381.004 (Fla. Stat. ch. 381.004) provides for civil and criminal penalties for wrongful disclosure of HIV testing results. Disclosure is permitted, however, in certain circumstances where lawmakers felt there was a compelling need to do so.

The exception carved out by section 455.674 (Fla. Stat. ch. 455.674) is directly applicable to this question. Section 455.674 allows a physician, who has confirmed positive test results for a patient under her care, to disclose HIV status in the following circumstances:

- for the purpose of diagnosis, care, and treatment of persons notified;
- for the purpose of interrupting the chain of transmission to the patient's spouse or to a person reasonably believed to be the patient's sexual partner.

To this end, the physician may disclose HIV status to the patient's spouse, sexual partner, or needle-sharing partner within the guidelines established by the Department of Health.

Before disclosing any confidential information, the physician must discuss the test results with the patient, recommend that the patient refrain from high-risk activity, advise the patient that he or she should inform the partner, and attempt to obtain the patient's consent to notify the partner. The physician must also tell the patient that she intends to notify the patient's contacts. Note that section 455.674 is permissive rather than mandatory. A physician does not have a duty to inform; while she may do so, and is excused from liability if she follows the statute's guidelines, the statute specifically provides that she will not get into trouble for failing to disclose a patient's positive HIV status.

The statute applies to all practitioners subject to regulation by the Division of Medical Quality Care Assurance, which is part of Department of Business and Professional Regulation. It seems reasonable to assume that if physicians may disclose this information, then non-M.D. mental health professionals—who may have equal or even better access to information about a patient's intentions—may do so as well. Only physicians, however, have the protection of a statute, and so only physicians may assume they are protected. Keep in mind that it is always best to work with your patient, and you should disclose information against his will only as an absolute last resort, to be used when all else fails. Also, think through carefully whether (1) it is necessary to disclose this information to protect a third party, and (2) disclosing the information has a reasonable chance of achieving your desired goal. If you are faced with the possibility of disclosing HIV status, get a consultation from a senior colleague, an attorney who is experienced in mental health law, or both; rarely will the importance of obtaining a consultation be greater. Be sure to document your consultation.

As part of your decision-making process, also consider whether any other statutes apply. If, for example, your patient has communicated a wish to infect a specific person, you might have the discretion to warn pursuant to the confidentiality statutes discussed in chapter 2, especially in a case where the partner has reason to believe your patient is HIV negative (such as a spouse who remains unaware of her husband's IV drug use or high-risk sexual activity). In addition, consider whether you might have the discretion to hospitalize your client, pursuant to the Baker Act. A duty to hospitalize might arise if you determine that, as a result of a mental illness, your patient's capacity to refrain from unprotected sexual activity, or to appreciate the consequences of engaging in unprotected sexual activity, has been significantly impaired. In such a case there might be a substantial likelihood that, in the near future, your patient will inflict serious bodily harm on another person, as evidenced by recent behavior (in this case, the refusal to use safety precautions or to refrain from sexual activity). Your final decision will depend upon the individual facts of the case.

177. From a professional liability perspective, what is the difference between a consultation and supervision?

The difference between a consultation and a supervision is the degree to which an individual, other than the treater, becomes involved in and responsible for a treatment. This difference in degree has significant liability implications.

A consultation consists of a treater bringing a specific question, or questions, to a consultant. A consultation is not open-ended or indefinite; the question is asked, a recommendation is made, and the treater is free to use the recommendation in whatever manner she feels will be most helpful to the treatment. The consultant assumes no responsibility for what the treater does, and makes a recommendation based only on what material the treater presents. When the consultant puts forth a recommendation, the consultant-consultee relationship ends. Because of the nature of this relationship, a consultant's liability is extremely limited. Consultants are rarely named as defendants in lawsuits.

From the perspective of risk management, supervision, which places an entire treatment under the scrutiny of another mental health professional, plays much the same role as a consultation. A supervision consists of an ongoing relationship in which an entire treatment, or significant aspects of a treatment, are placed under the scrutiny of the supervisor. If the supervisee is a trainee, and the supervisor has both clinical and administrative responsibility for the supervisee's work, the supervisor is nearly as responsible for the treatment as if the patient were the supervisor's own. In this sense, the supervisor is much "closer" to the patient than is the consultant. If the supervisee is a licensed clinician with experience, the supervisor's responsibility is less, yet still considerably more than that of a consultant. A supervisor will be held accountable for not actively exploring what the supervisee is doing, how the supervisee is handling the transference and countertransference, how the supervisee is addressing issues of safety, and the like. Because of their greater degree of involvement and responsibility, supervisors are more likely to be named in lawsuits than are consultants.

178. Is a trainee required to tell a patient that the treatment is being supervised?
Yes. Trainees must tell their patients that a treatment is being supervised.

179. What is negligent supervision? What would be an example of negligent supervision?
Negligent supervision is the failure to live up to the standard expected of you in the supervisory relationship. For this reason, it is important that

you define the frame of the supervision at the outset. You will want to be clear about how often you and your supervisee will meet; which cases your supervisee will bring to the supervision; which aspects of those cases you will supervise; who, if anyone, will cover for you during vacations; and so forth. Once you set the frame, you will then be responsible for providing *reasonable* supervision. The important question from a professional liability point of view: Given the frame, what would a reasonable supervisor do in these circumstances?

Here are three examples. First, you have agreed to meet with your supervisee once per month, and you miss three months without taking the time to "check-in" with your supervisee. An untoward event happens. Your supervision could be considered negligent, because a reasonable supervisor would have made sure to communicate with the supervisee in some way about the status of the cases. Second, a supervisee talks at length about how physically attractive he finds his new patient. You do not address the erotic countertransference, nor do you attend to how the supervisee is handling the countertransference. An affair results. Your supervision could be considered negligent, because a reasonable supervisor would have made sure that the countertransference was appropriately addressed. Third, your supervisee begins to treat a patient with a long history of suicide attempts. For a period of several weeks you do not ask your supervisee about her assessment of the patient's suicidality, and the patient makes a serious suicide attempt. You could be considered negligent, because a reasonable supervisor would have made sure that the supervisee was adequately assessing the patient's suicidality. Your touchstone is what a reasonable supervisor would do under the circumstances.

12

CHILDREN AND FAMILIES

Perhaps no area of mental health law generates more intense feelings than that of children and families. Clinicians will not find this surprising: The bonds that tie children to their parents, parents to their children, and partners and siblings to one another are the strongest that humans experience. When the state intrudes into the life of a family—for however good a reason—that intensity can be felt by all involved. The questions below address circumstances in which family life is touched by the law.

QUESTIONS DISCUSSED IN THIS CHAPTER

184. What if a minor requires medical treatment, but a parent or guardian is not available to provide the necessary consent?

185. What makes a minor "emancipated"?

186. Can a minor consent to treatment?

187. If a minor who is of the appropriate age—13 years or older—receives outpatient treatment, who is financially responsible for the services rendered?

188. Can a minor consent to an abortion?

189. What rules of confidentiality govern the treatment of minors?

190. How does a court decide on custody when the parents can't agree?

191. In deciding on custody, to what extent will a judge consider a child's wishes?

192. Is sexual orientation a factor in custody determinations?

193. Is domestic violence a factor in custody determinations?

194. What happens if a noncustodial parent wishes to have a child treated?

195. Can a parent who has *not* been awarded legal custody of a child obtain the child's school or medical records?

196. On what grounds may a court terminate parents' rights to their child?

197. Does a parent's mental illness provide a basis for terminating parental rights?

198. What is the standard of proof required to terminate parental rights?

199. What can Florida courts do to make testifying against an alleged perpetrator of sexual abuse easier for a child?

200. When can a minor be tried as an adult in Florida?

DISCUSSION

180. Under what conditions may a minor be placed in a psychiatric hospital?

According to section 394.459 (Fla. Stat. ch. 394.459[3][a]), each patient who enters a psychiatric hospital "shall be asked to give express and informed consent to treatment." If the patient is a minor, the minor's guardian (the parent, for example), along with the minor, will be asked to consent to the hospitalization. Thus, prior to hospitalizing the minor, the hospital will obtain the minor's consent. Section 394.459 goes on to state, "Express and informed consent for admission and treatment given by a patient who is under 18 years of age shall not be a condition of admission when the patient's guardian gives express and informed consent for the patient's admission" under the involuntary examination or admission provisions of the Baker Act (sections 394.463 and 394.467; see chapter 5). Thus, if a minor meets the criteria for involuntary examination or treatment, a parent or guardian may consent to have the minor admitted to a psychiatric hospital regardless of whether the minor consents.

181. What should I do if I recommend that a child be hospitalized and the parents refuse to follow my recommendation?

First, you should review the reasons behind your recommendation, ideally with a consultant. If, following the review, you continue to believe that failure to hospitalize places the child at risk of serious harm, you should attempt to persuade the parents to accept your recommendation. If the parents, in turn, continue to refuse the hospitalization, you should determine whether you have an obligation to file a mandatory report according to the child abuse and neglect mandatory reporting statute (see chapter 3). If the child is likely to suffer serious harm from lack of hospitalization, the child protective agency will assess the situation. If you decide that it is not necessary to file a mandatory report, you still have the option of initiating Baker Act proceedings for involuntary examination and placement. A mental health professional should proceed against the parents' wishes only after obtaining a consultation (see also the following question).

182. Can I hospitalize a child against the child's wishes and over a parent's objections?

Parental consent is generally required before a minor may be hospitalized. A treater may, however, proceed without the parents' consent if the child meets the statutory requirements for involuntary hospitalization and treatment (see chapter 5). It will be extremely important to obtain a consultation in this situation. In *Garcia v. Psychiatric Institutes of America*, 638 So. 2d 567 (Fla. App. 5 Dist. 1994), the Fifth District Court of Appeals ruled that confining a child and giving him drugs against his mother's express and written directions could constitute false imprisonment and battery. The lesson here is to proceed against a parent's wishes only when you have legitimate reasons to do so, when you have obtained a consultation, and when you have thoroughly documented both your reasons and your consultation.

183. Can a minor enter a psychiatric hospital voluntarily, without the consent of a parent or guardian?

Section 394.4625 (Fla. Stat. ch. 394.4625[1]) addresses the voluntary admission of a minor to a psychiatric facility. According to section 394.4625, a minor's parent or guardian must first apply for the minor's admission. The facility must then hold a hearing to verify that the minor's consent to treatment is truly voluntary.

184. What if a minor requires medical treatment, but a parent or guardian is not available to provide the necessary consent?

Section 743.0645 (Fla. Stat. 743.0645[2]) provides for a circumstance in which a minor needs treatment but a parent or guardian is not available to provide consent. In such a situation, the following individuals may provide consent to treat the minor: a person who possess power of attorney; a stepparent; a grandparent; an adult brother or sister; an adult aunt or uncle. The treater should document what attempts she made to reach a person with the legal power to consent to the minor's treatment.

Physicians, of course, may treat a minor in an emergency when a parent or guardian is not available.

185. What makes a minor "emancipated"?

By definition, minors—individuals under the age of 18—are subject to another's care. Courts can release a minor from the care of a parent or guardian through a process called "emancipation." In Florida law, emancipation is also referred to as removing the "disability of nonage." The idea is that certain minors are mature enough to take on adult responsibilities and therefore should be accorded adult rights.

Section 743.01 (Fla. Stat. ch. 743.01) and section 743.015 (Fla. Stat. ch. 743.015[1]) set forth the criteria for removing the disability of nonage. These criteria are:

- marriage of the minor; and
- when a parent, guardian, or guardian ad litem petitions the court to remove the disability of nonage, and the minor is 16 or 17 and resides in Florida.

When a court removes the disability of nonage, the individual is then considered an adult in the eyes of the law.

186. Can a minor consent to treatment?

Minors are generally not able to consent to treatment. A parent or guardian, the individual charged with the minor's care and upbringing, makes treatment and a host of other decisions for the minor. That said, important exceptions to this general rule may arise.

- A minor with the disability of nonage removed according to section 743.01 is considered an adult and is thus capable of consenting to treatment.
- Section 397.601 (Fl. Stat. ch. 397.601[4][a]) permits a minor of any age to consent to treatment for substance abuse.
- Section 394.4784 (Fla. Stat. ch. 394.4784[1]–[2]) permits a minor 13 years of age or older to consent to limited outpatient crisis intervention.
- Section 743.065 (Fla. Stat. ch. 743.065[1]–[2]) permits an unwed pregnant minor to consent to medical or surgical care or services that relate to her pregnancy, as well as to services for her child.

The law balances opposing values in allowing minors to consent to treatment. While the law generally deems minors not competent to consent to treatment, certain minors are especially mature. When we believe that a minor is mature, for example because he or she is married, or has had the disability of nonage removed by a court, the law allows that minor to make his or her own treatment decisions. Similarly, despite the presumption that minors are incompetent to make treatment decisions, they are unlikely to tell parents about drug use or certain emotional crises and so may not get treatment if their parents must first give consent. Because the law wants to encourage minors to get treatment in these circumstances, it makes a set of exceptions to the general rule.

187. If a minor who is of the appropriate age—13 years or older— receives outpatient treatment, who is financially responsible for the services rendered?

Section 394.4784 (Fla. Stat. ch. 394.4784[3]) says that a parent or legal guardian is not financially responsible for the treatment unless the parent or guardian participates. Even then, the parent or guardian is financially responsible only to the extent that he or she participates in the treatment. Note, however, that section 394.4784 (Fla. Stat. ch. 394.4784[4]) absolves licensed mental health professionals from any obligation to provide outpatient treatment to a minor; treatment is provided only when the mental health professional voluntarily agrees to do so.

188. Can a minor consent to an abortion?

Yes. In Florida an unwed pregnant minor can consent to any medical or

MINORS AND CONSENT TO TREATMENT

I. A minor is generally **not able to consent** to treatment.
   A. A minor is an individual **under 18 years** of age.
   B. A parent with legal custody, or a guardian, may consent to treatment for a minor.
   C. If parent or guardian unavailable, consent to treatment may be given by (Fla. Stat. ch. 743.0645[2]):
      1. person with power of attorney;
      2. stepparent;
      3. grandparent;
      4. adult brother or sister;
      5. adult aunt or uncle.

II. A minor may consent to treatment in the following circumstances:
   A. A court has removed the disability of nonage (Fla. Stat. ch. 743.01);
   B. A minor of any age may consent to treatment for substance abuse (Fla. Stat. ch. 397.601[4][a]);
   C. A minor 13 years of age or older may consent to limited outpatient crisis intervention (Fla. Stat. ch. 394.4784[1]–[2]);
   D. An unwed minor may consent to medical or surgical care or services that relate to her pregnancy (Fla. Stat. ch. 743.065[1]) or to services for her child (Fla. Stat. ch. 743.065[2]).

surgical care related to her pregnancy. The consent is valid, as though she had achieved majority (Fla. Stat. ch. 743.065[1]). In addition, section 390.0111 (Fla. Stat. ch. 390.0111[3]) states that an abortion may not be performed without the voluntary and written consent of the pregnant woman. Section 390.0111 is silent as to age. Thus, in Florida, minors may obtain an abortion according to the same restrictions as women who are 18 or older.

189. What rules of confidentiality govern the treatment of minors?

The rules of confidentiality that govern the treatment of minors are similar to the rules that govern the treatment of adults: Treaters are bound by confidentiality and testimonial privilege. Information about a minor's treatment can be shared with the minor or a parent or guardian (since a parent or guardian is legally the person who will provide consent to the treatment). To disclose material from or about the treatment to any other individual, an exception to confidentiality must apply. Note that when a minor is able to consent to treatment herself (perhaps, for example, because she has had the disability of nonage removed), the treater should not disclose information without the minor's consent, unless a statutory exception to confidentiality applies or a court has ordered the mental health professional to disclose the information.

190. How does a court decide on custody when the parents can't agree?

According to Florida law, the touchstone for deciding on custody is the "best interest" of the child. According to section 61.13 (Fla. Stat. ch. 61.13[3]) a court should consider a number of factors in determining what custody arrangement is in a child's best interest, including:

- the length of time the child has lived in a stable, satisfactory environment and the desirability of maintaining continuity;
- the performance, as a family unit, of the existing or proposed custodial home;
- the moral fitness of the parents;
- the mental and physical health of the parents;
- the reasonable preference of the child;
- the willingness and ability of each parent to facilitate and encourage a close and continuing parent-child relationship between the child and the other parent;
- evidence of domestic violence or child abuse;
- evidence that either parent has knowingly provided false information regarding a domestic violence proceeding; and
- any other factor the court considers to be relevant.

Section 61.13 leaves the court broad discretion in fashioning a custody arrangement that is in the child's best interest. At the same time, a custody determination is not left solely up to a judge's whim. Rather, a custody determination represents a balance of factors that the law deems relevant to the child's best interest. One final note: While Florida law presumes that shared legal custody is the most appropriate custody arrangement (see question 194), the actual custody decision is always subject to the overarching concern of the child's best interest.

191. In deciding on custody, to what extent will a judge consider a child's wishes?

The rule of thumb follows common sense—as the child gets older, her preferences matter more. Section 61.13 (Fla. Stat. ch. 61.13[3][i]) states that a judge shall consider and give due weight to the wishes of the child, if the child is of sufficient age and reasoning capacity to form an intelligent custody preference. If the child is actually called as a witness to indicate her preference about custody, the judge should take steps to make testifying easier. As examples, the judge could take steps to protect the child from undue harassment or embarrassment, to restrict the unnecessary repetition of questions, and to ensure that the questions are in a form appropriate to the child's age. If the best interest standard speaks against having the child actually testify in the custody proceeding, the judge is free to meet with the child "in chambers" (in the judge's office), or to accept written testimony.

192. Is sexual orientation a factor in custody determinations?
Judges are given a great deal of leeway in determining what custody arrangement is in a child's best interest. This leeway includes the discretion to consider a number of factors that a judge believes speaks to this question. In two Florida cases, *Packard v. Packard,* 697 So. 2d 1292 (Fla. 1st DCA 1997), and *Murphy v. Murphy*, 621 So. 2d 455 (Fla. 4th DCA 1993), Florida courts have held that the parent's sexual orientation cannot be the *sole* determinant of a custody arrangement. These courts have said, however, that judges are free to consider sexual orientation as *a* factor to be considered.

193. Is domestic violence a factor in custody determinations?
Section 61.13 (Fla. Stat. ch. 61.13[3]) states explicitly that "evidence of domestic violence or child abuse" is a factor to be considered in fashioning a custody arrangement. Several other factors named in section 61.13 might be relevant to a history of domestic violence as well, as a judge determines what arrangement would be in the child's best interest. For example, section 61.13 makes reference to the emotional ties between parent and child, the stability of the home, the functioning of the family unit, the moral fitness of a parent, and the mental health of a parent. A history of domestic violence could be relevant to all of these factors.

194. What happens if a noncustodial parent wishes to have a child treated?
If the situation is an emergency, no consent is necessary. You may go ahead and treat the child, regardless of who brought her to you.

If the situation is not an emergency, you must distinguish between "shared parental responsibility" and "sole parental responsibility." It is the policy of the state of Florida to assure that each child has frequent contact with both parents, which is why courts generally order shared parental responsibility (known as "joint legal custody" in other states). Section 61.046 (Fla. Stat. ch. 61.046[14]) defines shared parental responsibility as "a court-ordered relationship in which both parents retain full parental rights and responsibilities with respect to their child." When parents share parental responsibilities, all major decisions affecting the welfare of the child are made jointly. When, on the other hand, the court believes that shared parental responsibility would not be in the child's best interest, the court will order sole parental responsibility, and only one parent will be authorized to make decisions for the child.

195. Can a parent who has *not* been awarded legal custody of a child obtain the child's school or medical records?

Section 228.093 (Fla. Stat. ch. 228.093) provides that a "parent" has a right to his or her child's school records. Section 228.093 makes no distinction between a parent who has sole or shared custody. As a consequence, section 228.903 permits any parent the right to see the records from a child's school.

Section 455.667 governs the right to medical records. According to section 455.667 (Fla. Stat. ch. 455.667[4]), a health care practitioner must provide records, when requested to do so, to a patient or a patient's legal representative. Thus, only a parent who is a minor's authorized legal representative has the legal right to gain access to the minor's medical records.

196. On what grounds may a court terminate parents' rights to their child?

Section 39.806 (Fla. Stat. ch. 39.806[a–f]) sets forth the grounds on which a court may terminate parental rights. These grounds include:

• when the parents have voluntarily surrendered custody of their child;
• when a child's parents cannot be identified or located within 90 days;
• when a parent will be incarcerated for a substantial part of his son's or daughter's childhood, and the parent has been convicted of a serious felony;
• when the child is under the court's supervision and the parents continue to abuse, neglect, or abandon the child;

- when the parents have engaged in behavior that threatens the child's life, safety, or health;
- when the parents have sexually abused the child.

Parents have a fundamental right to custody of their children. That right will be terminated only in the most egregious circumstances, as this list demonstrates.

197. Does a parent's mental illness provide a sufficient basis for terminating parental rights?

The mere presence of mental illness is not a sufficient basis to terminate parental rights. In *Hroncich v. Department of Health and Rehabilitative Services*, 667 So. 2d 804 (Fla. App. 5th Dist. 1995), the Fifth District Court of Appeal stated:

> The mere affliction with a mental illness which produces behavior or symptoms harmful to a child for a limited period of time does not necessarily support a finding of prospective abuse or mean that a parent will never be able to care for his/her child . . . a parent's mental illness is but one factor to be considered: all other relevant facts must also be considered. (at 808)

A court cannot terminate parental rights solely on the basis of a parent's mental illness.

198. What is the standard of proof required to terminate parental rights?

Termination of parental rights, the very final step of the dependency process, severs all legal ties between a parent and a child. The United States Supreme Court has recognized the profound implications of such an action by the state: termination of parental rights impinges on the fundamental right of family integrity. Because a fundamental right is affected, the Supreme Court held in *Santosky v. Kramer*, 455 U.S. 745 (1982), that the standard of proof required to terminate parental rights is *clear and convincing evidence* (see question 4). Note that the clear and convincing standard is not our strictest standard of proof—*beyond a reasonable doubt* is the highest standard of proof in our legal system. Thus, the clear and convincing standard is a compromise: Because the Court gives great weight to a parent's right to raise a child, the Court "raises the proof hurdle" (see question 4) before those rights may be taken away. At the same time, however, the Court does not want to make it too difficult to remove a child from an unsafe environment. The clear and convincing standard recognizes the possible conflict between a desire to protect the rights of a parent and the desire to protect the safety of a child, and serves as a compromise between these two competing values. Section 39.809 (Fla. Stat. ch. 39.809) makes the clear and convincing standard for termination cases explicit.

199. What can Florida courts do to make testifying against an alleged perpetrator of sexual abuse easier for a child?

Any reasonable person would want to make testifying less stressful, burdensome, and traumatic for a child. Attempts to protect a child witness may, however, conflict with certain clauses of the State and Federal Constitution that provide criminal defendants basic rights at trial. The United States Constitution, for example, provides that a criminal defendant has the right to information that could help prove his innocence, as well as the right to confront face-to-face those who accuse him of a crime. These rights are balanced against the interests of victims and witnesses, who deserve sympathy, support, and justice. Florida's Legislature (and its courts) have recognized that when the victim testifying is a child, special supports may be needed.

Section 92.53 (Fla. Stat. ch. 92.53[1]–[7]) allows special arrangements for a witness who is either under 16 or is mentally retarded. Before the special arrangements in section 92.53 can be used, however, the court must find that there is a "substantial likelihood" that the witness would suffer "at least moderate emotional or mental harm" if required to testify in open court in the presence of the defendant. If the court does make this specific finding:

- the child's testimony may be videotaped, at a time before the actual trial takes place;
- the court may order that the defendant view the child's testimony from outside the child's presence, where the child cannot see or hear the defendant;
- the court may have a person who is able to formulate questions appropriate to the child's age and understanding, and capable of interpreting the child's responses, assist in eliciting the child's testimony.

If the child's testimony is videotaped, the defendant must be able to observe the child as the child testifies (for example through a two-way mirror) and he must be able to communicate with his attorney, who will be present in order to cross-examine the child, in a direct and immediate way. A videotape made in this manner may be admitted into evidence at trial.

Section 92.54 (Fla. Stat. ch. 92.54[1]–[5]) allows for a child's testimony to be taken live, by way of closed circuit television. The initial requirement of section 92.54 is the same as for section 92.53—the court must find a substantial likelihood that the witness would suffer at least moderate emotional or mental harm if required to testify in open court in the presence of the defendant. When the court makes this finding:

- the child's testimony may be transmitted live by closed circuit television into the courtroom;
- the defendant may be required to be in the actual courtroom, away from where the child is testifying, so that the child cannot see or hear him;
- in the room where the child testifies may be someone who the court feels "contributes to the well-being of the child."

The defendant must be able to watch the child's live testimony, and must be able to communicate in a direct and immediate way with his attorney, who will be in the room where the child is testifying.

Sections 92.53 and 92.54 balance the needs of the child witness against the constitutional rights of the defendant. Special needs of the child can be accommodated in order to protect the child's emotional or mental health. On the other hand, the defendant must be able to see the child's live testimony, to have his own attorney present in the room where the child testifies, and to communicate with his attorney while the child testifies.

200. When can a minor be tried as an adult in Florida?

Whether a minor is tried as an adult depends on the facts and circumstances of the crime and the minor's past criminal history. Florida statutes identify the various factors relevant to this determination. At times, the statutes give the state attorney discretion over whether to charge a minor as an adult, while at other times the statutes require the state attorney to do so. The state attorney is required to file charges in adult court when:

- a minor of any age is charged with a crime punishable by death or life imprisonment;
- a minor of any age is charged with a crime and the minor has been

adjudicated at least three times for crimes that, if committed by an adult, would be felonies;

- a minor is 16 or 17 years old at the time of committing a second alleged crime against a person and the minor has been previously found delinquent for any of various serious offenses (such as murder, sexual battery, and carjacking).

At other times the state attorney has discretion over whether to file charges in adult court. For example, section 985.227 (Fla. Stat. ch. 985.227[1][a–b]), gives the prosecutor discretion to file charges in adult court when a minor who was 14 or 15 at the time of the offense is charged with such serious crimes as arson, aggravated assault, murder, or armed burglary. In such an instance the prosecutor must decide whether the public interest requires adult sanctions (see Fla. Stat. ch. 985.227 [1][a][1–15]). In addition, a minor over the age of 14 at the time of committing any alleged delinquent act or violation of law can be involuntarily transferred to criminal court to be tried as an adult if the juvenile court authorizes the transfer following a request by the prosecutor. Again, the prosecutor has the option—not the obligation—of requesting that the case be moved to adult court.

Sometimes a minor may *voluntarily* elect to be tried as an adult in criminal court if the minor indicates his desire in writing and the minor's parent, guardian, or guardian ad litem joins the demand. This may occur because adult criminal court offers more elaborate procedural protections, including the right to jury trial (the juvenile court does not allow trial by jury).

AFTERWORD

The *Essentials of Florida Mental Health Law* has two important points. If we've made them, we'll consider our book a success. First, laws are not made in a vacuum. Behind each law there is a value or principle the law seeks to advance. Sometimes the value is straightforward. Communications between a patient and her therapist are confidential because we want to promote the mental health of our citizenry and because we respect an individual's right to decide with whom she will share sensitive and perhaps intimate information about her life. At other times the law must balance important goals against one another. While confidentiality is important, for example, confidentiality yields to matters of public safety. When you read a statute, regulation, or case, try to see what value the law seeks to promote or which values the law is balancing against one another. The law will make infinitely more sense if you are able to find the spirit behind its letter.

The second point follows from the first: When faced with a dilemma that has legal implications, the process by which you decide becomes as important as the decision itself. Don't begin by asking, "What specific statute or regulation do I need to follow?" Begin by asking, "What's at stake here? What values are at issue, and how can I act consistent with those values?" When uncertain, seek a consultation, and carefully consider the consultant's recommendations. The process you bring to bear on your decision-making will be your greatest protection against legal troubles.

Appendix A

FLORIDA STATUTES AND REGULATIONS GOVERNING PRIVACY, CONFIDENTIALITY, AND TESTIMONIAL PRIVILEGE

PRIVACY

ARTICLE I, §23 OF THE FLORIDA CONSTITUTION
Every natural person has the right to be let alone and free from governmental intrusion into the person's private life except as otherwise provided herein. This section shall not be construed to limit the public's
right of access to public records and meetings as provided by law.

CONFIDENTIALITY

§394.4615. THE BAKER ACT
(1) A clinical record shall be maintained for each patient. The record
shall include data pertaining to admission and such other information as
may be required under rules of the department. A clinical record is confidential . . . Unless waived by express and informed consent, by the
patient or the patient's guardian or guardian advocate or, if the patient is
deceased, by the patient's personal representative or the family member
who stands next in line of intestate succession, the confidential status of
the clinical record shall not be lost by either authorized or unauthorized
disclosure to any person, organization, or agency.
(2) The clinical record shall be released when:
  (a) The patient or the patient's guardian authorizes the release. The
guardian or guardian advocate shall be provided access to the appropriate clinical records of the patient. The patient or the patient's guardian or
guardian advocate may authorize the release of information and clinical
records to appropriate persons to ensure the continuity of the patient's
health care or mental health care.
  (b) The patient is represented by counsel and the records are
needed by the patient's counsel for adequate representation.
  (c) The court orders such release. In determining whether there is
good cause for disclosure, the court shall weigh the need for the information to be disclosed against the possible harm of disclosure to the person to whom such information pertains.
  (d) The patient is committed to, or is to be returned to, the Department
of Corrections from the Department of Health and Rehabilitivative Services,
and the Department of Corrections requests such records. These records
shall be furnished without charge to the Department of Corrections.
(3) Information from the clinical record may be released when:

(a) A patient has declared an intention to harm other persons. When such declaration has been made, the administrator may authorize the release of sufficient information to provide adequate warning to the person threatened with harm by the patient.

(b) The administrator of the facility or secretary of the department deems release to a qualified researcher as defined in administrative rule, an aftercare treatment provider, or an employee or agent of the department is necessary for treatment of the patient, maintenance of adequate records, compilation of treatment data, aftercare planning, or evaluation of programs.

(4) Information from clinical records may be used for statistical and research purposes if the information is abstracted in such a way as to protect the identity of individuals.

(5) Information from clinical records may be used by the Agency for Health Care Administration, the Department, and the human rights advocacy committees for the purpose of monitoring facility activity and complaints concerning facilities.

(6) Any person, agency, or entity receiving information pursuant to this section shall maintain such information as confidential . . .

(7) Any facility or private mental health practitioner who acts in good faith in releasing information pursuant to this section is not subject to civil or criminal liability for such release.

§455.671. CONFIDENTIAL COMMUNICATIONS AND PSYCHIATRISTS
See chapter 2, page 19, for the text of this statute.

§490.0147. CONFIDENTIAL COMMUNICATIONS AND LICENSED PSYCHOLOGISTS
Any communications between a [licensed psychologist] and his or her patient or client shall be confidential. This privilege may be waived under the following conditions:

(1) When the person licensed under this chapter is a party defendant to a civil, criminal, or disciplinary action arising from a complaint filed by the patient or client, in which case the waiver shall be limited to that action.

(2) When the patient or client agrees to the waiver, in writing, or when more than one person in a family is receiving therapy, when each family member agrees to the waiver, in writing.

(3) When there is a clear and immediate probability of physical harm to the patient or client, to other individuals, or to society and the [licensed psychol-

ogist] communicates the information only to the potential victim, appropriate family member, or law enforcement or other appropriate authorities.

§491.0147. CONFIDENTIAL COMMUNICATIONS AND LICENSED SOCIAL WORKERS, MARRIAGE AND FAMILY THERAPISTS, MENTAL HEALTH COUNSELORS, OR CERTIFIED MASTER SOCIAL WORKERS

Any communications between [one of the mental health professionals named above] and his or her patient or client shall be confidential. This secrecy may be waived under the following conditions:

(1) When the [licensed or certified mental health professional] is a party defendant to a civil, criminal, or disciplinary action arising from a complaint filed by the patient or client, in which case the waiver shall be limited to that action.

(2) When the patient or client agrees to the waiver, in writing, or when more than one person in a family is receiving therapy, when each family member agrees to the waiver, in writing.

(3) When there is a clear and immediate probability of physical harm to the patient or client, to other individuals, or to society and the [mental health professional named above] communicates the information only to the potential victim, appropriate family member, or law enforcement or other appropriate authorities.

§90.5035. CONFIDENTIAL COMMUNICATIONS AND SEXUAL ASSAULT COUNSELORS

(d) A communication between a sexual assault counselor and a victim is "confidential" if it is not intended to be disclosed to third persons other than:

    1. Those persons present to further the interest of the victim in the consultation, examination, or interview.

    2. Those persons necessary for the transmission of the communication.

    3. Those persons to whom disclosure is reasonably necessary to accomplish the purposes for which the sexual assault counselor is consulted.

§90.5036. CONFIDENTIAL COMMUNICATIONS AND DOMESTIC VIOLENCE ADVOCATES

(d) A communication between a domestic violence advocate and a victim is "confidential" if it relates to the incident of domestic violence for which the victim is seeking assistance and if it is not intended to be disclosed to third persons other than:

    1.   Those persons present to further the interest of the victim in the consultation, assessment, or interview.

    2.   Those persons to whom disclosure is reasonably necessary to accomplish the purposes for which domestic violence advocate is consulted.

§39.908. CONFIDENTIAL COMMUNICATIONS AND DOMESTIC VIOLENCE CENTERS

(1) Information about clients received by the department or by authorized persons employed by or volunteering services to a domestic violence center, through files, reports, inspection, or otherwise, is confidential . . . Information about the location of domestic violence centers and facilities is confidential . . .

(2) Information about domestic violence center clients may not be disclosed without the written consent of the client to whom the information or records pertain. For the purpose of state law regarding searches and seizures, domestic violence centers shall be treated as private dwelling places. Information about a client or the location of a domestic violence center may be given by center staff or volunteers to law enforcement, firefighting, medical, other personnel in the following circumstances:

    (a)   To medical personnel in a medical emergency.

    (b)   Upon a court order based upon an application by a law enforcement officer for a criminal arrest warrant which alleges that the individual sought to be arrested is located at the domestic violence shelter.

    (c)   Upon a search warrant that specifies the individual or object of the search and alleges that the individual or object is located at the shelter.

    (d)   To firefighting personnel in an emergency.

    (e)   To any other person necessary to maintain the safety and health standards in the domestic violence shelter . . .

(3) The restriction on the disclosure or use of the information about domestic violence center clients does not apply to:

    (a)   Communications from domestic violence shelter staff or volunteers to law enforcement officers when the information is directly related to a client's commission of a crime or threat to commit a crime on the premises of a domestic violence shelter; or

    (b)   Reporting suspected abuse of a child or a vulnerable adult as required by law. However, when cooperating with protective investigation services staff, the domestic shelter staff and volunteers must protect the confidentiality of other clients at the domestic violence shelter.

§397.501. CONFIDENTIALITY RIGHTS OF PERSONS RECEIVING SUBSTANCE ABUSE SERVICES
Clients receiving substance abuse services from any service provider are guaranteed protection of the rights specified in this section, unless otherwise expressly provided, and service providers must ensure the protection of such rights. . . .
(7) Right to confidentiality of client records
    (a) The records of service providers which pertain to the identity, diagnosis, and prognosis of and service provision to any individual client are confidential . . . Such records may not be disclosed without the written consent of the client to whom they pertain except that appropriate disclosure may be made without consent:
        1. To medical personnel in a medical emergency.
        2. To service provider personnel if such personnel need to know the information in order to carry out duties relating to the provision of services to a client.
        3. To the secretary of the department or the secretary's designee, for purposes of scientific research, in accordance with federal confidentiality regulations, but only upon agreement in writing that the client's name and other identifying information will not be disclosed.
        4. In the course of review of records on service provider premises by persons who are performing an audit or evaluation on behalf of any federal, state, or local government agency, or third-party payor providing financial assistance or reimbursement to the service provider; however, reports produced as a result of such audit or evaluation may not disclose client names or other identifying information and must be in accord with federal confidentiality regulations.
        5. Upon court order based on application showing good cause for disclosure. In determining whether there is good cause for disclosure, the court shall examine whether the public interest and the need for disclosure outweigh the potential injury to the client, to the service provider–client relationship, and to the service provider itself.
    (b) The restrictions on disclosure and use in this section do not apply to communications from provider personnel to law enforcement officers which:

1.   Are directly related to a client's commission of a crime on the premises of the provider or against provider personnel or to a threat to commit such a crime; and

2.   Are limited to the circumstances of the incident, including the client status of the individual committing or threatening to commit the crime, that individual's name and address, and that individual's last known whereabouts.

(c) The restrictions on disclosure and use in this section do not apply to the reporting of incidents of suspected child abuse and neglect to the appropriate state or local authorities as required by law. However, such restrictions continue to apply to the original substance abuse client records . . .

(e)(1) Since a minor acting alone has the legal capacity to voluntarily apply for and obtain substance abuse treatment, any written consent for disclosure may be given only by that minor client . . .

(j) A court may authorize the disclosure and use of client records for the purpose of conducting a criminal investigation or prosecution of a client only if the court finds that all of the following criteria are met:

1.   The crime involved is extremely serious, such as one which causes or directly threatens loss of life or serious bodily injury, including but not limited to homicide, sexual assault, sexual battery, kidnapping, armed robbery, assault with a deadly weapon, and child abuse and neglect.

2.   There is reasonable likelihood that the records will disclose information of substantial value in the investigation or prosecution.

3.   Other ways of obtaining the information are not available or would not be effective.

4.   The potential injury to the client, to the physician-client relationship and to the ability of the program to provide services to other clients is outweighed by the public interest and the need for the disclosure.

§455.674. SHARING OF INFORMATION ABOUT A CLIENT'S HIV STATUS
(1) A practitioner regulated through the Division of Medical Quality Assurance of the department shall not be civilly or criminally liable for the disclosure of otherwise confidential information to a sexual or a needle-sharing partner under the following circumstances:

(a) If a patient of the practitioner who has tested positive for human immunodeficiency virus discloses to the practitioner the identity of a sexual partner or a needle-sharing partner;

(b) The practitioner recommends the patient notify the sexual partner or the needle-sharing partner of the positive test and refrain from engaging in sexual or drug activity in a manner likely to transmit the virus and the patient refuses, and the practitioner informs the patient of his or her intent to inform the sexual partner or needle-sharing partner; and

(c) If pursuant to a perceived civil duty or ethical guidelines of the profession, the practitioner reasonably and in good faith advises the sexual partner or the needle-sharing partner of the patient of the positive test and facts concerning the transmission of the virus. . . . any notification of a sexual partner of a needle-sharing partner pursuant to this section shall be done in accordance with protocols developed pursuant to rule of the Department of Health and Rehabilitative Services . . .

(d) Notwithstanding the foregoing, a practitioner regulated through the Division of Medical Quality Assurance of the department shall not be civilly or criminally liable for failure to disclose information relating to a positive test result for human immunodeficiency virus of a patient to a sexual partner or a needle-sharing partner.

§627.4195. HEALTH INSURERS
An insurer must maintain strict confidentiality against unauthorized or inadvertent disclosure of confidential information to persons inside or outside the insurer's organization regarding claims for payment of psychotherapeutic services provided by psychotherapists [licensed: psychologists, social workers, marriage and family therapists, mental health counselors; and certified masters level social workers] and psychotherapeutic records and reports related to the claims. . . . A psychotherapist submitting records in support of a claim may obscure portions to conceal the names, identities, or identifying information of people other than the insured if this information is unnecessary to utilization review, quality management, discharge planning, case management, or claims processing conducted by the insurer. An insurer may provide aggregate data which does not disclose subscriber identities or identities to other persons to entities such as payors, sponsors, researchers and accreditation bodies. . . .

TESTIMONIAL PRIVILEGE

§90.503. PSYCHOTHERAPIST-PATIENT PRIVILEGE
(2) A patient has a privilege to refuse to disclose, and to prevent any other person from disclosing, confidential communications or records

made for the purpose of diagnosis or treatment of the patient's mental or emotional condition, including alcoholism and other drug addiction, between the patient and the psychotherapist, or persons who are participating in the diagnosis or treatment under the direction of the psychotherapist. This privilege includes any diagnosis made, and advice given, by the psychotherapist in the course of that relationship.

(3) The privilege may be claimed by:

(a) The patient or the patient's attorney on the patient's behalf.

(b) A guardian or conservator of the patient.

(c) The personal representative of a deceased patient.

(d) The psychotherapist, but only on behalf of the patient.

The authority of a psychotherapist to claim the privilege is presumed in the absence of evidence to the contrary.

(4) There is no privilege under this section:

(a) For communications relevant to an issue in proceedings to compel hospitalization of a patient for mental illness, if the psychotherapist in the course of diagnosis or treatment has reasonable cause to believe the patient is in need of hospitalization.

(b) For communications made in the course of a court-ordered examination of the mental or emotional condition of the patient.

(c) For communications relevant to an issue of the mental or emotional condition of the patient in any proceeding in which the patient relies upon the condition as an element of his or her claim or defense or, after the patient's death, in any proceeding in which any party relies upon the condition as an element of the party's claim or defense.

§90.5035. SEXUAL ASSAULT COUNSELOR–VICTIM PRIVILEGE

(2) A victim has a privilege to refuse to disclose, and to prevent any other person from disclosing, a confidential communication made by the victim to a sexual assault counselor or any record made in the course of advising, counseling, or assisting the victim. Such confidential communication or record may be disclosed only with the prior written consent of the victim. This privilege includes any advice given by the sexual assault counselor in the course of that relationship. . . .

§90.5036. DOMESTIC VIOLENCE ADVOCATE–VICTIM PRIVILEGE

(2) A victim has the privilege to refuse to disclose, and to prevent any other person from disclosing, a confidential communication made by the victim to a domestic violence advocate or any record made in the course

of advising, counseling, or assisting the victim. The privilege applies to confidential communications made between the victim and the domestic violence advocate and to records of those communications only if the advocate is [appropriately registered under the law] at the time the communication is made. This privilege includes any advice given by the domestic violence advocate in the course of that relationship.

Appendix B

SAMPLE FORMS AND LETTERS

Subpoena
Reply to a Board of Registration Letter of Complaint
Informed Consent Letter for a Psychodynamic
    Psychotherapy
Letter Terminating a Therapy Relationship

Subpoena

On the following page is an example of a subpoena. The subpoena has a somewhat intimidating quality; most probably because it is intended to intimidate. Remember, though, that a subpoena is a demand for your <u>appearance</u>. Once you have appeared, you have fulfilled your obligation. A subpoena does not allow you to release records or to discuss confidential information, and doing either without a court order or client consent—notwithstanding that you have received a subpoena—will expose you to liability for having breached your client's confidentiality.

SUBPOENA DUCES TECUM FOR DEPOSITION

THE STATE OF FLORIDA

TO: Dr. Richard Coyle:

YOU ARE COMMANDED to appear before a person authorized by law to take depositions at 1495 West Flagler Street in Miami, Florida, on July 18, 2000, at 10 A.M., for the taking of your deposition in this action and to have with you at that time and place the following: ANY AND ALL RECORDS PERTAINING TO YOUR DIAGNOSIS, ASSESSMENT, AND/OR TREATMENT OF JOSEPH DAVID HUBBS. If you fail to appear, you may be held in contempt of court.

You are subpoenaed to appear by the following attorney, and unless excused from this subpoena by this attorney or the court, you shall respond to this subpoena as directed.

Dated on June 15, 2000.

Will David
As clerk of the Court

By Greta Sanchez
As Deputy Clerk

Stephen Haggerty
Attorney for Joseph David Hubbs
14 Allen Street
Miami, Florida

Reply to a Board of Registration Letter of Complaint

On the following page is an example of a reply to a board of registration letter of complaint. Your initial response to a board of registration should be a request that the individual who made the complaint provide a release of information. Without a release, providing a substantive response—a response that discloses confidential information—could lay the basis for another claim against you, for breach of confidentiality.

Once you receive a release and are prepared respond to the complaint itself, be sure to consult with your malpractice carrier. Your response to the complaint is "discoverable," which means that if the matter goes to court, the other side's lawyer will have the opportunity to read your letter and possibly use it to your disadvantage. Also, a well-written response is likely to end the matter. For these reasons, it is wise to consult with your carrier as you draft your letter.

Ms. Curtiss
Board of Psychology

                              August 20, 2000

Dear Ms. Curtiss,

I have received your letter of August 12 that contained a complaint from Mr. Mark Foster. It is my understanding of patient-therapist confidentiality that I am required to have a consent from the patient before I may release any information concerning a treatment.* If you would forward a copy of Mr. Foster's consent giving me permission to discuss this matter with your Board, as well as to share his record with you, I will provide a response to the complaint.

I will assume that the 30-day period of time for my response will not begin to run until I have received Mr. Foster's consent to release information.

Thank you for your understanding in this matter.

                              Sincerely,

                              Dr. Saks

---

* The consent to release information should include *all* treaters involved in the patient's care. Thus, an additional paragraph might read:

> I note from my records that I consulted with Dr. Wizner and Dr. Hibbard during the course of Mr. Foster's treatment. Because it will be necessary for my response to include their input about Mr. Foster's treatment, I would ask that Mr. Foster also provide consent for Drs. Wizner and Hibbard to release information. Mr. Foster's consent for Drs. Wizner and Hibbard to release information may be sent to me directly, or to Dr. Wizner and Dr. Hibbard at the addresses below.

INFORMED CONSENT LETTER FOR A PSYCHODYNAMIC PSYCHOTHERAPY

Below is an example of an informed consent letter; this particular letter involves a psychodynamic psychotherapy, as the second paragraph explains. Clinicians have <u>very</u> different responses to the idea of using such a letter. While some clinicians find letters helpful in making the frame of a psychotherapy clear at the outset, other clinicians would not even consider using written material to start off a therapeutic relationship, mostly because of what they see as detrimental implications for the transference.

Most important is that at the beginning of your work, enough information is conveyed for your prospective client to make a reasoned judgment about whether to begin a therapy with you. Whether this information is conveyed in a letter, a form, or orally, is not as important as that your client understand the nature of what you do, as well as the essential elements of the frame. Note, however, that the letter contains a significant amount of information, probably more than can be absorbed in a single sitting, especially since most clients are somewhat anxious at a first session. From this perspective, a written explanation of how you work affords a client the opportunity to review what you've said in a more relaxed setting.

As this letter makes clear, important aspects of the therapy—such as what gets talked about, how often sessions are held, and how long the therapy lasts—are left to be decided as the psychotherapy progresses. In this sense, the letter does not constitute informed consent; rather, it informs the client about nonnegotiable aspects of your work, and encourages discussion of other important aspects of the treatment. An

*informed consent letter is therefore best understood as the beginning,
rather than the end, of a process.*

June 20, 2000

Dear Mr. Edwards,

I provide a letter when I first meet with someone interested in beginning therapy, to explain important aspects of how I work. I encourage you to read it before we meet next, so that you have the chance to ask any questions you have either about my way of working or about psychotherapy in general. Please feel free to bring the letter to our session.

The work I do is best described as psychodynamically-oriented psychotherapy.* Sessions consist of my listening to what a client has to say and then responding with a comment or question. Sometimes I simply remain silent, in order not to interfere with what a client is thinking or feeling. It is natural and expected for very strong feelings to arise during the course of a psychotherapy; coming to understand such feelings is an important part of the work. While not all psychotherapies meet a client's expectations, and a client's symptoms may become more pronounced during the course of therapy, many psychotherapies do help with painful feelings, difficult memories, or conflicts in relating to others. Clients should always feel free during the course of a session to discuss their experience of how the psychotherapy is going.

I hold 45-minute sessions, in my office. The frequency of sessions and the length of the psychotherapy are aspects of the work that the client and I decide together. Generally, a psychotherapy will continue until the client and I decide our work is complete. It is important to begin sessions on time; my schedule requires that I end sessions promptly, which means that a client who arrives late for an appointment will not have a full 45-minute session.

Messages for me can be left with my answering service (734-1300) at any time. Although I check my answering service several times each day, I cannot be sure of receiving a message immediately, so that arrangements must be in place should an emergency arise. In an emergency clients may go to the emergency room of any hospital or call 911. The time to use an emergency room or "911" is when physical safety is at risk.†

---

* Some clinicians may want to provide information about their training and background (e.g., Ph.D. or M.D.).
† Therapists who have contracts with managed care companies will need to make sure that nothing in an informed consent letter is inconsistent with their contract. Thus, therapists should be sure to read provisions of the contract which concern availability during emergencies, coverage during vacations, billing, and the like.

My fee is $110 per session. I bill once per month, on the final session of the month. I ask that the bill be paid by the final session of the following month. If more than two months worth of unpaid payments accumulate, it is necessary to discuss and agree upon a payment plan before the psychotherapy can continue.

Clients who use insurance are responsible for co-payments. I encourage clients to read their insurance policies with care; many policies place significant limitations on mental health benefits, and it is important to know what these are. It is also important to know that using mental health benefits may have implications for future insurance coverage. I ask that clients please let me know if it would be helpful to discuss such implications; I am happy to do so.

I do not charge for sessions that are missed because of an emergency or ill health when I have at least 24 hours notice. I do charge for sessions missed with less than 24 hours notice.* Because insurance companies do not cover missed sessions, clients who miss sessions without 24 hours notice are responsible for the full session fee. I ask that clients give at least one week notice of their vacation.

I take approximately four weeks vacation each year. When I am away, another clinician will provide coverage. I will share with the covering clinician any important issues the client and I agree the covering clinician should know about, in case the client needs to contact that person in my absence. The clinician covering for me can be reached through my answering service.

I have both a legal and an ethical duty to ensure that what a client and I talk about remains confidential. In addition, both law and ethics require that I discuss circumstances in which aspects of the work may *not* be kept confidential. If I have reason to believe that a child, or an elderly or disabled person is being abused, neglected, or taken advantage of, I am legally obligated to disclose this information to a state agency. I may choose to disclose confidential information if I believe someone's safety is seriously at risk. In addition, if a client's mental status or emotional condition is introduced at a legal proceeding, I may be required to turn records over to a court or to testify. For clients who would find it helpful, I can provide a copy of the actual laws and regulations governing confidentiality. Should the necessity of releasing confidential information arise, I make every reason-

---

* Clinicians who work with individuals struggling with substance abuse may want to explain their policy should a client show up for an appointment under the influence. Some clinicians will treat this circumstance as a missed session, which seems perfectly appropriate from a legal, ethical, and clinical point of view.

able effort to discuss this matter with the client first; it is my preference to make any such disclosures together with the client, from my office.

I consult with other professionals in the field when I judge that doing so would be helpful to the psychotherapy. When speaking with other professionals I will attempt to disguise any identifying information about a client. Any professional with whom I speak is, like me, bound by confidentiality.

I am not an expert in matters involving the law, and do not conduct evaluations ordered by a court. If a client is involved in, or intends to commence, a legal proceeding in which any aspect of his or her mental or emotional functioning will be examined, it is essential that this matter be discussed as soon as possible.

I am sometimes asked to provide documentation when clients belong to an HMO or are using their insurance. If I receive such a request, it is my policy not to release material until the client and I have discussed the matter. Although certain confidentiality laws apply to HMOs and insurance companies, once material is released I no longer control who may have access to this information.

Finally, it is important to know that other therapies are available. Clients should feel free to explore other therapies if they find this therapy not as helpful as they would like; I can provide referrals to therapists whose way of working is different than my own.

When we next meet I will leave time for you to ask questions you may have about anything in this letter, or about psychotherapy in general.*

I look forward to our next session,

Dr. Elyn Saks

While this letter covers a great deal of material, two points should be emphasized. First, the letter, in and of itself, does not constitute informed consent. Rather, the letter begins a <u>process</u> of discussing with your client the nature, purpose, and intended outcome of the psychotherapy. Second, in regard to a letter, what's most important is not the substance of your policies concerning billing, missed sessions, emergencies, and the like, but rather <u>that you make your policies clear to your client.</u> Adopt whatever policies make most clinical sense to you—but be sure to make those policies clear as you begin your work.

* Some clinicians may want to mention the law concerning access to records; whether to do so will, of course, entail a good deal of thinking about the clinical implications of raising this issue (see chapter 10, Records and Record-Keeping).

Letter Terminating a Therapy Relationship

In a letter of termination, be sure to state clearly: the reasons for termination; your assessment that the treatment is no longer viable; a plan for termination sessions; any conditions that would precipitate a deviation from the plan for termination sessions; a plan for referring the patient to other treaters; and ways in which the patient may obtain treatment on an emergency basis.

Below is an example of a termination letter written by a therapist who has been harassed by a patient. By including each of the elements listed above, the therapist has protected herself from a claim that she abandoned the patient.

September 10, 2000

Dear Mr. Sheridan,

I am writing this letter to confirm our understanding that our work together will stop as of the first week in October. I realize that we discussed the reasons for stopping when we met this afternoon for your weekly session, but I wanted also to write them down in case you had any questions or wished to review what had been said.

In our first session, we went over how our work together would proceed. My letter of September 17, 1998, in which I outlined our treatment agreement, said that messages could be left with my answering service outside of our regularly scheduled meetings. We also discussed ways to handle emergencies: by going to an emergency room or calling 911.

This past spring, beginning in March, you began to call me at night, sometimes as late as 11 P.M. I reminded you that you could leave messages with my answering service outside of our regularly scheduled appointments and that I did not accept calls at home at that hour. You said that you understood and would not call me at home again. In late June I received numerous late-night calls from you. I told you that you must stop calling me at home and again reminded you how you could leave messages outside our scheduled session times. While you said that you understood our agreement, and assured me that you would not call me at home again, during the first three weeks of August you called me at home no less than 20 times. One call came at 3 A.M. In early September, you stopped your car and came to my front door. To the person who answered the door you appeared upset and angry that I was not available to see you. You left only when that person threatened to call the police. At that time I said that a similar incident would result in the need for our work together to end. Unfortunately, two days ago you again came to my house, and left only after my husband did call the police. I am sorry that you are either unable or unwilling to abide by the agreements we established during our initial sessions.

It has become clear to me that we will no longer be able to work together. For this reason, our work will stop in three weeks. Our work will stop immediately should you again come to my house or disturb my family.

I am enclosing the names of five clinicians and their phone numbers. I have spoken with the first two, Dr. Ronald Smith and Dr. Judith Barney. Both have said that they have times available in their schedules. In addition, you may seek treatment at the Mental Health Center downtown. I would encourage you to begin contacting possible treaters immediately. I will speak with a treater of your choosing and then send your records to that individual as soon as you sign a release for me to do so. Also, as we have discussed, emergency treatment is available at any hospital emergency room or by calling 911.

If you have any questions, please bring this letter with you when we next meet so that we may discuss them. I hope that our sessions can focus on how to make this transition go as smoothly as possible for you.

Sincerely,

Dr. Elyn Saks

BIBLIOGRAPHY

Appelbaum, P. S., & Gutheil, T. G. (1991). *Clinical handbook of psychiatry and the law* (2nd ed.). Baltimore: Williams & Wilkins.

Appelbaum, P. S., & Roth, L. H. (1981). Clinical issues in the assessment of competency. *American Journal of Psychiatry, 138,* 1462–1467.

Appelbaum, P. S., Lidz, C. W., & Meisel, A. (1987). *Informed consent: Legal theory and clinical practice.* New York: Oxford University.

American Psychiatric Association. (1994). *Diagnostic and statistical manual of mental disorders* (4th ed.). Washington, DC: Author.

American Psychiatric Association. (1995). *The principles of medical ethics, with annotations especially applicable to psychiatry.* Washington, DC: Author.

American Psychological Association. (1992, December). Ethical principles of psychologists and code of conduct. *American Psychologist,* 1597–1611.

American Psychological Association Ethics Committee. (1992, December). Rules and procedures. *American Psychologist,* 1612–1628.

Bray, J. H., Shepherd, J. N., & Hays, J. R. (1985). Legal and ethical issues in informed consent to psychotherapy. *The American Journal of Family Therapy, 13,* 50–60.

Berkowitz, S. (1979-1996). Legal briefing [column]. *Massachusetts Psychological Association Quarterly.*

Clark, D. C., & Fawcett, J. (1992). An empirically based model of suicide risk assessment for patients with affective disorder. In D. Jacobs (Ed.), *Suicide and clinical practice* (pp. 55–73). Washington, DC: American Psychiatric Press.

Clark, D. C., & Fawcett, J. (1992). Review of empirical risk factors for evaluation of the suicidal patient. In B. Bongar (Ed.), *Suicide: Guidelines for assessment, management, and treatment* (pp. 16–48). New York: Oxford University.

Gabbard, G., & Lester, E. (1996). *Boundaries and boundary violations.* New York: Basic.

Grisso, T. (1986). *Evaluating competencies: Forensic assessment and instruments.* New York: Plenum.

Handelsman, M. M., & Galvin, M. D. (1988). Facilitating informed consent for outpatient psychotherapy: A suggested written format. *Professional Psychology: Research and Practice,19,* 223–225.

Handelsman, M. M., Kemper, M. B., Kesson-Craig, P., McLain, J., & Johnsrud, C. (1986). Use, content, and readability of written informed consent forms for treatment. *Professional Psychology: Research and Practice, 17,* 514–518.

Katz, J. (1984). *The silent world of doctor and patient.* New York: Free.

Keith-Speigel, P., & Koocher, G. P. (1985). *Ethics in psychology. Professional standards and cases.* New York: Random House.

Millstein, B., Rubenstein, L., & Cyr, R. (1991, March). The Americans with Disabilities Act: A breathtaking promise for people with mental disabilities. *Clearinghouse Review,* 1240–1249.

Nolan, J. R., Nolan-Haley, J. M., Connolly, M. J., Hicks, S. C., & Albrandi, M. N. (1990). *Black's law dictionary: Definition of the terms and phrases of American and English jurisprudence, ancient and modern* (6th ed). St. Paul: West.

McBeth, J. E., Wheeler, A. M., Sither, J. W., & Onek, J. N. (1994). *Legal and risk management issues in the practice of psychiatry.* Washington, DC: Psychiatrists' Purchasing Group.

Petrila, J., & Otto, R. K. (1996). *Law and mental health professionals: Florida.* Washington, DC: American Psychological Association.

Physicians' desk reference. (1997). Montvale, NJ: Medical Economics.

Rozovsky, F. A. (1990). *Consent to treatment* (2nd ed.). Boston: Little, Brown.

Soler, M. I., Shotton, A. C., Bell, J. R., Jameson, E. J., Shauffer, C. B., Warboys, L. M., & Dale, M. J. (1998). *Representing the child client.* New York: Matthew Bender.

Tribe, L. H. (1999). *American constitutional law* (3rd ed.). Mineola, NY: Foundation.

Winick, B. J. (1997). *Therapeutic jurisprudence applied: Essays in mental health law.* Durham, NC: Carolina Academic.

Winick, B. J. (1997). *The right to refuse mental health treatment.* Washington, DC: American Psychological Association.

Winslade, W. J., & Ross, J. W. (1983). *The insanity plea.* New York: Charles Scribner's Sons.

Woodward, B., Duckworth, K. S., & Gutheil, T. G. (1983). Pharmacotherapist-psychotherapist collaboration. In J. M. Oldham, M. B., Riba, & A. Tasman (Eds.), *American Psychiatric Press review of psychiatry* (pp. 631–649). Washington, DC: American Psychiatric Press.

INDEX

INDEX OF CASES

INDEX OF STATUTES

INDEX OF REGULATIONS*

INDEX OF RULES

INDEX OF SUBJECTS

*Florida Administrative Code Annotated